T0331993

Capacity beyond Coercion

MODERN SOUTH ASIA

Ashutosh Varshney, Series Editor
Pradeep Chhibber, Associate Series Editor

Capacity beyond Coercion

Regulatory Pragmatism and Compliance along the India-Nepal Border

SUSAN L. OSTERMANN

OXFORD
UNIVERSITY PRESS

OXFORD
UNIVERSITY PRESS

Oxford University Press is a department of the University of Oxford. It furthers
the University's objective of excellence in research, scholarship, and education
by publishing worldwide. Oxford is a registered trade mark of Oxford University
Press in the UK and certain other countries.

Published in the United States of America by Oxford University Press
198 Madison Avenue, New York, NY 10016, United States of America.

© Oxford University Press 2023

Library of Congress Cataloging-in-Publication Data
Names: Ostermann, Susan L., author.
Title: Capacity beyond coercion : regulatory pragmatism and compliance along the India-Nepal border /
Susan L. Ostermann.
Description: New York, NY : Oxford University Press, [2022] |
Series: Modern South Asia | Based on author's thesis
(doctoral - University of California, Berkeley, 2016) issued under title:
Rule of law against the odds : legal knowledge, poverty & compliance along the India-Nepal border. |
Includes bibliographical references and index.
Identifiers: LCCN 2022027412 (print) | LCCN 2022027413 (ebook) |
ISBN 9780197661116 (hardback) | ISBN 9780197661123 | ISBN 9780197661130 |
ISBN 9780197661147 | ISBN 9780197661130 (epub)
Subjects: LCSH: Law—India. | Law—Nepal. |
Conservation of natural resources—Law and legislation—India. |
Conservation of natural resources—Law and legislation—Nepal. |
Educational law and legislation—India. | Educational law and legislation—Nepal. |
Child labor—Law and legislation—India. | Child labor—Law and legislation—Nepal.
Classification: LCC KNC95 .O78 2022 (print) | LCC KNC95 (ebook) |
DDC 349.54—dc23/eng/20220801
LC record available at https://lccn.loc.gov/2022027412
LC ebook record available at https://lccn.loc.gov/2022027413

DOI: 10.1093/oso/9780197661116.001.0001

1 3 5 7 9 8 6 4 2

Printed by Integrated Books International, United States of America

Contents

Acknowledgments

Though it is certainly a cliché to say so, it is no less true that this book would not have been possible without the sustained efforts of an enormous number of people. The name that sits on the front of it simply belongs to the ringleader.

For her role in my discovery of the empirical puzzle at the heart of this border design project, I thank Inga Schmoldt. She thought she was accompanying me on a trip to Nepal and, therefore, the Himalaya. Little did she know that I was interested in Madeshi politics and had planned to head to the Terai. In my efforts to keep her nevertheless entertained, I took her to Chitwan National Park for an elephant ride in the jungle. And, while walking away from the meeting point for said ride, I saw a map depicting Chitwan National Park on one side and Valmiki on the other. The excellent methodological training I received at UC Berkeley kicked in, and I dropped my plans for the day in favor of speaking with the park warden. During our conversation, he mentioned a surprising level of wood-taking across the border in Valmiki. I asked him what he thought explained it and he said he had no idea. As they say, the rest is history.

My family, regardless of whether they understand what I am up to, has always been supportive and engaged with the work. My partner, Stuart Pilorz, has put up with incredible amounts of travel, but also contributed materially to the satellite imagery analysis in the volume. Portulaca, Tom, Jackson, Leo, and Rani have all been present and responsible for various typos over the years, each maintaining somewhat of a love-hate relationship with the project. I am also indebted to my Nepali host family, whom I have stayed with since 2001, whenever I am in Kathmandu. In particular, Ram Kumar Pandit Chettri provided research assistance on this project and drove me, on the back of his motorcycle, to myriad government offices and even down to Birgunj and to a whole host of brick kilns.

At Berkeley, this book was incredibly well supported. Pradeep Chhibber and Bob Kagan were both instrumental throughout the project, from grappling with the initial ideas and providing funding for fieldwork, to taking concerned calls from the field, to providing manuscript feedback long after

I had graduated and Bob had shifted to emeritus status. Sean Farhang, David Rogel, and Alex von Rospatt, as committee members, were outstanding and ensured that the manuscript spoke well to many different audiences.

Adding no less to the quality of the manuscript were my friends and fellow graduate students Vasundhara Sirnate, Adnan Naseemullah, Francesca Jensenius, Rahul Verma, Tanu Kumar, Matt Baxter, and Nafisa Akbar. Their lighthearted commiseration and honest feedback were invaluable. In the wings, my longtime coauthor Amit Ahuja has always provided his ear and the right advice throughout this project.

Without Sitansu Amar, the folk at MORSEL, and Birendra Mahato in the field, data collection would not have happened.

At Notre Dame, the university and my colleagues have always prioritized the book and provided the resources, including both time and money, necessary to make it happen.

Finally, it has been a pleasure to work with Dave McBride at OUP and I am very grateful to my reviewers, whose comments contributed to a dramatic improvement in the quality of the text you are about to read.

1

Coercion meets Pragmatism

State capacity is an overutilized term and underconsidered concept. To date, those writing about and seeking to measure state capacity have largely concerned themselves with the coercive apparatus of the state and its ability to achieve its objectives—typically through compliance with legal mandates—by threat or use of force. But as Max Weber himself pointed out in *Politics as a Vocation*, states do not always rely on coercion. This is true even of states with significant coercive power. We know that states sometimes reduce their coercive burden by making the law seem legitimate, relying instead on the sense of duty of those targeted by regulations to motivate compliance. States also reduce their coercive burden by converting existing customary or social norms to law and largely relying on societal mechanisms to achieve compliance. The choice to rely on a non-coercive means of securing compliance is sometimes purely convenient, as when the state's goals and those of society are aligned. At other times, it is pragmatic. This is true when the state is attempting to alter behavior but simply cannot muster the force necessary to do so. This book examines weak-state compliance and the state and societal behaviors associated with it. The primary focus of this inquiry is on accurate legal knowledge, the role it plays in fostering compliance, and how it comes about under adverse circumstances.

The Neglected Role of Legal Knowledge

While the legal maxim *ignorantia legis non excusat* holds that ignorance of the law does not excuse one from blame for violating its dictates, it also admits, albeit somewhat inadvertently, that many do remain unaware of applicable laws. The law literature has often assumed that the law is "widely known and understood" (Carothers 1998; Polinsky 1989; Priest 1981; Shavell 1980a, 1980b) and/or that it generates "implicit general deterrence" (Thornton, Gunningham & Kagan 2005; *contra* Feest 1968; Winter & May 2001). These assumptions are not always accurate, and this is important because law is the

Capacity beyond Coercion. Susan L. Ostermann, Oxford University Press. © Oxford University Press 2023.
DOI: 10.1093/oso/9780197661116.003.0001

primary means by which states create order within their territories and shift individuals from social norms to legal rules or from old legal rules to new ones. If individuals are unaware of a legal rule, they are less likely to comply with it and the state's project may fail. Knowledge of the law is, therefore, essential to compliance in the many situations in which law does more than simply codify social norms. Simply put, accurate legal knowledge is essential to any state project that involves norm change.

However, before we can consider norm and/or rule change and projects that aim to achieve same, it is important to be clear about norms and rules themselves. In her 2005 book *Understanding Institutional Diversity*, Elinor Ostrom suggests just how difficult this can be. Here I adopt Christina Bicchieri's definition of norms, as elucidated in *Norms in the Wild* (2016): according to Bicchieri, norms exist "when a number of individuals prefer to act in a certain way because they expect others to do the same (empirical expectations) or/and because they think that others expect them to act in this way (normative expectations)." With respect to rules, I adopt Ostrom's definition, with rules being the hidden structure underlying games. Taking this a step further, in the case of legal rules, these are the not-so-hidden structures of the game that the state hopes to create and impose throughout its jurisdiction.

It follows that we must also be clear about accurate legal knowledge. As the above definition of legal rules suggests, there is often a gap between the letter of the law and that which exists in practice (Ostrom's rules). Oliver Wendell Holmes considered this gap at length in *The Theory of Legal Interpretation* (1898), arguing that the law, by virtue of its being encoded via language, is inherently unclear. Because it is unclear and must be applied to factual scenarios in the real world, some interpretation regarding its meaning is required. And it is through interpretation and application that we slowly, over time, learn about the law. But Holmes was writing about ideal conditions. On the ground in the developing world, where courts are sometimes unable to fulfill this role and rule of law is not firmly established, the gap between the law on the books and law as practiced can be very large. Arguably, those seeking accurate legal knowledge under these conditions might focus on the practice of the law, rather than words on pages in a law library somewhere that may never be interpreted by judge or bureaucrat and, thus, have almost no relationship with the state's actual enforcement behavior on the ground. This legal knowledge is certainly valuable information. It is not, however, how I invoke accurate legal knowledge here. Instead, this book takes up some of the central questions of the ongoing law and development debate (Trubek 1996), inquiring as to the conditions under which social norms shift toward legal norms and "rule of law" starts to take shape, as well as how various actors might affect these conditions. Thus, for the present purposes, those with accurate legal knowledge are those who know, with reasonable certainty, what behavior the law requires or prohibits in a variety of simple and straightforward situations. This is the knowledge that must somehow pass from state to society if norms are to shift in the direction the state wants. Or, put differently, this is the knowledge that must pass from state to society if the state is to get relevant actors to play the game of its choice.

For evidence that this particular type of legal knowledge is a prerequisite for compliance, we need look no further than behavior surrounding the US tax code, particularly when it is applied to forms of income and deductions that are not encompassed by employer withholding. While knowledge of the code itself is certainly not widespread, tax preparation services and lawyers increase the dissemination of this information (Klepper & Nagin 1989; Klepper, Mazur & Nagin 1991). Ordinary individuals and businesses alike make decisions and change their behavior in an effort to both minimize their tax burden and achieve compliance (Posner 2000). Some even over-comply in response to uncertainty about legal requirements (Alm, Jackson & McKee 1992a, 1992b).[1] They do so despite the fact that the likelihood of an Internal Revenue Service (IRS) audit for all but the wealthiest individuals is exceedingly unlikely[2] (Posner 2000; Andreoni, Erard & Feinstein 1998; Feld & Frey 2007; Hofman, Hoelzl & Kirchler 2008).

In general, information helps to foster compliance. This is perhaps why we often assume people know the law when we see them comply with it (Carnes & Cuccia 1996; Webley, Robben, Elffers & Hessing 1991; *contra* Hofman, Hoelzl & Kirchler 2008; Feest 1968). As Feest explains, when someone stops at a stop sign, we often assume she is doing so because she is aware that *not* doing so is illegal, even if she stopped for other reasons (cross-traffic, for instance). Similarly, when we see non-compliance, we often assume it is willful (Feest 1968; *contra* Sorg 2005; Brehm & Hamilton 1996). If someone renovates her home without securing approval from the appropriate authorities, we often assume that she did so intentionally, perhaps to avoid an outlay of both time and money, even if she was actually unaware of the requirement. These inferential problems highlight a fact first brought to the fore by Winter and May (2001): that many do not actually know what the law requires of them and some fail to comply as a result.

This prompts an important question: how do those who have accurate legal knowledge learn about the law? Information about the law is thought to be transmitted in three ways: (1) by the state, directly, through printed materials, including statutes and case law, or through public awareness campaigns (Feest 1968; Zago 2016); (2) by experts or other interested parties, including lawyers (Muir 1973; Klepper & Nagin 1989; Klepper, Mazur & Nagin 1991; Hillman 1998; Zago 2016); and (3) by the state, indirectly, through its actions and those of its agents, which target populations can observe and use to deduce legal requirements (Thornton, Gunningham & Kagan 2005).

But in order to fully understand legal knowledge acquisition, we need to consider the circumstances under which legal information transmission breaks down. Here an analogy is helpful: the assumption that the law is "widely known and understood" is similar to the assumption of perfect information in economics. As the economics literature has demonstrated at length, asymmetries of information exist and undercut the efficient markets hypothesis, as well as some of the other bedrock principles of modern economic theory (Akerlof 1970; Stiglitz 1975a, 1975b; Rothschild & Stiglitz 1976; Radner & Stiglitz 1984; Arnott & Stiglitz 1988; Greenwald & Stiglitz 1987; Greenwald & Stiglitz 1988). As Joseph Stiglitz explains, information asymmetries can be exacerbated by agency problems (Stiglitz 2000; Stiglitz 2002). In economics, this is the idea that the person who owns the land is different from the one who works the land and that they behave differently as a result of their different positions. In political science, a principal-agent problem exists between the state and its agents, those who do its bidding and through whom it accomplishes its prerogatives (McCubbins, Noll & Weingast 1987). Most agree that the state's agents are distinct from the state and have their own set of motivations (Weingast 1984; Cook 1988; Prendergast 2007; Gailmard 2010). As a result, the state's agents can create and perpetuate information asymmetries regarding what exactly the state is demanding with its laws and the penalties associated with non-compliance. This is true in almost any legal context, but it is particularly true when the state is weak and cannot properly train its agents, or when corruption is rampant.

When target populations have little ability to learn about the law on their own, a condition that is common when the state is weak, agency problems are compounded. As the economics literature did earlier, the literatures that examine compliance and rule of law often assume perfect information,[3] largely because this assumption greatly simplifies analysis. Stiglitz writes that, in economics, it was hoped that "the same optimality properties . . . that held for economies with perfect information would hold for economies with imperfect information" (Stiglitz 2000). There was, however, empirical evidence that this was not the case. The same is true with respect to compliance (Snortum, Berger & Hauge 1988; Beck, Ogloff & Corbishley 1994; Kim 1998). The basic demographics of places where the state tends to be weak, including lack of education and poverty, suggest that the costs of acquiring legal knowledge—information about what the state is demanding and the penalties associated with non-compliance—from the state directly remain high. In addition, anyone who has tried to discern what the law is, even when armed with a law degree, knows that it is a costly endeavor under the best of circumstances. When legal experts are poorly trained, limited in number, or very costly, the cost of acquiring legal knowledge becomes untenable for the average person. That is, unless that person can learn about the law by observing the state.

When the state's agents have reason and ability to transmit accurate information about the law to target populations and to behave consistently with respect to enforcement, they communicate information about the law in the same way that economic actors transmit information: through their observable behavior (Stiglitz 2002). If principal and agent—state and bureaucrat—share similar interests, principal-agent problems are far less likely to develop and state behavior will be consistent, leading to fewer information asymmetries. For instance, in the United States, with respect to the tax code, it is assumed that everyone knows roughly what the law is, whether they acquire their knowledge by reading about the law, through experts, or by observation; it is also assumed that the interests of the state and IRS agents are similar.[4] As a result, information asymmetries with respect to the tax code are limited and the surprisingly high levels of compliance we see seem to bear this out.

But what happens when the cost of acquiring legal knowledge is high and the interests of the state and its agents vary enormously? In such a situation, target populations are reliant on observation of bureaucrat actions for information about the law and the principal-agent problems that are well recognized in both the political science and economics literatures come to the fore (Ross 1973; Stiglitz 2002; Moynihan 1998; Weingast 1984; Cook 1988; Prendergast 2007; Gailmard 2010). When principal-agent problems exist, whether they result from poor training or corruption, communication of legal information can get muddled. Some agents, by their actions, send one message, while others, by behaving differently, send a different one (Stiglitz 2002). For instance, enforcement of a law that *does not* exist can lead target populations to believe that it does, while frequent non-enforcement of laws that *do* exist can lead to the opposite result. As a result, asymmetries of legal information grow and target populations often end up with inaccurate information about the law. If individuals do not know what the state's demands are, as well as the penalties associated with non-compliance, they cannot make decisions about whether or not to comply.

These parameters are commonplace in many parts of the world, especially where coercive state capacity is weak. Populations have limited education and cannot read the law themselves; lawyers are poorly trained and often too expensive to provide advice to average people; corrupt officials enforce the law capriciously, resulting in a lack of consistent behavior to watch and learn from. We, therefore, are unlikely to see compliance with the law in weak states unless those states are able to increase education, the availability of affordable lawyers, or the consistency with which their agents enforce the law. These are tall, rigid demands for states with limited capacity and, at least at first glance, it appears as if we might as well wait for Godot.

Interestingly, corruption is not the only explanation for the inconsistent behavior of bureaucrats. The pressure to secure compliance with limited capacity can also lead street-level bureaucrats to behave inconsistently in order to *further* state interests. Tendler (1997) documents how street-level bureaucrats in Ceara, Brazil, did so, they used discretion to find compliance-consistent paths forward for both state and target population in the very specific circumstances that these entities found themselves. As Tendler notes, this could have easily been construed as corruption and could, indeed, have undermined the state's efforts, had it not been for two things: (1) bureaucrats' desire to perform better in order to live up to societal and government expectations; and (2) citizens' demands for accountability. Ceara's success is fantastic, but such approaches are not entirely cost-free. While bureaucratic discretion may generate compliance among specific actors, overall inconsistency may, at the same time, be perpetuating inaccurate legal knowledge and the non-compliance of others.

Do such circumstances and capacity constraints suggest that non-compliance is inevitable? There is evidence to suggest it is not. There are areas where laws, including ones that run counter to customary norms, are followed, despite bureaucratic inconsistency, regardless of whether that inconsistency derives from corruption of discretion. Take, for instance, compliance with wood-collection prohibitions in Nepal's Chitwan National Park ("Chitwan") and India's Valmiki National Park and Tiger Reserve

("Valmiki"). Individuals living in this region need fuelwood in order to cook and heat their homes, have been sourcing it for centuries from what is now parkland, and have few other sources of fuel. Wood-taking prohibitions are, thus, an attempt by the Nepali and Indian states to shift individuals from social norms to legal norms. Unlike areas where the state is strong, however, the states on either side of the India-Nepal border simply do not have the resources to engage in large-scale enforcement, nor have they conducted massive public awareness campaigns regarding these regulations. There has also been no concerted state effort and concurrent accountability drive, as in Tendler (1997), to foster compliance. The populations living in this area have, for their part, little means to learn about wood-collection prohibitions on their own, as education levels are low and competent lawyers are expensive and few in number. Despite this, in Nepal in particular, we see surprisingly high rates of both legal knowledge and compliance.

Given that wood-taking prohibitions require behavior that differs from that dictated by both social norms and self-interest, and given the massive information asymmetries that exist between the Indian and Nepali states and relevant target populations, how do those living near Chitwan and Valmiki come to know that wood collection in national parks is prohibited?

Pragmatism as a Regulatory Strategy

Many are able to learn about the law because of the Nepali state's use of *regulatory pragmatism*, a flexible—rather than legally doctrinaire or dogmatic—approach to the design and implementation of a regulatory system that is specifically adapted for the context in which regulation will occur. Such an approach prizes effectiveness and durability over all other goals and typically takes into account on-the-ground realities of state capacity, the irregular behavior of state agents, and the needs of populations targeted by particular regulations. In the United States, regulatory pragmatism is behind the employer income tax withholding requirement and the use of grandfather clauses for new regulations (Huber 2011). Approaches that do not employ regulatory pragmatism are those that largely rely on threat of legal sanctions and fail to design for regulatory context. Examples of this latter category include regulations that require individuals to desist from activities necessary to their basic survival (Ostermann 2016) or the persistence of 55 mph speed limits on interstates in rural areas of the United States (Keeler 1994) long after the 1970s oil crisis had ended and despite dramatic improvements in both highway and vehicle safety.

Though law has long been a province of absolutes and ideals, regulatory pragmatism suggests a middle path. According to William James (1907), pragmatism is a method of settling metaphysical disputes that otherwise might be interminable. Descended etymologically from the Greek word for action, *pragma*, it has made inroads in law more recently. Though the classical view of law emphasizes argument by analogy and the need for judges to follow an abstract and consistent jurisprudence when making decisions, legal pragmatism emphasizes the need to include a more diverse set of data and claims. For the legal pragmatist all legal issues are grounded in a specific context. As Posner (1995) explains, avoiding context "disconnects the whirring machinery of philosophical abstraction from the practical business of governing our lives and our societies." Thus, legal pragmatists like Thomas Grey, Daniel Farber, Richard Posner, and Margaret Radin emphasize: (1) the importance of context; (2) the instrumental nature of law; (3) the unavoidable presence of alternate perspectives; and (4) the problematic nature of utilizing any particular foundation for legal reasoning.

Regulatory pragmatism is an extension of this line of reasoning beyond the judge's chambers. An effective regulatory system need not be backed by a coercively strong state. It must, however, be grounded in a specific regulatory context and respond to on-the-ground realities and challenges. It must recognize that law is instrumental and that the purpose of law, from the state's perspective, is to produce particular behavior. It must account for alternative perspectives, including those of individuals who believe the law should require entirely different behavior. And, finally, it must be designed to be effective, first and foremost, rather than to be consistent with a particular theory or set of foundations.

The image on the cover of this volume contains an excellent example of this. For many years, while working on my PhD and the manuscript for this book, I would go for long walks in the nearby park to clear my head. As I did so, I would walk right by the fence depicted in the photo. It would regularly collect graffiti. The graffiti would then be painted over, as in the left side of the image. This cycle went on for years. The fines for defacing property with graffiti are not insignificant in San Francisco, where the fence is located. For some time the nearby school of the arts posted a security guard to prevent their students from involvement. None of these appears to have had any effect whatsoever on the return of the graffiti after the fence had been freshly painted. If anything, the strategy followed was a smart one, informed by research (Wilson & Kelling 1982) that suggests that the appearance of neglect, in the form of persistent graffiti, invites further graffiti and, potentially, other crime. Unfortunately, graffiti abatement just didn't work in this case. One day, though, a new strategy seemed to materialize. Students from the art school started painting the mural you see depicted in the right side of the image. When I saw it, I thought, "Now that may actually work." There was clearly a desire to have something on the fence that wasn't brown paint, as evidenced by years of tagging. And graffiti artists would likely not want to paint over someone else's art. This might be particularly true if the artists, in both cases, were from the art school. I waited and regularly walked, curious to see what would become of the mural. As it turns out, the mural, a pragmatic regulatory strategy that accounted for on-the-ground realities, *did* work. The left side of the fence continues to get the occasional tag, while the right side has been brightening the entrance to the park and art school it sits beside for years now, tag free.

This is, of course, just one example. The private rights of action that Sean Farhang discusses at length in "The Litigation State" (2006) are another. For instance, the environment cannot advocate for itself or hire its own lawyer, and it isn't clear that a bureaucracy would cheaply and effectively fill that role. A private right of action in this context gives lawyers an incentive to act as environmental advocates; if they win the cases they bring, they are paid for the time they spend on them. Lawyers rather than bureaucrats become the state's agents, and the interests of both are aligned. Regulatory pragmatism is also behind the Amber Alert system used in the United States to crowd-source information about child abductions. The time and effort required for law enforcement to track down a missing child is enormous and costly. The population at large, however, is well positioned to do so and, importantly, has an incentive to assist. Few are opposed, ideologically or otherwise, to resolving missing child cases, and providing information is quick and easy. Principal-agent problems are, thus, unlikely. In the forested borderlands between India and Nepal, where populations are poorly educated and lack access to legal services and where bureaucrats are often corrupt and/or poorly trained, regulatory pragmatism necessarily involves designing for legal knowledge transmission. This means resolving principal-agent problems by designing around anyone or anything that prevents diffusion of accurate legal information (e.g., bureaucrats who behave inconsistently), as well as designing for observational learning, since education is limited and acquisition from legal experts is unrealistic.

Knowledgeable Compliance

Once individuals know what the law demands of them, they are in a position to choose whether or not to comply. To a great degree it goes without saying that if the law requires behavior that aligns with cultural norms or self-interest, many will comply. Thus, the real questions, for those who want to understand the extent to which the state can achieve compliance, are: Can law be used to change norms? And under what circumstances will people comply with law when compliance requires a costly, non-habitual, or non-customary behavior?

The socio-legal compliance literature takes up these questions, examining the circumstances under which law can be used as an instrument of change when the individuals or entities targeted by it are not particularly receptive to the change required. Early figures like the sociologist William Graham Sumner (1907) stated that the law must always reflect social practice and predicted that if law-ways were to come into conflict with folkways, the latter would surely win. For example, the fact that murder is almost universally categorized as illegal is not problematical because nearly everyone agrees that murder is "wrong" and should be illegal. Meanwhile, the "wrongness" of alcohol consumption in the United States has been a far more contested matter. While some segments of the population have always found it to be reasonable and permissible adult behavior, others have found it damaging to public health and/or morality. When the latter group won and the Eighteenth Amendment ushered in the Prohibition era, the state struggled to enforce this new law. By all accounts, alcohol remained readily available and large swaths of the population continued to consume it, albeit slightly less openly and with greater risk than before. And, eventually, the Twenty-first Amendment served as an admission of the failure of this seemingly well-intentioned project. So, was Sumner right, that law-ways can't change folkways? This particular example seems to support Sumner's position. However, other scholars have pointed to situations in which law *has* changed individual behavior.

For instance, Prothro and Matthews (1966) found that law, in this case state laws that removed poll taxes and literacy tests, did have a positive influence on black voter registration in the South, even before the intrusive remedies provided by the 1965 Federal Voting Rights Act. Later, Orfield (1987) found that the exclusionary rule, which bans improperly collected evidence from a trial record, effectively deterred narcotics officers in Chicago from illegal collection of evidence. Kagan and Skolnick (1993) examined no-smoking ordinances in US cities in the late 1980s and early 1990s and found that compliance without enforcement was common, but only as abetted by certain circumstances—in this case, infractions were highly visible; cost of compliance was low (which was only temporary); there was not a strong culture of resistance among smokers (by then, generally aware smoking was dangerous to themselves as well as others); non-smokers and businesses, rather than the state, could and would carry out much of the enforcement. Later, Gunningham, Kagan & Thornton (2003) examined corporate performance vis-à-vis environmental regulation in Australia, New Zealand, Canada, and the United States and found that the behavior of businesses like paper mills—which are highly visible and, thus, their infractions easily detectable—is fairly susceptible to change by regulation, but that social pressures were instrumental as well. That study and others (for a summary, see Kagan et al. 2011), found that, in addition to fear and social pressure, a sense of duty to comply with law, or with the norm underlying the law in question, often provides a significant incentive to comply. Meanwhile, in contrast, Pager, Western, and Bonikowski (2009), who took an experimental approach to examining patterns of discrimination in the low-wage labor market in New York City, found that compliance with civil rights and anti-discrimination laws was poor, suggesting that businesses and organizations are not as willing to comply with laws if infractions are not readily detectable and enforcement is difficult and minimal. In such situations, Winter and May's (2001) work on the compliance of Danish farmers with agricultural/environmental regulations suggests that peer pressure, when set against a legal backdrop, may also foster compliance. In sum, according to the compliance literature, the answer to the basic question of whether law can generate compliant social practice despite adversity is: yes, under certain conditions.

According to the standard deterrence model, three main factors drive compliance: fear (Gibbs 1968; Jensen 1969; Tittle 1977; Friedman 1975), duty (Braithwaite & Makkai 1994; Scholz & Pinney 1995; May 2005), and social license pressure (Gunningham, Kagan & Thornton 2003). There are then a host of other factors that enhance or detract from the power and effectiveness of these main three. Among them are likelihood of detection (of non-compliance) (Klepper & Nagin 1989); severity of penalty (Klepper

& Nagin 1989; Scholz & Gray 1990); cost of compliance in both time and money (Gerstenfeld & Roberts 2000; Yapp & Fairman 2004; Hillary 1995; Bowman, Heilman & Seetharaman 2004); knowledge of the law and of enforcement odds (Gerstenfeld & Roberts 2000; Hillary 1995; Hutchinson & Chaston 1995; Petts 1999, 2000; Yapp & Fairman 2004; van der Wal et al. 2006); attitude toward and/or treatment by regulators (Braithwaite & Makkai 1994; Yapp & Fairman 2004); attitude toward regulation (Bardach & Kagan 1982; Gunningham, Kagan & Thornton 2003; Tyler 1990; Makkai & Braithwaite 1996; Kagan & Scholz 1984); formal management systems in the cases of businesses, organizations, or governments (Palmer & van der Vorst 1996); social pressure (Gunningham, Kagan & Thornton 2003); the belief that others are complying (Coleman 1996; Gunningham, Kagan & Thornton 2003); the saliency of the need for compliance (Gray & Scholz 1991; Siskind 1980; Weil 1996; Ko et al. 2010; Bowman, Heilman & Seetharaman 2004); and formal allowances for self-regulation (Rees 1994). Yet the evidence for these factors comes largely from places where the state is strong—places where traditional legal enforcement, even if largely not used in practice, retains its deterrent value.[5] In light of this fact, what should we expect to find in areas of state weakness, where principal-agent problems often limit effective and predictable enforcement?

Limited research has examined compliance in such contexts. Gezelius and Hauck (2011), in their examination of compliance with fishery regulations in Norway, Canada, and South Africa, explain that the source of a motivation to comply with the law can vary from context to context and, as a result, a state's strategy for ensuring compliance must change accordingly. Boittin (2013), in her study of sex workers in China, reveals that many individuals who break laws prohibiting prostitution often do so out of necessity, but, interestingly, that poverty-driven non-compliance does not imply rejection of the legal system in other contexts. James Scott (1987) and Mauricio Villegas (2012) find that attitudes toward the law and the state are often different in areas of state weakness and that responses to same reflect this fact.

Against this backdrop, Gunningham, Kagan & Thornton (2003), Thornton, Gunningham & Kagan (2005), and Kagan, Gunningham & Thornton (2011) tell us that enforcement, even if only used against a small percentage of the regulated, is important for getting the rest of a given target population to comply. This assertion suggests that state capacity need not be terribly great in order for deterrence-based enforcement to work. But it also, I believe, assumes that deterrence works similarly for all individuals and organizations, an untenable assumption in contexts in which many of the individuals in the population targeted by a particular regulation desperately need the very resource they are prohibited from taking from a relatively accessible source. Sibley (2005), Pogarsky (2009), Piquero et al. (2011), and, in particular, Christine Parker's (2013) recent work on cartel compliance with financial regulation suggest as much. Parker finds that elite and non-elite actors are situated differently with respect to the law, at greater or lesser distance from it, and, as a result, are more or less susceptible to deterrence. Parker (2013) builds on Peter May's (2005) conclusion that individuals are often differently motivated toward compliance, Tetty Havinga's (2006) finding that private entities can have more of a deterrent effect than public ones, Judith van Erp's (2011) argument that corporate perceptions of sanctions are socially embedded, and her own work with Vibeke Nielsen (2011), which suggests that a "business case" for compliance can be as important as deterrence in terms of determining behavior. Each of these pieces suggests that deterrence is in the eye of the beholder. And, yet, none of these authors considers cases in which enforcement is nearly impossible given resource and other constraints. This book takes up this latter issue: what happens when limited coercive state capacity means that enforcement is nearly nonexistent and when target populations have little to lose and quite a bit to gain from non-compliance? Are there ways to overcome the poverty problem (i.e., target populations situated in such a way that deterrence, even if it existed, would likely not work) and generate compliance against the odds?

A growing literature suggests that developing-world actors still conduct cost-benefit analyses when considering compliance, but that their analyses may have more and different factors, particularly with respect to environmental issues, than those of their developed-world counterparts. In a study of illegal pesticide use in China, Yan, van Rooij, and van der Heijden (2015a) find that farmers are more likely to respond to operational costs and benefits than deterrence when considering non-compliance. Schmidt and McDermott (2015) add that non-compliance with deforestation laws in the Amazon basin is associated with both stress and the perception that legal processes are contradictory, often because of inconsistent local law enforcement. Tacconi (2007) finds that the subjective interpretation of which forest practices are "harmful" can lead to non-compliance with related laws. Along the same lines, Pendleton (2007) shows that non-compliance with conservation regulations was only subjectively considered illegal when it met certain community-level, extra-legal criteria. This may be because, as Yan, van Rooij, and van der Heijden (2015b) point out in a separate paper on compliance with pesticide regulations, motivations for compliance are not necessarily different from those for non-compliance, but that deterrence may be more important to the former than the latter.

Despite the complicated cost-benefit analysis that developing-world actors must consider when choosing whether or not to comply with conservation regulations, a number of papers suggest that compliance with these types of regulations is possible (Barr 2000; Contreras-Hermosilla 1997, 2000, 2007). This literature, however, provides limited empirical evidence for the claims it makes and instead relies largely on "best practices" evidence derived from years of policy-promotion work.

The commons literature, however, goes further, examining this very topic. After William Forster Lloyd's original 1833 essay on this topic, academics, pundits, and policymakers alike assumed that the widespread plundering of the commons areas of the Great Britain and Ireland that Lloyd had observed was inevitable. Coase (1960) , Hardin (1968), and others then fleshed this out using increasingly sophisticated economic models. Starting in the 1980s, however, and led largely by Elinor Ostrom—a political scientist who eventually received a Nobel prize for her work—academic thinking shifted in the face of new evidence. Ostrom (1990) demonstrated that the tragedy of the commons was not inevitable and could be avoided by way of social institutions. Baland and Platteau (1996) then integrated Ostrom with field experiences among so-called traditional societies in the developing world. Their field data suggest conditions—co-management and early integration of resource users into the management/regulatory process, in particular—under which collective action around common pool resources is possible. Agrawal and Ostrom (2001) echo these ideas, suggesting that compliance with forest regulations is possible when the institutional context is conducive. In particular, they find that decentralization of forest management to forest users and other local-level actors via collectively or individually held property or forest access rights allows these group to act collectively and in a way that is consonant with both compliance and effective forest management. Gibson et al. (2005) find that, while the specific institutions may vary, "regular monitoring and sanctioning of rules—rule enforcement" is positively associated with ecological/forest management goals and that local actors seem to be better placed to effectively enforce forest rules. But local actors can be a diverse set and are not always similarly situated when it comes to a particular resource. Indeed, inequality sometimes exacerbates environmental problems by making cooperation in the design and enforcement of measures to protect natural resources more challenging (Baland et al. 2006).

The above suggests that decentralization and collective action with respect to the commons is possible and may help explain observed cross-border variation in compliance with wood-taking prohibitions in place in Chitwan and Valmiki National Parks. However, it doesn't explain unexpected compliance—compliance in the absence of significant coercive capacity—in other regulatory contexts. Nor does it suggest how states in the developing world might translate regulatory success with respect to the commons into regulatory success in non-commons arenas.

Compliance along the India-Nepal Border

The India-Nepal border runs through hills and mountains to the west and east, but the longest portion of it runs across the Terai, the plains—at a height of only 220 to 984 feet above sea level. It is bisected by six large rivers—the Yamuna, Ganges, Sarda, Karnali, Narayani, and Kosi—that originate in the high Himalaya and feed the plains, tropical forests, and fertile farmland below. Historically, the region tended much more toward forests than farmland, but in the face of population pressure the jungle—which included large stands of *sal*, or teak—has retreated. With the retreat of the forests and as a result of hunting, biodiversity has also dwindled. The Terai is known for its charismatic megafauna: elephants, tigers, rhinoceros, bears, etc. But it is also home to incredible bird populations, endangered insects, and a whole host of aquatic life.

In the eighteenth and nineteenth centuries, when the British entered the region, it was officially controlled by a variety of different *rajas* (monarchical rulers), but their control was largely concentrated in populous areas. The forests themselves were sparsely inhabited, but not *un*populated. For hundreds of years, the Tharu and Dhimal people have made their homes in and around this forested area and have maintained a close relationship with the land. So much so that many present-day Tharus are not sickened by the parasite that causes malaria, which used to be common in this region. It was only after a large-scale, DDT-based malaria eradication program in the 1950s and 1960s that individuals from other communities started inhabiting the Terai in large numbers.

Today the Terai is an important and productive agricultural region. Rice, wheat, maize, mustard, and sugar cane dominate, with more rice in Nepal and sugar cane in India. Other crops include potatoes, lentils, turmeric, ginger, chilis, mangoes, bananas, papayas, guavas, jackfruit, and tea. Despite its agricultural importance, poverty is endemic in the Terai. At the time of data collection, World Bank data indicated that average per capita income in India and Nepal was $1,503 and $690, respectively. However, my own data indicate that 73 percent of respondents were living on less than $1/day. Education levels the area are relatively low. Overall literacy rates in India and Nepal are 74.0 percent and 66.0 percent, respectively. However, my own data indicate that the numbers are not this high in the Terai. Despite these lagging social and economic indicators, the region has also long been considered politically peripheral to both Indian and Nepali politics.

Though getting leverage over the question of whether and how weak states generate compliance in spite of widespread poverty and in a wide variety of regulatory contexts is challenging, the Terai is an excellent place to do so. This is in part because the Indian and Nepali states have relatively weak deterrence-based enforcement capacity in this region. What this means on the ground is that this area is one in which the *a priori* likelihood that members of a target population will feel a strong duty to obey state-propounded regulations is low. Legal institutions' chances of fostering compliance, vis-à-vis social norms, are quite unfavorable, making the Terai a so-called hard case.

The Terai is also an excellent place to explore how coercively weak states generate compliance because of the border itself, which is, and always has been, open. This book utilizes the border to consider the compliance consequences when different design and implementation strategies are associated with the same basic regulation. Its openness, and the lack of distinction between populations living on either side of it, allows me to study regulatory pragmatism and determine whether strategies consistent with this approach bring about legal knowledge and compliance more effectively than do legally doctrinaire tactics.

The border depicted in Figures 1.1 and 1.2 was first formally delineated like many other colonially drawn borders: on a semi-random basis by the British when they ceded back territory that they took from Nepal during the Anglo-Nepal War (1814–1816). Due to the subsequent India-Nepal Peace and Friendship Treaty, residents of this region have been permitted to cross the border, unimpeded by legal restrictions, for as long as it has existed.

Figure 1.1 Satellite Map of the Study Region

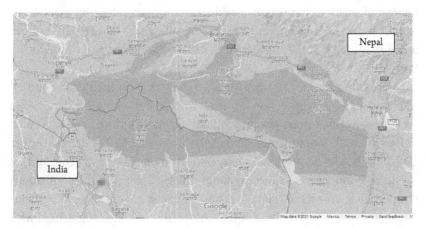

Figure 1.2 Map of Settlements and Road Networks in the Study Region

Indians and Nepalis need not present documentation to cross and they do so to work, shop, and marry. As a result of the unusual relationship that India and Nepal have enjoyed along their border, the populations living on either side of it do not differ significantly in this particular area: the same ethnic group (Tharu) is dominant, individuals generally speak the same set of three languages (Bhojpuri, Nepali, and Hindi), and people are generally poor and uneducated. Many of those living in Nepal are originally from India. Some Nepalis also live across the border in India.

In addition, the India-Nepal border is a region in which the *a priori* likelihood that members of the target population will have knowledge of those state-propounded laws that differ from customary norms and feel a strong duty to obey the former is low. This is, in part, because coercive state capacity—at least at the local level—does not vary as one travels across the border. Up until recently, this border region was plagued, both in India and Nepal, by Maoist insurgencies. During these conflicts, the state almost ceased to exist at the local level. In the intervening time, the Nepali and Indian states have re-entered the region, but only minimally: signs of the state remain limited.

The most notable state projects in this region are Chitwan National Park, in Nepal, and Valmiki National Park, in India. Contiguous and divided only by the border, these parks are ostensibly managed for the same purposes: to protect endangered big-game species and to protect the environment in which they reside. Both parks employ the same total prohibition on wood collection, a prohibition that runs counter to both customary norms[6] and the self-interest of many in the region. Residents have been collecting wood from what is now park area for centuries, if not millennia—and refraining from doing so means that they have difficulty cooking and keeping warm during the winter.

Distributing legal knowledge is challenging on both sides of the border. Implementation budgets are limited and do not allow for large-scale awareness-raising campaigns. Individuals generally lack the means to read the law themselves or to acquire knowledge from experts. The states on either side of the border do not consistently punish wood collection, behavior that would communicate information about this legal norm to the populations targeted by it. Agents of the Indian and Nepali states are charged with enforcement across thousands of square kilometers of jungle augmented with only minimal infrastructure. Whether because of the difficult terrain, lack of will, poor training, or corruption, these agents, regardless of the state that employs them, often behave inconsistently when enforcing wood-taking prohibitions.

Some individuals living in this area have, however, been exposed to an implementation strategy that embodies regulatory pragmatism. In Nepal, the state has delegated management of some government-owned forest land just outside Chitwan to "User Groups," groups of citizens who come forward with an approvable plan to sustainably manage nearby forest resources. Nepal's Community Forestry Program allows citizens to create consistency where the state struggles to do so, thus communicating legal norms more effectively than that state might do on its own. The contrast between the state's inconsistent enforcement of wood collection prohibitions in Chitwan, where wood collection is illegal, and the consistent, penalty-free access to wood in Community Forests, where wood collection is allowed, may allow target populations to develop more accurate understandings of the law. This strategy should, at least *ex ante*, foster accurate legal knowledge. India, in contrast, has used a more traditional, deterrence-based approach. I exploit this variation in policy implementation strategy to discern whether policies consistent with regulatory pragmatism can improve legal knowledge and lead to higher compliance rates.

It is important to note at the outset that the research presented in this book flows from a least favorable case research design; as such, I examine only one case in geographic terms: the cross-border region of India and Nepal that I describe above. I selected Chitwan and Valmiki and *not* other parks in India and Nepal because of the border that runs through them, providing methodological traction (see Dunning 2012). With the culture, income, and education of ordinary individuals being similar across this region, I was not forced to control for these potentially important causal variables.[7] I did, however, measure each of these variables in order to be reasonably confident that cross-border differences in compliance stem from variation in the independent variables I measure and discuss in the third chapter of this book.

It is also important to note at the outset that the conservation case at the heart of this book could be anomalous. To deal with this concern and to explore regulatory pragmatism more deeply, I introduce two additional "shadow" cases in Chapter 7 that are drawn from different layers of Indian and Nepali society: businesses and organizations. The first involves compliance with teacher-student ratio regulations in private schools, while the second involves compliance with child labor regulations in brick kilns. These shadow cases are drawn from a similar location to the conservation case, but also provide an opportunity to observe the effects of varied state behavior. Education and brick manufacturing are present on both sides of the border and are economically important. In addition, the states on both sides of the border use regulations governing these activities to try to change behaviors that are perceived to be harmful. Further, the behavior required by law in each case stands in contrast to social practice and to self-interest. Most important, the efforts made by the Indian and Nepali states vary distinctly with respect to the implementation of teacher-student ratio regulations in schools, but not with respect to child labor in brick kilns. This allows me to determine whether strategies consistent with regulatory pragmatism are capable of fostering accurate legal knowledge and compliance across multiple regulatory contexts. Collecting data on the compliance behavior of two additional commonly regulated target populations allows me to provide deeper analysis of the conditions under which coercively weak states are nevertheless able to generate compliance.

Summary of Findings

I generally find support for four important compliance-related relationships. The first runs between consistent state action and accurate legal knowledge; the second runs between accurate legal understandings and compliance; and the third runs between poverty and non-compliance. I also find that, in the absence of consistent state action or when large-scale poverty may lead to significant non-compliance, a fourth relationship is important: the positive relationship between regulatory pragmatism and compliance. I examine each of these relationships briefly below and in individual chapters later in the book.

The first relationship (see Figure 1.3), between consistent state action and accurate legal understandings, is perhaps the most crucial in the chain and the one most often absent when the state is generally weak. In the absence of accurate information, individuals and entities struggle to shift from cultural norms to legal norms, or from old legal norms to new ones, even if they are

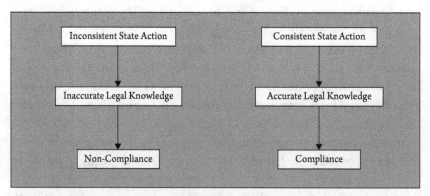

Figure 1.3 Relationships between Consistency of State Action, Accuracy of Legal Knowledge, and Compliance

motivated to comply with government-propounded rules and regulations. I found this to be particularly true in a context in which the availability of information about the law is low, due either to illiteracy or to poor communication of legal or regulatory norms on the state's behalf. Interestingly, in such a context, individuals still look to the state, even if only observationally, when forming legal understandings. In situations in which the state has behaved consistently—regularly and visibly punishing a particular illegal behavior—target populations observe the state's actions and infer that punished behavior is illegal. However, when the state behaves inconsistently, target populations receive mixed messages, depending upon what they observed and what those whom they know observe. For instance, those who knew someone who took a particular action and was punished believed that behavior to be illegal, while those who knew someone who took the same action and was not punished believed that behavior to be legal. The Indian and Nepali states, at least in the region in which I conducted my research, suffer from principal-agent problems and tend to behave inconsistently. It is, therefore, not surprising that my respondents' legal understandings were often inaccurate.

As illustrated in Figure 1.4, inconsistent state action and the resulting absence of accurate legal knowledge can be overcome, however, if states let regulatory pragmatism guide their legal design and implementation strategies. I examine two such strategies: delegated enforcement and information dissemination through local leaders. With respect to the first, I was able to demonstrate that delegated enforcement plays an important role in fostering accurate legal knowledge. The Nepali state was consistent in its noninterference in delegated Community Forest management, allowing many of those living near these areas of self-regulation to develop the understanding that taking wood from Community Forests is legal, while taking wood from Chitwan National Park is illegal. In particular, those with Community Forest access were able to observe the contrast between the state's consistent non-interference in Community Forests and inconsistent enforcement of wood-taking prohibitions in the National Park. Observation of this contrast helps those who have Community Forest access to arrive at more accurate legal understandings than their counterparts who lack access. Of those who report having access to a Community Forest, 74.6 percent hold an accurate understanding of the wood-taking prohibitions in place in Chitwan National Park; the same number amongst those who do not have access to a Community Forest is 53.2 percent.

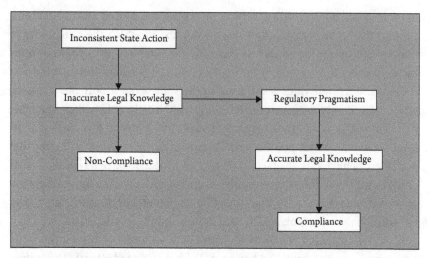

Figure 1.4 Role of Regulatory Pragmatism in Altering the Relationship between Inconsistent State Action, Inaccurate Legal Knowledge, and Non-Compliance

A similar pattern has developed in the private schools case in India. While the District Education Officers in both India and Nepal are largely absent and only occasionally engage in enforcement action, delegated enforcement is in place in India. The 2009 Right to Education Act in India empowers parents to remove their children from schools that they believe are performing poorly by allowing parents to take state funding with them to whichever school, public or private, their children ultimately attend. It is essentially a voucher program. And school administrators on the Indian side of the border have generally taken note. When asked whether a parent would remove a student from his or her school if the teacher-student ratio exceeded legal limits, 22.2 percent of administrators in India stated that parents "sometimes" do so and another 19.4 percent stated that parents "often" do so. Across the border in Nepal, 33.3 percent of administrators stated that parents "sometimes" do so and no administrator stated that parents "often" do so. In other words, the enforcement of teacher-student ratio regulations in India, even if achieved via delegation, is more consistent than that in Nepal. And, importantly, delegated enforcement is associated with more administrators holding accurate legal understandings. I find that 83.3 percent of private school administrators in India hold accurate legal understandings of the maximum teacher-student ratio proscribed by law, while only 59.0 percent of their counterparts in Nepal hold the same.

My experimental findings with respect to information dissemination through local leaders are similar. The data indicate that local leaders, who often act as a conduit for communication from the state and/or local bureaucrats, are an important vector for legal knowledge. This is consistent with the psychology literature that indicates that length of relationship is predictive of whether individuals will find a source of information trustworthy (Levin, Whitener & Cross 2006). More specifically, I find no significant differences in terms of the pre- and post-treatment accuracy of legal understanding in either of the control of "flier" villages. However, in the "local leader" village, there was a significant difference (p = 0.017). Before my intervention, about 58.8 percent of my semi-random sample of villagers knew that collecting wood in Chitwan is illegal. After my intervention, this number jumped to 78.7 percent, suggesting that local leaders can be effective conduits for Accurate Legal Knowledge. Local leaders are widely believed to be an accurate source of information about the state. Thus, what they say matters and villagers update their understandings of the law accordingly, with many seemingly privileging this information over both firsthand observation and information received from other sources like printed materials or neighbors, family, and friends. As with my findings with respect to delegated enforcement, these findings regarding information dissemination through local leaders suggest that even a coercively weak state, so long as it employs regulatory pragmatism when considering how to disseminate information about the law, may be able to achieve accurate legal understandings.

The accuracy of the legal understandings that target populations hold are important and relate to the second relationship I mention above, the one between legal knowledge and compliance. In the conservation case, as well as in my two shadow cases, when I subset by accurate legal understanding, I find significant differences in compliance behavior. In the conservation case, those who hold accurate legal understandings, on either side of the border, report behavior consistent with compliance 70.2 percent of the time. Meanwhile, those of their counterparts who hold inaccurate legal understandings comply 39.1 percent of the time. In the private schools these numbers are 72.5 percent and 30.8 percent; and in the brick kilns, they are 70.6 percent and 43.8 percent. Yet members of these subsets are not differentially motivated toward compliance. I find no significant differences across groups in terms of either fear of being punished or the felt sense of duty to obey the law. This suggests that many of those who are not complying are doing so unintentionally—many of them likely believe they are complying—and that, if those holding inaccurate understandings of the law were provided with accurate information, quite a few of them would be motivated to alter their behavior in the direction of compliance.

But my data suggest that not all of them would ultimately comply. Even those who hold accurate legal understandings and report being motivated, by either fear or duty, to comply with the law, sometimes fail to comply. This begs the question of whether something else is going on or whether my respondents were simply being disingenuous about their motivations when responding to survey questions. I am confident it is the former. Unlike their counterparts in developed countries, many of my respondents must overcome a difficult hurdle in order to comply with the regulations I examine: the cost of compliance. Each of the regulations I examine imposes a cost on its target population, and many of my respondents are extremely cost-sensitive. Most of them live below the poverty line and, when a regulation imposes a cost, many of those who cannot afford such a cost, even if aware of the particular regulation and otherwise motivated to comply with it, will choose satisfaction of their basic needs—fuel for cooking and heating in the conservation case—over compliance. When I subset my conservation case respondents into two groups, those living above the poverty line and those living below it, I find significant compliance differences. Compliance among the former is 64 percent, while among the latter it is 49 percent.[8] The same basic relationship exists among respondents in brick kilns and schools facing tight margins, though, interestingly, I find that the elite schools, those that can easily afford to comply with teacher-student ratio regulations, are rarely in compliance, a fact I will discuss later in terms of the limitations of accurate legal understandings. But the broader point remains: poverty, something that is often endemic in places where the state is generally weak, can drive individuals who are aware of the law and otherwise motivated to comply with it towards non-compliance.

Thus, if one is trying to regulate in areas plagued by poverty and one wants individuals to comply with laws that impose costs on them, one has to lower the cost of compliance to one that the poor can bear. This is exactly what regulatory pragmatism demands, and it is also precisely what Nepal's Community Forests do. They provide those who have access to them with an alternative source of fuelwood, thus allowing these individuals to both comply and meet their basic needs. I find that when I subset my data by "access to a Community Forest," respondents living below the poverty line are much more likely to be in compliance than their counterparts without such access: 79 percent vs. 39 percent. This is fascinating because a second regulation that is seemingly orthogonal to the wood-taking prohibition in place in Chitwan National Park, one which permits conduct that is prohibited in the park, appears to be aiding compliance with wood-taking prohibitions in the park. It also suggests, as illustrated in Figure 1.5, that regulatory design and implementation strategies that are consistent with regulatory pragmatism— ones that take care to lower the cost of compliance for those who can least afford it—can result in significantly higher compliance rates than can regulations that simply impose a cost.

While staying within the border region, I also examined—as mentioned above—two additional types of behavior in terms of regulatory subject-matter and target population: (1) compliance with teacher-student ratio regulations in private schools; and (2) compliance with child labor regulations in brick kilns. These "shadow cases" help to illuminate one of the more interesting findings of this book: that when the coercive capacity of the state is weak, but the social fabric at the local level is strong, states can delegate enforcement to interested parties, those who have both an incentive to get involved and act according to law, and achieve significantly higher rates of compliance. In the conservation case, the Nepali government adopted a policy that fosters accurate legal knowledge through the delegation of regulatory responsibility to User Groups that then manage Community Forests.

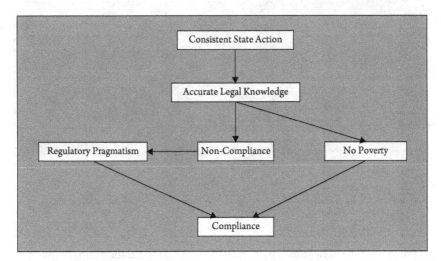

Figure 1.5 Role of Regulatory Pragmatism in Altering the Relationships between Accurate Legal Knowledge, Poverty, and Non-Compliance

User Group members have reason to get involved because they are able to secure access to an important resource and are continually incentivized to comply with the law and encourage others to do so by the threat that the state could reassert its right to the land on which the Community Forest is located. In the schools case, it is the Indian government that delegated enforcement. The 2009 Right to Education Act in India allows individuals (parents) to take an active role in enforcing teacher-student ratio regulations by removing or threatening to remove their students from schools with high ratios and send them to presumably better schools with lower ratios. Meanwhile, in the brick kilns case, neither government has done much to enforce child labor regulations, nor have they adopted strategies consistent with regulatory pragmatism.[9] We should therefore expect to find little cross-border variation in both consistency of enforcement and rates of compliance. Exploring these shadow cases allowed me to confirm my findings regarding regulatory pragmatism and accurate legal knowledge from the conservation case.

When looked at together, the data indicate that coercively weak states *can* generate compliant behavior so long as they can: (1) substantially increase the number of individuals who hold accurate legal understandings; and (2) lower the cost of compliance for those who will be forced to choose between complying with the law and meeting their own basic needs. This is consistent with the integrated set of relationships indicated in Figure 1.6. My findings also

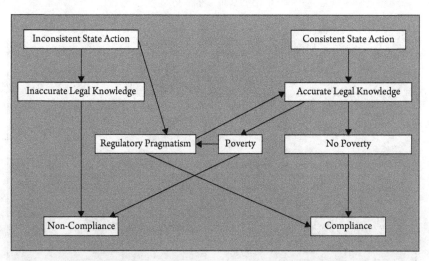

Figure 1.6 Role of Regulatory Pragmatism in Altering Relationships between Consistency of State Action, Accuracy of Legal Knowledge, Poverty, and Compliance

suggest that, when principal-agent problems result in inconsistent state action, states can still achieve accurate legal knowledge (and compliance) if they allow regulatory pragmatism to guide their actions: delegated enforcement and information dissemination through local leaders are just two examples of implementation strategies that can accomplish this goal. This information not only adds to the existing academic understanding of compliance by exploring the circumstances under which it can be brought about in areas generally associated with limited state capacity, it also goes a long way toward providing information to governments and non-state actors in developing and/or coercively weak states about strategies they can adopt to foster compliance, even if they cannot muster the capacity necessary to do so by force.

Organization of the Book

This book is organized as follows. After this introductory chapter, I turn, in Chapter 2, to the long intellectual lineage of pragmatism, focusing in particular on legal pragmatism, before developing the concept of regulatory pragmatism.

In Chapter 3, I describe research design and methodology. I provide some historical and anthropological background on the region in which I conducted this research and substantiate the manner in which the border was delineated. I then turn to a thorough explication of my hypotheses and specific information about data collection and analysis.

In Chapter 4, I present descriptive findings for the three different regulatory projects I explore throughout the rest of the book: (1) wood-collection prohibitions in national parks; (2) teacher-student ratio regulation in private schools; and (3) child labor law, as applied at brick kilns. As the region in which the data were collected is understudied, I present more data than is strictly necessary for an understanding of the trends discussed in this book.

In Chapter 5, I examine the relationship between consistent state regulatory action and the accuracy of individually held legal understandings in the region surrounding Chitwan and Valmiki National Parks. I then turn to the positive externalities associated with accurate legal knowledge, demonstrating that knowledge of the law, so long as it is accurate, is a useful predictor of compliance with wood-taking prohibitions.

In Chapter 6, I explore two distinct regulatory strategies that a pragmatic state can use to foster accurate legal knowledge even if it cannot behave consistently itself. In particular, I examine the roles of delegated enforcement and information dissemination through local leaders in fostering accurate legal knowledge, even when state enforcement capacity is low. I also examine a second compliance barrier, poverty-driven non-compliance. This phenomenon occurs when those who have accurate legal understandings and are otherwise motivated to comply with the law are forced by their economic circumstances and the high cost of compliance to continue their illegal behavior. I then demonstrate how states, guided by regulatory pragmatism, can lower the cost of compliance for the poor and allow these individuals to behave in a manner that is consistent with the accuracy of their legal understandings and their motivation to comply with the law.

In Chapter 7, I turn to my shadow cases, teacher-student ratio regulations governing private schools and child labor regulations in brick kilns. In the former, I demonstrate that the 2009 Right to Education Act effectively delegates enforcement to parents of enrolled children, much as with Community Forest management in the conservation case, and this allows for consistent enforcement by non-state actors. This regularity, in turn, fosters both more accurate legal understandings among administrators and higher observed rates of compliance. After further developing the concept of delegated enforcement in dialogue with evidence from the conservation case, I explore its limits. On both sides of the border, the schools with the most resources are the least likely to be compliant. Here I argue that while poverty-driven non-compliance, akin to that seen in the conservation case, continues to drive the behavior of administrators at the poorest schools. Administrators at schools with the most resources behave differently. They remain unconcerned about enforcement of any variety and also believe that their schools are above the law due to the high-quality education they provide. In other words, administrators at these schools feel neither a sense of fear nor a sense of duty, and as a result, it is hardly surprising that their schools are non-compliant. Finally, I examine compliance with child labor law in brick kilns. Here I argue that inconsistent state action on both sides of the border has led to widespread misunderstandings of the law and that, as a result, non-compliance is common among those with inaccurate information. Those who do have accurate information and are motivated to comply often do so, but, as with the poor in the conservation case, brick kiln managers who face tight margins engage in poverty-driven non-compliance, whereas their counterparts, at more economically viable kilns, do just the opposite.

Finally, in Chapter 8, I attempt to tie all three cases together, offering my thoughts about observed variation and associated effects across all of them. I then explore the implications of these findings for other countries and regions and provide some concluding remarks focused on important areas of future research.

2

From James to Regulatory Pragmatism

The concept at the core of this book is *regulatory pragmatism*: a flexible—rather than legally doctrinaire or dogmatic—approach to the design and implementation of a regulatory system that is specifically adapted to regulatory context. Pragmatic regulatory approaches prize effectiveness and durability over other goals and account for on-the-ground realities of state capacity, the irregular behavior of state agents, and the needs of target populations. It is important to note up front, for the sake of conceptual clarity, that those deterrence-based regulatory programs that overcome no known compliance barrier and happen to be effective do not represent pragmatic regulatory strategies; instead, they embody a default approach to regulation.

The law has long been a province of absolutes and ideals. Against that backdrop, regulatory pragmatism suggests a middle path that is, nevertheless, consistent with philosophical and theoretical developments across a variety of different fields. It is not so much a break with the past as an extension of it. William James's (1907) work on pragmatism represents a point of origin for the conceptual lineage of regulatory pragmatism.[1] The concept is also in keeping with the legal pragmatists of the late twentieth century. In this chapter, I will review these authors' contributions before moving on to a detailed theoretical mapping of regulatory pragmatism itself.

Pragmatism

Descended etymologically from the Greek word *pragma*, for action, pragmatism, according to William James (1906), is a method of settling metaphysical disputes that might otherwise be interminable. James's work on pragmatism, as revealed in his famous series of seven lectures, is even pragmatic itself. He starts by recognizing a particular problem in the first of his lectures: that the world of philosophy is "simple, clean and noble," while the world of "concrete personal experiences to which the street belongs is multitudinous beyond imagination, tangled, muddy, painful and perplexed"

Capacity beyond Coercion. Susan L. Ostermann, Oxford University Press. © Oxford University Press 2023.
DOI: 10.1093/oso/9780197661116.003.0002

(James 1906: 17–18). And, yet, the two must relate to one another if philosophy is to be anything other than refined artifice. Pragmatism is James's resolution of this problem: the articulation of a philosophical position that is in "cordial [] relation with facts" (James 1906: 26). In short, an approach that considers context to have some import, some value.

Pragmatism as a concept, according to James, was nothing new. Aristotle, Locke, Berkeley, and Hume all used it—they just didn't have a name for it. In later lectures, James goes on to articulate what he calls "the pragmatic method": "a method of settling metaphysical disputes that otherwise might be interminable" (James 1906: 28). Doing so involved an "attitude of looking away from first things, principles, 'categories,' supposed necessities; and of looking towards last things, fruits, consequences, facts" (James 1906: 32). It also involved an instrumental conception of truth, as first articulated by Schiller and Dewey: the notion that our ideas are true only to the extent that they work in the real world. The result was a concept that was "completely genial" (James 1906: 44). Pragmatism, according to James, "will entertain any hypothesis, she will consider any evidence."

By nature, then, pragmatism takes alternate perspectives seriously. While rationalists insist upon a single, abstract truth, James argues that, for pragmatists, "our duty to agree with reality is . . . grounded in a perfect jungle of concrete expediences" (James 1906: 111). Moreover, the manner in which we come to truth, often through scientific inquiry or rational thought predicated on known fact, allows for multiple reasonable conclusions to be drawn. As James explains, "sometimes alternative theoretic formulas are equally compatible with all the truths we know, and then we choose between them for subjective reasons" (James 1906: 104). Truth here matches reality, which is how we know truth when we see it, even if different individuals hold different ideas of what is true. This does not take James into a fully subjective conception of reality, however. "Truth with a big T," James writes, "and in the singular, claims abstractly to be recognized, of course; but concrete truths in the plural need to be recognized only when their recognition is expedient." Put differently, we must, of course, seek a singular truth, but if concrete truths help us to navigate the world as we do so, pragmatism suggests we should allow them to.

James also goes on at length, across several of his lectures, about the problematic nature of using any particular foundation when seeking truth. As James demonstrates, if we are to choose among various approaches, we need criteria, but these criteria do not produce the same answer across a variety of different fact patterns or "spheres of life." As James explains:

There is no ringing conclusion possible when we compare these types of thinking, with a view to telling which is the more absolutely true. Their naturalness, their intellectual economy, their fruitfulness for practice, all start up as distinct tests of their veracity, and as a result we get confused. Common sense is better for one sphere of life, science for another, philosophic criticism for a third; but whether either be truer absolutely, Heaven only knows. (James 1906: 93)

While seemingly admitting that a single truth may be knowable to God, James also argues that mere mortals struggle to determine which approach is best. The same criteria suggest that one approach is better in one set of circumstances, but worse under a different set of constraints. "There is no simple test available for adjudicating offhand between the divers types of thought that claim to possess it" (James 1906: 93). Indeed, the criteria themselves and the circumstances to which they are applied determine the answer. In light of this, James finds pragmatism to be the most reasonable way forward.

Legal Pragmatism

Since James, pragmatism has made inroads across a variety of fields, including in legal theory and practice. The classical, formal view of the law emphasizes argument by analogy and the need for judges to follow an abstract and consistent jurisprudence. In particular, "all versions of formalism have in common an insistence that certain specifically legal virtues be honored when they compete with substantive considerations of fairness and utility" (Grey 2003). *Legal pragmatism*, in contrast, and especially the recusant variety described by Posner (and by Grey), emphasizes the need to include a more diverse set of data and claims throughout the legal process. Legal pragmatists like Dewey, Grey, Farber, Posner, Radin, and Sullivan emphasize context as well as law's instrumentality and subjectivity.

For the legal pragmatist, all legal issues are grounded in a specific context, whether those attempting to resolve them realize it or not. The "contextualist thesis," as described by Grey (2014), is the simple "idea that thought is essentially embedded in a context of social practice." It involves the recognition that law is "contingent not just upon the acts of legislatures or other authoritative entities, but also upon the surrounding social context, the content of an entire form of life" (Radin 1989). Legal thought, say the legal pragmatists, is no different, even if legal formalists choose to pretend otherwise. Legal thought must necessarily come from somewhere and legal pragmatists suggest that the formalists, whose epistemology leans heavily on philosophy for credence, are denying the role that contextual experience played in the development of particular philosophical traditions. By adhering to this "myth" of pure thought, completely untouched by context, formalists were in danger of being theoretically wrong, say the legal pragmatists, but perhaps more important, empirically wrong. As Posner (1995) explains, avoiding context, as legal theorists and some practitioners had so long done, "disconnects the whirring machinery of philosophical abstraction from the practical business of governing our lives and our societies." Indeed, Dewey (1924) , writing much earlier than Posner, argued that the "infiltration into law of a more experimental and flexible logic is a social as well as an intellectual need," and that general rules and principles should be treated as "working hypotheses, needing to be constantly tested by the way in which they work out in application to concrete situations." The implication here is that judges were sometimes getting it "wrong"; formalist legal theory, no matter how beautifully and carefully constructed, did not always deliver justice. The contextualist thesis that legal pragmatists have sought to advance suggests that theory and practice should be brought into dialogue with one another, that theory should inform practice, and vice versa. Cold abstraction in law, they argue, a discipline that necessarily involves public interaction, can insulate from the law from critique, but it can also undermine the legitimacy and social underpinnings of rule of law itself.

In addition to their focus on context, legal pragmatists, often borrowing from the legal realist tradition, tend to emphasize the instrumental nature of the law. As Farber (1988) argues: "Too often, judges seem unconcerned about the societal effects of constitutional rules." After all, the state and all those individuals and entities that comprise it make law, at least in part, to change behavior. Judges, at least in a common law system, also make law, and to believe they have no agenda whatsoever is to deny a great body of evidence that suggests the opposite. In his 2003 work on the subject, Grey borrows from policy jurisprudence and explains that "law [i]s a means to social ends, the fulfillment and the accommodation of the interests of those the law is meant to serve. Interests give rise to policies, which are balanced against each other in the formulation of legal rules, standards and principles. Interpretation of legal enactments tends to be purposive, with an eye on the relevant interests and policies, rather than confined to plain meaning." Sullivan (2007) extends this logic even to the special case of rights—legal instruments demanded by society and acquiesced to by the state: "rights must be understood pragmatically, that is as self-conscious, social efforts to foster individual growth. As such, rights are both means and ends. They are means in that they are tools by which a society protects its citizens against unwarranted interference from the state or tyrannical majorities. As a proper result of legislation, rights are also ends to be defended as such." These legal pragmatists and others suggest that—in contrast with the abstract accounts provided by philosophers and legal formalists who seemingly see the law as existing in a vacuum—law is created by people for particular ends and that recognition of this fact is important for the resolution of legal disputes. Radin even takes the instrumental aspects of legal pragmatism one step further by articulating how pragmatic critical practitioners might contribute by showing how other "analysts seem either not to notice or not to care that the 'political' processes" they cast aside as "obstreperous value issues (including issues of justice in distribution)" may actually be quite central. The implication here is that all practitioners within the legal system, even scholars, can be pragmatic in their approach and the way in which they do so is by recognizing the instrumental nature of law in their thinking and work, whatever form that may take (legal brief, judicial decision, or journal article).

Given the emphasis legal pragmatists place on context, it should not be surprising that most also tend to highlight the unavoidable presence, when attempting to resolve legal issues, of alternate perspectives. Farber, in his 1988 piece "Legal Pragmatism and the Constitution," identifies the nature of the problem and the pragmatist solution quite succinctly: "Foundationalist analysis supposes that the genuine conflicts that underlie many constitutional cases will dissolve. Pragmatism, however, acknowledges that there are real conflicts that have to be squarely confronted rather than finessed." While limiting himself to the case of the United States, Posner (2005) takes Farber's line of thinking one step further, arguing that diversity of thought and perspective makes pragmatism unavoidable. "[I]n twenty-first-century America there is no alternative to legal pragmatism. The nation contains such a diversity of moral and political thinking that the judiciary, if it is to retain its effectiveness, its legitimacy, *has* to be heterogenous; and the members of a heterogeneous judicial community are not going to subscribe to a common set of moral and political dogmas that would make their decisionmaking determinate." Meanwhile, Radin once again includes in the resolution of legal issues scholars grappling with them outside of the court-room. Writing about the role of legal pragmatists as scholars who provide a critical perspective, Radin explains that "[f]or purposes of critical insight and incision, the field of legal thought contains-arguably-not one norma-tivity, but many normativities. The styles of scholarly activity that currently and colloquially fall under the heading of normative legal thought are diverse and in some respects incompatible" (Radin 1991). Thus, the consensus we get from the legal pragmatists on this particular aspect of the theory is quite clear. Legal pragmatism acknowledges, as pragmatism did before it, that rea-sonable minds, developed within different contexts (or similar ones), can differ on what the law is, what behavior constitutes compliance, what the law does, how the law is practiced, and even on what the law should be. The em-phasis of the legal pragmatist, therefore, must be placed on "reasonableness," as Posner (2005) explains, as a means by which legal issues can, nevertheless, be resolved.

While legal pragmatists do place emphasis on the need for reasoned judg-ment when resolving legal issues, they also tend to acknowledge the prob-lematic nature of utilizing any particular foundation for their legal reasoning. This approach, of course, stands in stark contrast to that of the rest of the legal academic establishment, which has largely emphasized grand theory and the need for a single explanation for the behavior of legal actors, judges in particular. Grey (2003), writing about Langdell, the first dean of Harvard Law School, and the "legal scientist" project, recognized the problem of using grand theory to explain the functioning of the law. Langdell and his compatriots were attempting to create a single theory that was comprehen-sive, complete, formal, conceptually ordered, and broadly acceptable, but, as Grey writes: "All this was aspiration; the actual state of the common law was such as to leave the legal scientists a great deal to do. Judges often did not accurately state the rules on which they decided cases. Further, the basic principles had not been properly formulated and arranged. The law consisted of a mass of haphazardly arranged cases: a 'chaos with a full index.'" Farber (1988), writing about constitutional law, explains the legal pragmatist posi-tion quite bluntly:

If judges needed a sound theoretical foundation before proceeding, *Marbury v. Madison* would still be on the Supreme Court docket, having been reargued at the beginning of each term but never actually decided.

Presumably, the rest of the Court's constitutional docket of the last century would be on the weekly conference list, with the notation "held pending decision in *Marbury v. Madison*." In reality, of course, the Court's need to decide actual cases has prevailed over any desire for theoretical justification. . . . Constitutional law needs no grand theoretical foundation. None is likely ever to be forthcoming, and none is desirable. Instead, legal pragmatism is a sufficient basis for constitutional law.

As Farber seems to suggest, if judges are pragmatic in action and, over time, eschew conformity to any particular line of legal reasoning or jurisprudence, those seeking to explain the functioning of legal systems should not contort their theories to encompass the full range of observed behavior. Radin (1991) echoes Farber's sentiments and goes one step further, explaining that: "In the pragmatic moment of critical practice, one may understand the structural weakness of a target discourse not as its already fatal flaw, but as its working interface with surrounding cultural dispositions." In other words, in the legal pragmatists' world, structural weakness is inherent and to be expected of any grand theory, particularly when such a theory is applied in new contexts and is met with alternative perspectives. Moreover, these so-called weaknesses are not essentially problematic; they actually help chart the boundaries of different modes of thinking.

Following in the footsteps and intellectual tradition of Peirce, James, Rorty, etc., the legal pragmatists have—in fits and starts—made a space for pragmatism in the legal world. Previously a sphere reserved for grand theory and absolutes, the law did not exactly welcome pragmatism. Instead, the legal pragmatists had to fight to be taken seriously. Over time, however, the intellectual purchase of their arguments, particularly in terms of their explanatory power, demanded attention and careful consideration. Judges *do* appear to behave in ways that fit the pragmatic model. Arguably, they are not the only legal actors who do so.

Regulatory Pragmatism

Regulatory pragmatism is an extension of legal pragmatism's line of reasoning *beyond* the judge's chambers. Judges, after all, are not the only actors empowered to shape the law. After a law has been passed, bureaucrats often have substantial discretion to choose the character of associated regulations: how both executive and legislative prerogatives are accomplished. Sometimes this involves choices about the penalties associated with proscribed behavior; other times bureaucrats decide what resources will be used to implement a particular regulatory project. To be sure, bureaucratic discretion is more limited than that of judges, who are, in most cases, considered independent and not subject to executive or legislative oversight. Bureaucrats cannot change the law, but they can dramatically alter how the implementation of a particular regulation looks and feels on the ground. Frontline bureaucrats also have quite a bit of discretion, to issue a citation for a regulatory violation or not, but this type of discretion is distinct from that discussed in this chapter and throughout the rest of this book. Indeed, regulatory pragmatism is largely practiced by higher-level bureaucratic officers who make *systemic* choices about how a particular regulatory project will be handled by the administration.

When a bureaucrat or group of bureaucrats is exercising this latter, systemic type of discretion, shaping the implementation of a regulatory project, he or she or they are, *functionally*, the state. How they choose to accomplish a state prerogative is how the state will act, unless they are later overridden by the legislature or the executive. This does not mean that these bureaucrats are all powerful. Quite the opposite. They are limited by the capabilities and power of other aspects of the state. If they choose to focus on enforcement of a particular aspect of a larger regulatory project— let's say securing access for disabled persons to restaurants, as opposed to workplaces or housing or other stores—they do not do so in a vacuum. They must have the staff necessary to accomplish this goal. Not only must they have bodies on the ground, these frontline bureaucrats must be competent and effectively trained; they must also faithfully carry out orders from their higher-ups. Finally, members of the public or other members of the administration may not approve of this choice and apply pressure in order to change the focus of enforcement to other tasks, regardless of whether the budget or staffing are adequate to accomplish everything the state has said—through its regulations—that it will do. Imagine for a second that the state in this case is a strong, Weberian one, that monopolizes force over its territory and has limitless resources, competent staff, etc. Under such circumstances, the bureaucrat or bureaucrats in charge of ensuring equal access for disabled persons to public spaces can readily ensure compliance with law by using or threatening to use force against anyone or anything that denies access.

But what happens when the coercive apparatus of the state is weak or poorly formed, as is the case in many parts of the developing world and even in isolated pockets of the developed world as well? In many such cases the state, through the choices made by its bureaucrats, will forge ahead anyway, attempting under-resourced enforcement. Under these circumstances, and when the bureaucracy is nevertheless well disciplined, the most likely outcome is that bureaucrats will simply fail to detect all violations. If the bureaucracy is instead poorly trained, it may detect the wrong violations or punish the wrong actors. If the bureaucracy is corrupt, it will detect quite a few violations, but only enforce the law when it is in the interests of individual bureaucrats or small groups of aligned bureaucrats to do so. And, in each of these cases, the errant or poor behavior of state representatives not only serves to undermine the efficacy of a particular state project, it also undercuts rule of law and popular perceptions of the competence of the state itself. Populations targeted for enforcement, be they individuals, corporations, etc., are then less likely to engage in "voluntary compliance." Many academics and practitioners would observe such a self-reinforcing cycle and prescribe "capacity building," seemingly suggesting that the state simply needs to become stronger and then all will work as expected. This is not false, but few states have pulled it off over short- to medium-term time frames. It's also true that those of us in academia have leaned quite heavily and for quite some time on the coercive apparatus of the state when thinking and writing about state capacity. We have only learned to recognize state capacity when we see enforcement, so we often call states that do not appear to be actively enforcing their own regulations weak.

It may be time, however, to recognize other markers of state capacity and other means of securing compliance with regulations. While bureaucrats in some weak states recognize the weakness of the state's coercive apparatus and plow ahead with traditional enforcement-based implementation strategies anyway, as described above, others sometimes come up with different, more creative ways of achieving the state's goals. For instance, if a state has a largely poor population spread over a territory with wildly different climate, geography, etc., and wants to get students into the classroom, what can it do? Many states might make school attendance mandatory and attempt enforcement, but doing so is often colossally expensive. There is another path, however. If a state has neither the resources nor the personnel to enforce a mandatory school attendance policy, it can instead provide, as the Indian government does, an inducement to get many students to school: a free midday meal. The meal does have a cost, but it is far less than what it would cost to send state representatives out to individual homes across all of India and demand that children go to school, something that it might have to do repeatedly for some children, given their poverty and the relative benefits of child labor. The meal, in contrast, is a cheap and durable draw that, incidentally, fosters a positive relationship with the state rather than a negative one. Such an approach is qualitatively different from the shifts in enforcement style described by Kagan & Scholz (1984) or by Parker & Nielsen (2011), in particular because it is not *enforcement*-based. Its success also comes from a different kind of state capacity, one that does not rely on coercion.

When bureaucrats know that the state will struggle with traditional enforcement and compensate for this weakness in practical ways that further state prerogatives, they are behaving much like the judges that the legal pragmatists write about. They are engaging in *regulatory* pragmatism. Borrowing from the core aspects of legal pragmatism discussed above, we can expect that bureaucrats engaging in regulatory pragmatism will do the following: (1) recognize that the regulatory system must operate in specific contexts and, if it is to be effective, respond to on-the-ground challenges; (2) recognize that regulation is instrumental and that its purpose is to produce particular outcomes; (3) account for alternative perspectives, including those of individuals who believe regulations should be different; and (4) design implementation strategies for effectiveness rather than consistency with a particular theory or set of foundations.

But what might a pragmatic regulatory strategy look like in practice?

In the United States, regulatory pragmatism is behind income tax withholding requirements and the use of grandfather clauses for new regulations (Huber 2011). Regulatory pragmatism is absent from those approaches that largely rely on threat of legal sanction and fail to design for context. Examples of this latter category might include rules that were made for conditions that no longer exist, such as the persistence of 55 mph speed limits on rural interstate highways in the United States long after the oil crisis ended and despite dramatic improvements in highway and vehicle safety (Keeler 1994). It might also include regulations that require individuals to desist from activities necessary to their basic survival (Ostermann 2016).

For a more extended look at a pragmatic regulatory strategy, consider cap-and-trade schemes—as opposed to strict pollution controls—as a means of reducing pollution. Cap-and-trade, so long as it is used where target populations are reasonably sophisticated, is consistent with regulatory pragmatism. It responds to on-the-ground challenges, particularly those from the business community, by allowing those who can most cheaply reduce pollution to do so, while other actors can "pay to pollute." Cap-and-trade recognizes that the law is instrumental and that the end goal is emission reduction, regardless of reduction source. It also accounts for alternative perspectives by allowing those who do not think there should be emission reductions to pay and continue their behavior. Finally, cap-and-trade is designed for effectiveness, in that it provides individuals or entities that might not comply with a relatively affordable way to keep their behavior within regulatory bounds while also reducing state monitoring expenditures (Schmalensee & Stavins 2017). Under a strict actor-level pollution control regime, there are often regular challenges to the law, both formal (attempts to change it) and informal (willful non-compliance), monitoring costs are higher, and overall reductions in pollution are often not as significant (Hahn & Hester 1989).

A smaller-scale example of pragmatic regulatory behavior can be seen on the cover of this volume. On the left-hand side of the picture one can see the effects of anti-graffiti enforcement in the relatively wealthy city of San Francisco. While it's true that if the state in San Francisco wanted to prioritize enforcing anti-graffiti regulations, it could, even a well-resourced city would struggle to defend devoting the resources necessary to enforce such regulations when far more pressing issues exist and dominate public consciousness. As a result, the city has largely relied on a policy of trying to remove or cover up graffiti, something that is known to reduce further incidents. Recently, however, there has been experimentation with a new approach, which you can see on the right-hand side of the image: covering graffiti-prone surfaces with art.[2] Such an approach responds to context and on-the-ground challenges by forcing graffiti artists to cover up someone else's art with their own, something that many are reticent to do. It recognizes the instrumentality of anti-graffiti regulations and the fact that they are designed to prevent graffiti and not necessarily to keep large urban surfaces as empty canvases. In this same vein, this approach recognizes alternative perspectives, particularly those of individuals and/or groups who prefer a more colorful, art-filled urban landscape. Finally, this particular anti-graffiti approach is designed for effectiveness, in that both the approach and compliance with relevant regulations are relatively low-cost. A particularly pragmatic state might even reach out to previous offenders and offer them the opportunity to be involved in covering graffiti-prone surfaces with works of art.

Clearly there are many possible forms that a pragmatic regulatory strategy might take. In this book, I consider one of the many problems states face, principal-agent problems between itself and some of its bureaucrats, and how pragmatic states respond to this particular problem. One response to principal-agent problems that is already being used by numerous states is to empower diverse, non-traditional actors as "bureaucrat-alternatives." A state that proceeds in this manner must be careful to avoid replacing one principal-agent problem with another and must choose agents whose interests align with or can be made to align with its own, but doing so is feasible. For instance, in the United States, the "private rights of action"—discussed at length in "The Litigation State" (Farhang 2006)—are a paradigmatic example. In conservation, the environment cannot advocate for itself or hire a lawyer and a bureaucracy might not fill that role as effectively (or cheaply) as other actors. A "private right of action" in this context gives lawyers an incentive to act as environmental advocates; if they win, they are paid for time spent. Lawyers rather than bureaucrats become the state's agents and the interests of both are aligned. Regulatory pragmatism is also behind the United States' amber alert system, which crowd-sources information about child abductions. The time and effort required for law enforcement to track down a missing child is enormous and costly. The population at large, however, is well positioned to help and has reason to assist. Few are opposed, ideologically or otherwise, to resolving missing child cases and providing information is easy. Principal-agent problems are, thus, unlikely.

The above-described scenarios are, in many ways, relatively easy cases, however. It is useful, therefore, to consider regulatory pragmatism at its margins. How do we know regulatory pragmatism when we see it? Is the avoidance of traditional enforcement in challenging contexts always pragmatic? Not necessarily. I will elaborate below.

In theory, regulatory pragmatism exists whenever a state considers context, recognizes that law is instrumental, accounts for alternative perspectives, and designs for effectiveness. In an ideal world, we would be able to observe a state's regulatory approach and discern whether it behaved pragmatically in advance of implementation by determining whether its behavior satisfied all four of the required elements. I call this *ex ante* regulatory pragmatism. However, with the possible exception of courts, which regularly publish the reasoning behind their decisions, we rarely have access to the internal deliberations of the government and the thought processes used by decision makers. *Ex ante* regulatory pragmatism is, thus, rarely discernable, except to the most careful and well-connected observers. Given this, it is important to find a way to identify regulatory pragmatism *ex post*.

When we are trying to determine whether regulatory pragmatism has been used in the much more likely *ex post* scenario, additional consideration is required, as seen in Figure 2.1. Compromising on traditional enforcement is only "pragmatic" when a compliance barrier exists, when non-deterrence methods are used, and when the state's original regulatory purpose is achieved. If we, for instance, look at the midday meal program used in India's government schools discussed above, each of these elements is present. The compliance barriers in this case are multiple: poor parents see little benefit in sending their children to school when they could work instead and the government simply does not have the resources to determine which children are not in school and go door-to-door handing out fines or other sanctions, which further harm the population they are trying to help by providing free schooling in the first place. The midday meal program, in contrast, in an inducement rather than a deterrence-based method. Poor students are drawn to school with the offer of free food, something they (and their parents) need and want; threat of sanction is not part of the policy. Finally, the midday meal program, while not 100 percent successful, has resulted in a significant increase in

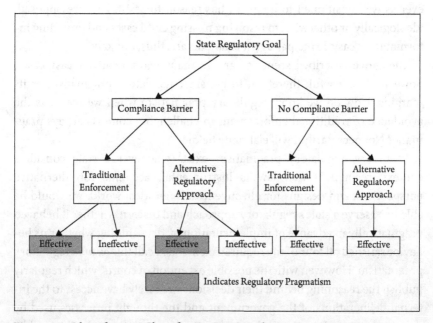

Figure 2.1 Identification Chart for *Ex-Post* Regulatory Pragmatism

school enrollment/attendance (Dreze & Goyal 2003; Afridi 2011; Jayaraman & Simroth 2015). To be sure, anyone who has spent time in rural India knows that some poor students come to school shortly before lunchtime and leave not long afterward, but the habit of going to school has at least been formed and some socialization and, perhaps, learning occur even during this short window. Thus, while imperfect, India's midday meal program has achieved the state's original regulatory purpose, increased school enrollment/attendance, and is a good example of *ex post* regulatory pragmatism.

Relatedly, traditional enforcement in a challenging context that nevertheless works likely also involves regulatory pragmatism, but of a different variety. The pragmatic choice in this latter category is often to forgo traditional enforcement of other regulations. This is something we do see in the developing world from time to time. For instance, in Kathmandu, of late, a surprising number of motorcyclists are complying with helmet laws. Nepalis, for the most part, have not been particularly inclined to wear helmets, even though many are aware that doing so might save their lives. This was reflected, in the past, by flagrant helmet law violations, even in the capital city. What changed? The bureaucracy made enforcing helmet laws a priority, likely at the expense of other law enforcement priorities. Police are now visible at numerous major and minor intersections and can be seen handing out tickets for violations. The police force in Kathmandu has not expanded significantly, so the recent high rates of helmet law compliance have been achieved with traditional methods, but almost certainly at a cost, to the state, and possibly to the public: the traditional enforcement of other laws. In this case the compliance barriers were multiple, including low awareness of helmet laws, a customary norm (of no helmet use) that was in conflict with a legal norm, and very limited state resources for enforcement. The state's chosen strategy overcame these barriers using traditional enforcement, something that we would not ordinarily expect to be effective. The state did manage effectiveness, however, and it did so by prioritizing enforcement in highly visible spaces, which increased awareness of helmet laws, dedicating an unusually large number of police to this task, at least for some time, and, finally, by levying penalties that are stiff enough[3] that many motorcyclists are willing to forgo the customary norm in favor of the legal one, especially in urban areas where the probability of detection was higher. This second form of *ex post* regulatory pragmatism is no less important than the first, but its use is even harder to detect.

Finally, the use of traditional or alternative methods when no known compliance barrier exists is not regulatory pragmatism because, by definition, the state did not have to design for context or around a known compliance barrier. Instead, the state was able to choose a method of convenience, knowing that it would be effective regardless of its choice. A good example of such an approach would be the security measures put into place in the United States and in many other places around the world in the aftermath of 9/11 to prevent air-related terrorism. Air travel is highly regulated to begin with, and it is relatively easy for a competent state and its agents to ensure that certain people, objects, and substances remain off of planes. Access to aircraft was already quite limited. Add to this the fact that the vast majority of people who fly on planes or work with them do not want them to be used for the purposes of terrorism and you have a favorable regulatory environment. Compliance in this case is largely voluntary and detecting non-compliance is, for the most part, a technological issue. Any state that can acquire the necessary technology, competently train agents to use it, and ensure that they do so faithfully should effectively stop all or nearly all air-related terrorism. There is nothing pragmatic about such an approach as there are no true compliance barriers, it makes use of traditional enforcement, largely centered on the detection of possible violations, and seems to have been remarkably effective, especially considering the number of passengers processed and successful flights completed in the time since 9/11.

Having explored a range of different regulatory strategies and where they fit with respect to regulatory pragmatism, it is worth considering what a pragmatic regulatory strategy might look like given the case at hand. In the forested borderlands between India and Nepal, where populations are generally poor, uneducated, and lack access to legal services, where bureaucrats are often poorly trained and principal-agent problems manifest themselves as petty corruption, and where populations largely prefer to avoid the arbitrary and sometimes heavy hand of the state, a pragmatic regulatory strategy might involve a design that will enhance legal knowledge transmission and account for poverty. The first is especially true in those contexts in which legal norms differ from social norms, and the second is important because poverty can make the cost of compliance unattainably high.

Contextualizing Regulatory Pragmatism

Regulatory pragmatism insists that we think about context. When considering pragmatic ways to govern forest areas in South Asia, it is impossible to sidestep the stream of literature that has flowed from Elinor Ostrom's (1990) pathbreaking book *Governing the Commons*. Decentralized forest management (DFM) is one of the dominant mechanism by which governments and climate/environment-focused non-governmental organizations have sought to preserve forest resources (Agrawal et al. 2008).

But what is DFM, exactly? Broadly speaking, it encompasses a variety of different institutional arrangements between citizens/forest users and state. In some cases, tenure rights or property rights are devolved from the state to individuals, usually to those who have traditionally used the forest for their livelihood, customs, etc. In others, these rights are devolved to groups and held collectively. Once again, the groups that receive devolved rights are customarily those who have traditionally had a strong relationship with the forest. The idea behind this transfer of rights from the state to those who make use of the forest is that if these individuals or groups have stable rights to make use of the forest, they will also take responsibility for its care and management.

In theory, DFM is a pill that can cure several diseases at once. It improves forest management by empowering local actors, who are thought to be most connected to their nearby forests and have the best knowledge of local conditions and needs (Van de Sand 1997; Blackman et al. 2017). These local actors are also thought to be close enough to the ground that they can be held accountable by other forest users with relatively minimal top-down oversight at the national or regional level (Vermillion 1997; Ribot 2008; *contra* Koch 2017 and Ribot et al. 2006). Under DCM, the incentives of local actors can be relatively well aligned with those of the state (Barbier & Burgess 2001) and managing forests in this way can achieve state objectives while also lowering costs (Somanathan et al. 2009).

In practice, recent experimental evidence suggests that, while DFM is not a panacea, it is a valuable tool for policymakers trying to achieve both ecological and socioeconomic objectives. A recent special issue of *World Development* that highlighted a variety of different impact evaluations found that DFM "clearly improves ecological and/or socioeconomic outcomes" in some cases (Velez et al. 2020; Okumu & Muchapondwa 2020; Gelo 2020), while less so in others (Sills et al. 2020, Miteva & Pattanayak 2021). These benefits are not without limit, however. Indeed, governance itself can act as an intervening variable capable of moderating DFM's success (Blackman & Bluffstone 2021), in particular, in the areas of local leader turnover (Kahsay & Medhin 2020), outside oversight (Turpie & Letley 2021), strong cooperative behavior (Bluffstone et al. 2020), and strong forest governance institutions (Gebreegziabher et al. 2020).

Any pragmatic regulatory approach to increasing compliance with wood-taking prohibitions in the forested areas along the India-Nepal border should at least take under advisement the prescriptions of the DFM literature. As it turns out, integrating the two is not challenging. The DFM literature suggests that accountability close to the ground is important. Thus, designing for legal knowledge transmission necessarily involves working around any obstacle to accurate legal knowledge—including bureaucrats who lack accountability and behave inconsistently for their own material benefit. It also implies that relying on local actors for legal knowledge transmission may be more effective. Along these same lines, the DFM literature suggests that effect forest management must ensure the livelihoods of those living near or dependent on the forest. Designing for target population livelihoods in the forested areas along the India-Nepal border means acknowledging poverty and considering the relative cost of compliance for poor populations whose existence is often tenuous enough that they have few options but to break the law in order to survive. Finally, though the DFM literature doesn't specifically speak to this issue, regulatory pragmatism demands that education levels and access to legal advice be taken into account. As literacy and access to competent lawyers are both limited in this region, pragmatism may mean designing for observational learning or legal knowledge transmission via trusted/embedded local sources.

In summary, in light of both regulatory context and existing literature, a pragmatic regulatory strategy might include: (1) recruiting unorthodox, non-state agents who have reason to behave in accordance with state principles and who are embedded in local forest-using communities; (2) delegating some enforcement (and legal knowledge transmission) authority to them; and (3) providing target populations with some alternative means of meeting their basic needs. Such a regulatory strategy would, in theory, work around three interrelated compliance barriers, principal-agent problems between the state and some of its bureaucrats, lack of accurate target population legal knowledge, and the relatively high cost of compliance often faced by poor populations.

3

Examining Regulatory Pragmatism along the India-Nepal Border

Many states forgo coercion and appear to regulate pragmatically. Therefore, in theory, one could explore regulatory pragmatism in a whole host of different locations all over the globe. The research presented in this book was conducted in the Terai region in the South of Nepal and in the North-Indian state of Bihar. I chose this location principally because it fit squarely within a least favorable case research design: the states on both sides of the border are, especially in this area, coercively weak at the local level. Under such circumstances, if individuals, businesses, or organizations are complying with laws that run counter to customary norms and their respective self-interests, fear of the state's use of force was necessary but not sufficient to explain their behavior.

At the time of data collection, Bihar, more generally, and the districts of Paschim and Purba Champaran, in particular, were just emerging from the severe law-and-order problems they experienced under Lalu Prasad Yadav's corrupt tenure as chief minister, as well as from the problems associated with a long-running, but now largely on-the-run Maoist insurgency. For instance, the police post just outside of Valmiki National Park and quite near to the village of Singhai, where I stayed during part of my fieldwork, was largely destroyed by a bomb almost a decade ago, yet it was only in 2015, after data collection was complete, that the government started building a new one alongside the broken concrete and rebar shell of the old. Nepal, too, has recently experienced a protracted Maoist conflict, during which the government largely withdrew from Maoist-held areas outside of the capital city of Kathmandu. The only presence locals living near Chitwan remember was the occasional army patrol and a bare-bones National Park staff. Otherwise many government offices and schools closed for months and even years at a time. This is on top the fact that the Indian and Nepali states, particularly in this area, were largely acknowledged to be weak at the local level before these insurgencies. Under this set of circumstances, the literature suggests that we

Capacity beyond Coercion. Susan L. Ostermann, Oxford University Press. © Oxford University Press 2023.
DOI: 10.1093/oso/9780197661116.003.0003

should not expect to see compliance on either side of the border. Yet there is some compliance occurring. And, more important, there are cross-border differences in compliance, which help to reveal the factors that contribute to this surprising behavior.

The fact of weak governance at the local level is not the only factor that makes the research location a hard case. In addition, the populations on either side of the border are generally poor and uneducated and the literature suggests that such conditions do not lend themselves to compliance. According to my own survey data,[1] in Paschim Champaran, the primary district in which I conduct research in Bihar, 73 percent of respondents living near the border in this region live on less than $1 per day. On the face of it, Purba Champaran, where I conducted additional data collection, is not different. Meanwhile, in the four districts in which I conducted research in Nepal, the percentage of respondents living on less than $1 per day is the same as it is in India, 73 percent. By way of comparison, according to World Bank data, average per capita income in India and Nepal at the time of research was $1,503 and $690, respectively: far more than $1/day and quite unevenly distributed between the two countries, suggesting that the districts I study are more like each other than like other parts of their respective countries. Moreover, literacy in the two districts[2] surrounding the park on the Indian side of the border is 56 percent. On the Nepal side of the border literacy in the four districts[3] surrounding the park ranges from a high of 77 percent to a low of 55 percent.[4] Meanwhile, the overall literacy rates in India and Nepal are 74.0 percent and 66.0 percent, respectively.[5] In other words, income and literacy do not differ substantially across the border in this region, suggesting that variation in either of these two variables is not responsible for cross-border variation in compliance. This region is also not particularly well-off or well-educated when compared to the broader populations of the two countries in which it lies, making compliance with government-propounded regulations somewhat unlikely. This is compounded by the fact that the state, as mentioned above, remains locally weak in this region.

Additional data on the region are scant and unreliable. As of 2011, the percentage of households in Paschim Champaran that had a computer with an internet connection was 0.49 percent, though a far greater percentage had mobile phones, at 48.97 percent. And it is perhaps telling that data on the percentage of households with electrical connections and with improved sources of drinking water were missing (not available) for

Paschim Champaran. Across the border in Nepal, 7.20 percent of Chitwan District households had internet in 2011; the same figure was 1.48 percent in Parsa, 2.37 percent in Makwanpur, and 1.93 percent in Nawalparasi. In terms of drinking water sources, 69.95 percent in Chitwan had an improved source, while the percentage was 14.36 percent for Parsa, 73.46 percent for Makwanpur, and 40.25 percent for Nawalparasi. Finally, as of 2011, 85.93 percent of Chitwan residents had access to electricity, while the same statistic was 71.42 percent for Parsa, 72.59 percent for Makwanpur, and 80.93 percent for Nawalparasi. Realistically speaking, on both sides of the border, an electrical connection did not indicate regular access to electricity during this time period. Regular load shedding and other grid-related problems resulted in very irregular supply. And, when taken together, the above should suggest that poverty and related resource issues were varied, but endemic in the region at the time of research, thus making it an excellent place to explore compliance dynamics under adverse-but-typical developing world circumstances.

The India-Nepal border region is also ideal for research in that it is dominated by the same geography and culture. Indeed, the same ethnic group—the Tharus—and dominant "culture" is present on both sides of the border. This has been so for as long as memory and record books bear witness, and it is not incidental. Prior to malaria eradication in the region, which occurred in the 1960s, geography made it difficult for any other groups to settle here. At the time, the area was a vast swath of mostly uncleared tropical jungle and it was literally deathly to anyone but the Tharus, who do not typically get malaria due to a natural—or more likely, evolved—resistance. Thus, on both sides of the border, one will find large numbers of Tharus and Tharu culture, which even newcomers to the region adopt, celebrating Magi (the Tharu New Year) in droves. Language is also similar on both sides of the border. Most speak Tharu or Bhojpuri, which are closely related, at home, while Hindi and Nepali are both understood on either side of the border. With the geography and culture being so similar throughout this region, the *a priori* likelihood that these factors explained variation in compliance was minimized.

Finally, the India-Nepal border in particular makes an excellent research location because this border: (1) was not delineated with special attention to culture or geography; and (2) is and has been open as far back as records bear witness. Prior to the East India Company's ("the Company") advances across the subcontinent, this region was part of two different kingdoms or areas of control: to the North, the region was controlled by the King of Nepal and to the South by the Champaran Raj. But thinking of this area as having been split into two kingdoms is a bit misleading, as I have found no evidence of actual delineation during this period or prior.

Subsequently, starting in the late eighteenth century, the King of Nepal's territory crept southward, mainly by peaceful occupation rather than by forceful taking of land, but the Company, which had made agreements with all of the surrounding fiefdoms, took notice. In 1814, after a long diplomatic correspondence in which the Company requested that the King of Nepal withdraw from all territories taken during the previous twenty-five years, the little-known Anglo-Nepal War broke out. Though it took some time, the Company won fairly handily and took not only the territory that Nepal had encroached upon in the late eighteenth and early nineteenth centuries, but all of Nepal's "lowlands," the Terai.[6] The King of Nepal negotiated fiercely to keep that part of the Terai that had "historically" been Nepali territory,[7] not on ethnic grounds, but seemingly because he had used gifts of this land, which was thought to be unlivable much of the year,[8] as pensions for high-level government bureaucrats and military officers.[9] Unfortunately, his intense interest in retaining control over the Nepali Terai appears to have spurred the Company's interest in same[10] and in 1816 the two parties finally signed and ratified the Sugauli (sometimes "Sugowlee") Treaty, leaving the Nepali Terai in British hands, but allowing for the free movement of people between the territories.

The Company did not forget the King of Nepal's interest in the Terai, however, and, when Gurka troops sent to the Company by the King of Nepal remained loyal and helped to put down the Sepoy uprising in 1857, the Company decided to reward this show of trust and loyalty by granting back to Nepal "the whole of the former Ghoorkha possessions below the Hills,"[11] an action that was problematic only in the particulars, as it wasn't clear exactly where Nepal's territory had been. Ultimately both parties agreed that the cession back to Nepal would include "[t]he whole of the lowlands between the rivers Kali and Raptee, and the whole of the lowlands lying between the river Raptee and the district of Goruckpore"[12] and that "[w]here the line traverses cultivated land, it should not be carried through, but should follow the village boundaries in the principle of giving and taking. . . . But where the line runs through forest, it should pass straight from Pillar to Pillar."[13] Moreover, since the 1860 treaty that finally "fixed" the India-Nepal border in this seemingly random manner, it has remained open to both Indians and Nepalis who, to this day, can legally cross it without paperwork and can even legally take up work and/or residence in either country. It is hard to imagine a better location in which to test whether compliance with regulations has resulted from differential state action.

The Freedom of Movement Problem

The fact that Indians and Nepalis can move freely across the border between the two countries is both a boon and a potential problem for this project because rational individuals from either side of the border with information about compliance patterns could, in theory, seek out low law enforcement and/or low-compliance areas for non-complying activities, while complying with regulations in their own village, or similar. In other words, a Nepali from an area in which compliance is high, but who nevertheless wants or needs forest products, might travel to a low-enforcement and/or low-compliance area, either in Nepal or across the border, to collect wood. It is difficult to account for such patterns with the survey data I collect. However, I spent nearly two years in this region and spoke with many people about where and how they collect firewood, in addition to observing it being done. Based on this qualitative data, I do not believe that potentially confounding cross-border strategic behavior is happening on a large scale, at least not when it comes to firewood collection by ordinary individuals. And, while I did get a sense that the situation is quite different when it comes to the felling of live trees and timber smuggling, this is an altogether different set of activities (sophisticated/organized and specifically criminal) and not one that I am trying to explain here.

Forests, Regulation, and Politics in the Terai

For many centuries, the forests of the Terai were managed by forest-dwellers, to the degree that they were "managed" at all. Subsequently, this land was officially controlled by monarchs, *rajas*, on both sides of the border. As best as we can tell, this involved very little management, at least initially. The various Kings of Nepal and the rulers of Bettiah Raj and Ramnagar Raj, however, used present-day Chitwan and Valmiki National Parks as their own private hunting reserves. Subsequently, law and regulation crept in.

On the Indian side, the British formalized control over Indian forests by way of the Indian Forests Act of 1865. This was then replaced by the Forest Act of 1878, which severely limited forest rights of use by communities that traditionally relied on Indian forests for their livelihood. This was then replaced by the Indian Forest Act of 1927, which consolidated state control and taxation of forest products. Though the 1927 Forest Act remains in force to date, other legislation has modified its mandate. Focusing on the case at hand, the Bihar state government took over the management of Ramnagar Raj forests in 1950 and the Bettiah Raj forests in 1953 and 1954 under the Bihar Private Protected Forests Act (1947). Valmiki Wildlife Sanctuary was formed in 1978 and then officially notified as a national park in 1990. Later that decade, Joint Forest Management (JFM) programs allowed for communal management of government-owned forest land, placing a strong emphasis on the need for consent of local governments (Gram Sabhas). These were seemingly never implemented in the area surrounding Valmiki, however. More recently, the Minor Forest Produce Act of 2005 (MFPA) and the Scheduled Tribes and Other Traditional Forest Dwellers (Recognition of Forest Rights) Act of 2006 (FRA) modified the 1927 Forest Act's prohibition on the removal of all forest products from national parks. In particular, the MFPA and FRA extended individually and communally held forest resource rights to forest-dwelling Scheduled Tribes occupying specific tracts of land before October 1980. They also recognize women as having rights to forest land and related resources that are equal to those held by their male counterparts. Notably, however, the MFPA and FRA do not extend forest use rights into Critical Wildlife/Tiger Habitat areas,[14] and "minor forest produce," which includes a variety of items ranging from bamboo, to honey, to medicinal plants, does not include timber. In addition, the MFPA and FRA have not been implemented in the area surrounding Valmiki.[15] Indeed, Nitish Kumar's state level government was still refusing to allow villagers to enter Valmiki for collection of any forest produce at all as late as 2015.[16] Thus, at the time of research, wood collection in Valmiki National Park was—for nearly all intents and purposes—prohibited.

On the Nepali side, prior to democratization, much of the country's land, including forest land, was property of the monarchy under birta tenure (Joshi 1993). After the initial 1950 democratization, all forest lands were then nationalized under the 1957 Private Forests (Nationalization) Act, ostensibly for conservation purposes. This was followed by the Forest Act of

1967 and the Forest Protection (Special Provision) Act of 1967. Though these acts ostensibly strengthened the state's hand with respect to forest conservation, they were largely unsuccessful in this regard (Wallace 1981). Reportedly it was in part because of this continued degradation that King Birendra worked to turn one of his private hunting grounds into a conservation area in 1970, making Chitwan Nepal's first national park. As part of Chitwan's formation, the Tharus who had been dwelling in the park were kicked out and made landless. Subsequently, in 1977, the 1961 Act was amended to facilitate community management of forests, though community forest remained marginal for many years after the fact. Nepal's 1993 Forest Act then solidified community forestry as one of the primary means of managing Nepal's forests. Importantly, however, forests located in national parks are not subject to community management or forest-use rights. Thus, collecting wood in Chitwan National Park is prohibited to all.[17]

Existing in dialogue with the formal legal regulatory apparatus in both India and Nepal is a fairly robust civil society. Though the presence of NGOs working on environmental issues is thicker on the ground in Nepal than it is in India, it is important to note that civil society has been active in both countries. This presence takes many forms. There are NGOs dedicated to wildlife preservation, park-people relations, the livelihood and uplift of indigenous groups, forest access, etc. Some of these organizations, like World Wildlife Fund Nepal, got off the ground by way of external (non-local and both domestic and international) impetus and funding. Others, like the Tharu Cultural Museum and Research Center, in Sauraha, Nepal, or the Trayi Vikas Manch, in Narkatiaganj, India, arose organically and tend more toward local funding. Perhaps because of this diversity, there are a number of non-governmental conduits for information, as well for aggregating interests to advocate politically or to push back against the existing regulatory apparatus.

Also existing in dialogue with the formal regulatory apparatus in both India and Nepal is a set of highly local leaders. The status of many of these leaders, as leaders, does not depend upon electoral results. Most are simply acknowledged to be such by the communities in which they live and work. They might be the acknowledged leader of several villages or sometimes just one. Some might run local NGOs, others run businesses. Some receive a direct salary for the leadership they provide, to the degree that they do so through the local panchayat in India, or the local Village Development Committee (at the time of research),[18] in Nepal. But others have no such formal position. Still, if you walk into any village in this region and ask for the leader, there will be widespread agreement and you will find him or her quite readily. Importantly, these are not the *naya netas* written about in the literature on Indian politics, though it's possible some *naya netas* got their start in this manner. This is a more traditional form of leadership, with more in common with that highlighted—albeit in an urban context—in Adam Auerbach's (2019) book *Demanding Development*. Importantly, for purposes of this book, local leaders are respected and, therefore, influential. If they are made aware of government behavior, including government-propounded laws and regulations, they can transmit that information to those they lead. They can also transmit their views on the appropriateness of government behavior. If local leaders view particular government projects negatively, these projects may face headwinds.

In theory, NGOs, other civil society groups, and local leaders could foster and instrumentalize a politics related to wood collection in the area surrounding Chitwan and Valmiki. Up through the period of data collection for this book, however, the politics of wood collection largely remained individual, rather than aggregate. Though numerous respondents expressed frustration with park regulations that they viewed as unreasonable, few reported taking any steps to work together with others to change the rules that frustrated them. Instead, what can be seen on the ground is consistent with James Scott's (1987) "weapons of the weak." Some people knowingly go into the forest and take wood, despite this act being prohibited. One respondent regretted being forced to "steal" firewood from the nearby national park. She viewed the park as a public resource and her actions as being harmless. Another respondent spoke of wood collection as a right, one that members of tribal group naturally hold; she referred to the park as "our land." The state is also part of this politics. A conversation with a high-ranking official in Chitwan National Park revealed that park officials have occasionally traded illegal grazing rights in the park for information on poaching operations in the area, looking the other way when helpful communities are clearly in violation of the law. Notably absent from all of this is contentious politics directed at political office and legal change. Since data collection, the beginnings of such a politics has started to develop on the India side of the border, but it remains nascent. If it develops further, there may come a time when compliance and non-compliance will be viewed as political acts by broad swaths of the public. Importantly, however, these dynamics were not at play during or in the lead-up to data collection.

Variables and Hypotheses

Regulatory pragmatism suggests that even when the state is coercively weak, it *can* still generate compliance in some circumstances and without great expenditure. Legal institutions can work in such a context if the state chooses legal design and implementation strategies that help target populations to overcome compliance barriers, in this case lack of accurate legal knowledge and poverty-driven non-compliance.

Compliance

The major dependent variable at issue in this book is compliance.[19] Compliance occurs when an individual acts or refrains from acting in such a way that his or her behavior is consistent with that required by law. In the main conservation case, this involves refraining from taking wood out of either Chitwan National Park or Valmiki National Park and Tiger Reserve. I measure compliance by asking respondents whether they need wood and where they source it.[20]

However, self-reporting is not without its problems. To allay any concerns about social acceptability bias and to capture widespread non-compliant behavior, I also include, in Appendix 3, an analysis of Forest Canopy Density (FCD). This analysis clearly demonstrates greater FCD on the Nepal side of the border and within park boundaries. It is important to note here, however, that, while deforestation is certainly a problem in both India and Nepal and illegal logging, which seems to be carried out by criminal gangs, does threaten the large stands of lucrative teak trees that are indigenous to these parks, it is not clear that the non-compliant wood collection of ordinary individuals living just outside of them is causing deforestation. It is the non-compliant wood collection of regular Indians and Nepalis that I seek to explore in this book.

Independent Variables

To determine the circumstances under which institutions are associated with compliance in areas of state weakness, I examine, as noted above, a region that is characterized by the same rules (both legal and customary), the same culture and, seemingly, the same basic incentives to comply with or break the law. With many of the variables that are customarily used to explain rule-following behavior held constant, I am able to focus on one key factor that does vary across the border: the use of legal design and implementation strategies that are consistent with regulatory pragmatism. In the main conservation case, I explore three different implementation strategies that are consistent with regulatory pragmatism: delegated enforcement, information dissemination through local leaders, and amelioration of poverty-driven non-compliance.

Beforehand, however, I focus on two important intervening variables that represent some of the most important hurdles any weak state must overcome if it hopes to achieve widespread compliance: (1) the accuracy of individually held legal knowledge; and (2) the amelioration of poverty driven non-compliance, which, in this case, I consider to be proportion of individuals for whom compliance with formal legal rules and institutions remains incompatible with basic survival.

Accurate Legal Knowledge

The often unstated assumption embedded in much of the socio-legal compliance literature is that before individuals can choose whether or not to comply with a given regulation they must first be aware that the regulation exists at all and have a decently accurate understanding of what compliance would entail. This seemingly common-sense assumption, however, is problematic, even in the strong-state contexts on which the socio-legal compliance literature has largely focused its inquiries. When the state is strong and capable, coercively and otherwise, the job of disseminating legal knowledge is often associated with the state and/or lawyers, with more emphasis on the state in civil law jurisdictions and on lawyers in common law jurisdictions, respectively.

But reality is more complicated. People tend to get information about the law from many different sources: the media, friends and family, government publicity, etc. They then distill this information with other information they have, for instance, about whether they've ever heard of or seen someone getting punished for a particular behavior and the state's known actions in other analogous situations, into a legal understanding. They then update this understanding from time to time when they come across new information. Certainly a sophisticated individual or corporation might consult a lawyer or a regulatory body if the legal issue was unclear and important enough to merit such an effort. But this happens less often than the literature would have us believe. Still, where the state is strong, coercively and otherwise, people, corporations, organizations, etc. do seem to develop a fairly accurate understanding of the regulations that govern their respective existences. This is less often the case in places where the state is weak.

Though I do not think individual actors behave differently in the way that they attempt to arrive at an accurate legal understanding depending upon the context of a locally strong or weak state, the outcomes of their efforts sometimes differ sharply. Where the state is strong, it often behaves consistently and, thus, the information that individual actors receive about the state's treatment of particular behavior tends to be fairly consistent and accurate. Legal understandings in areas of state weakness are sometimes wildly inaccurate. Here the state either does not appear to be present or, due to inconsistent enforcement, does not behave like a single entity. In such environments, in which the state makes little or no attempt to communicate legal requirements with target populations and in which one bureaucrat never enforces a particular law, the next enforces only when a bribe hasn't been paid, and a third always enforces, the information that filters down to individual actors is fuzzy at best. Yet, this information is all individuals have to go on, so they form legal understandings and continue to update them, just as their counterparts do when dealing with much stronger states. But, in the absence of consistent state action, these legal understandings can sometimes be quite inaccurate when measured against the law in the codebooks or even informal legal norms. The behavior predicated on these inaccurate legal understandings, not unsurprisingly, can then undercut the very purpose for which the regulation was put in place.

To understand the power of consistent state action, consider an example from an area where the state is strong, coercively and otherwise. At the time of writing, I lived in San Francisco and had reason to drive I-280 down to Silicon Valley on many occasions over a sixteen-year period. When I first drove this stretch of interstate, I observed the posted speed limit—which is, incidentally, 65 mph. I was fearful of what I knew from the media, past experience, and information provided by acquaintances to be an expensive violation. Thus, I kept my driving speed within the legal limits. But, over time, I observed that many of the other individuals driving on this road felt comfortable going well over the posted speed limit. Knowing that this is a commute road for many, I intuited that they must have known something from experience that I didn't know: that enforcement was unlikely. Observing their behavior, I noted that most drivers still kept their speed below 80 mph. I also noted that those who were in a real rush, flying by the crowds of 80 mph drivers, did often end up pulled over on the side of the highway a few miles later. This allowed me to update my legal understanding to reflect the realities of driving on I-280 in this particular corridor: stay below 80 mph and the likelihood that you will be punished for a violation of the speed limit is minimal. Even though this legal understanding is at odds with the law on the books, it remains useful and accurate because of the *consistency* of state action.

Now consider an example from an area in which the state is coercively weak, like that found along the India-Nepal border near Chitwan and Valmiki. A woman I met, who could not read and had never attended school herself, went down to the district office to try to enroll her child in school because this is what one of her neighbors said she had done to get her own child admitted to the local government school.[21] When this woman arrived at the district office, she found some staff on site, but the District Education Officer (DEO) was not in and she was told to come back another time. One of the staff members also told her that she could simply bring her child to the local government school. Thinking that this was all that was required, she returned home and brought her child to school the next day. When she arrived, the staff told her that her child had to have a uniform in order to attend. Seemingly updating her legal understanding as she went, she did not bother to return to the DEO, and used what little money she had to have a uniform tailored and then once again brought her child to school. The uniform seemed to work and the woman's child was admitted to the classroom; yet, two weeks later the woman's child was sent home for lack of appropriate paperwork. Weeks passed as the woman struggled to collect the necessary paperwork and had to eventually pay small bribes to get what she needed. Having finally done so, she returned with her child to school and was told that her papers were in order but that she had illegally been keeping her child out of school and would have to pay a fine before her child could be readmitted. Despairing, the woman returned home with her child. Some months later, having saved enough to pay the fine she had incurred, she then returned to the school and her child was admitted without incident and, perhaps more important, without her having had to pay a fine. She felt lucky for having gotten away without paying the fine, but she did not get away with an accurate legal understanding. The state behaved so inconsistently that she came away with little idea of what was required for school enrollment. Instead, she held the inaccurate understanding that enrollment is compulsory in Nepal when, in fact, it is not. Setting aside the fact that it might be normatively useful for the rural poor to think that school is compulsory, the troubling fact is that, when this woman relates her story to neighbors, friends, and family, as she did with me, others will likely end up with inaccurate legal understandings as well. And when they attempt to comply with what they believe the law to be, they may run into further trouble.

How do populations that live along the India-Nepal border know that wood collection in national parks is prohibited, particularly when it differs from the social/cultural norm that permits wood collection in these areas? The simple answer is that many of them do not. I find that, overall, 61.5 per-cent of my respondents hold *inaccurate* understandings of the wood-taking prohibitions in place in Chitwan and Valmiki. Yet, many individuals seem to want to avoid legal penalties—and the state more generally. This motivates them to try to determine the legal requirements that affect their lives in what-ever way they can, using whatever resources available to them.

But what does this mean in practice? Individuals improve their guesses by constructing and iteratively reconstructing what the law "must be" based upon the information available to them at any particular moment. Individuals seem to draw information for updating from many different sources, ranging from prior interactions with the state, to their beliefs about what types of regulations the state might make, to what amounts to rumors circulated by neighbors and friends regarding legal requirements. The result is an individually held understanding of what type of behavior is required or prohibited in a given situation that may or may not be accurate depending upon the pattern of observations and interactions that individual has witnessed. The state and its actions are important sources of information re-garding the law. In my open-ended interviews, I asked respondents how they determine whether something is illegal. The overwhelming sentiment was that something that incurs a negative government reaction is illegal. Along the same lines, those who knew someone who took a particular action and was punished tended to believe that the punished behavior was illegal, while those who knew someone who took the same action and was not punished believed it to be legal. States that employ regulatory pragmatism and avoid both principal-agent problems and the resulting inconsistency stand a much better chance of doing the opposite. I develop this idea more fully below.

In a low-information environment and when target populations are poorly educated, one would expect that principal-agent problems and the resulting inconsistent behavior ensure that misunderstandings of legal requirements remain pervasive. When the state punishes or appears to punish a particular action some of the time, while failing to punish the same behavior at other times, these mixed signals propagate through the legal understandings of the relevant target population. Those who have been punished or have seen or heard about others being punished receive information that suggests that the punished behavior is illegal. Many of these same individuals will later receive conflicting information, and this may cause them to question their original assumptions, as well as to update them based upon new information. In this way, when principal-agent problems result in inconsistent state behavior, inaccurate legal knowledge can be widespread.

In light of the above, where state action is consistent and/or where alternative systems to disseminate accurate legal information have developed, I expect to find that locally held understandings of what constitutes compliance are, for the most part, consistent with legal requirements. In all other areas, I hypothesize that locally held legal understandings will be largely inaccurate. Moreover, because accurate information about the law is required before individuals can *choose* between compliant and non-compliant actions, I anticipate that those who have accurate information about what constitutes compliance will be more likely to comply than those of their counterparts whose legal understandings are inaccurate.

This latter hypothesis requires a bit more explication. First, I do not mean to suggest that accurate information about the law is required for behavior that looks like compliance. In fact, it is not. A person who has an inaccurate legal understanding of whether a particular behavior is required or prohibited can still appear to comply if ostensibly compliant behavior is in his or her self-interest; as in, this person may actually believe that he or she is not compliant but, because of a happy coincidence, his or her behavior looks compliant when viewed from the outside. Still, if we assume that the distribution of similarly situated individuals is random, then the remainder of the population must fit into three categories: (1) those who have inaccurate understandings of the law and appear to be non-compliant; (2) those who have accurate understandings of the law and appear to be compliant; and (3) those who have accurate understandings of the law and appear to be non-compliant. If we further assume that once aware of a legal requirement individuals on both sides of the border will be similarly motivated (or unmotivated) to comply, then it follows that we should see higher rates of compliance in those locations in which legal understandings are more accurate.

That is, unless something like poverty-driven non-compliance, which I discuss below, pushes the cost of compliance to untenable heights for a substantial proportion of the population, effectively preventing individuals who are both aware of the law and motivated to comply with it from doing so.

I test the hypothesis that more widespread accurate legal knowledge leads to higher rates of compliance directly, by measuring legal knowledge among my respondents and determining whether it is correlated with compliant behavior. If accurate legal knowledge is predictive of compliance, we should expect to see higher levels of compliance when accurate legal knowledge is more widespread, regardless of whether accurate legal knowledge results from consistent state action, delegated enforcement, information dissemination through local leaders, or some other source. Along these lines, variation in the proportion of the relevant target population holding accurate legal knowledge should explain a significant amount of cross-border variation in compliance with wood-taking restrictions around Valmiki and Chitwan, as well as the magnitude of compliance found in different locations on the same side of the border.

I measure accuracy of legal knowledge by asking members of each target population true-false questions regarding the conduct required or prohibited by law and then by aggregating their responses geographically. For instance, in the conservation case, I ask ordinary individuals whether it is true that "[p]eople must not collect fallen wood." I also ask, among other things, whether it is true or false they "must stay on roadways at all times." By asking these questions of target population members, questions that pertain to both regulated and unregulated conduct and require individuals to recognize both false statements about the law and true ones, I am able to get a fairly clear picture of what individuals believe is required or prohibited by law. Then, by aggregating their responses geographically, I am able to see the proportion of people in a given location who hold an accurate understanding of the law and whether higher or lower proportions are associated with compliance.

Cost of Compliance

The cost of compliance is an important intervening variable. Not all actors face the same costs when it comes to compliance. While a speeding ticket may be "pocket change" for a famous Hollywood actor, it is substantial for the average person. Along the India-Nepal border, the cost of compliance with wood-taking prohibitions is extraordinarily high for those who depend upon wood to cook and keep warm during the winter; this population is also often quite poor and not able to afford alternative fuel. The wealthy in this region typically cook with gas. As a result, the cost of complying with wood-taking prohibitions is much higher for the poor than for the wealthy, who are less reliant on wood as a fuel source.

In this situation and ones like it, I posit that an individual is less likely to comply with a particular regulation, even if he or she knows a particular action is required or prohibited, if compliant action undercuts that individual's pursuit of her/her self-interest.[22] For instance, at least in theory, an individual who has ample material resources is less likely to break a law that prohibits stealing than is an individual who has few resources and is desperate for, say, food. This means that all individuals are not similarly situated to engage in compliant behavior. Some have powerful, perhaps overwhelming, incentives to break the law in order to survive, while others can easily afford to comply. Put another way, the cost of compliance with a regulation that prohibits stealing is relatively low for an individual who can afford to buy food, while for someone who is poor, it is quite high.[23]

Throughout much of the developed world, poverty-driven non-compliance is relatively low and, therefore, manageable. To foster compliance, some states manipulate the incentives that individuals face so that individual pursuit of self-interest and compliant behavior are not mutually exclusive. In so doing, states act to align the self-interest of a larger swath of the population with compliant behavior. Examples of such efforts include tax breaks or credits, subsidized government loans to cover the cost of compliance, certification regimes that help consumers identify compliant organizations (possibly generating higher revenues), payouts for compliant behavior, etc. (Huber 2011). We have seen a number of these types of efforts used to promote Covid-19 vaccination throughout the world, everything from lotteries for vaccinated individuals to payment for vaccination to privileges for the vaccinated that are denied to those who remain unvaccinated; to make sure the poor, who often cannot take time away from work or cannot afford transport to a vaccination center, still receive shots, various governments have implemented efforts to vaccinate at work places or to create mobile vaccine clinics that travel to poorer neighborhoods. States also use such approaches when the underlying behavior the state wants to change is legal, but remains, in the eyes of many, against the public interest or public health. In the United States, steep taxes on cigarettes and gun buy-back programs would be examples of this type of approach to behavioral change. But all these are programs and approaches that are far more easily carried off by governments with substantial state capacity, coercive and otherwise, and when targeting relatively small percentages of the population.

In the developing world, poverty is widespread and poverty-driven non-compliance can be endemic. Along the India-Nepal border, where most live at or below the poverty line and where many struggle to feed and clothe themselves, it is difficult to imagine compliance with regulations that run contrary to the self-interest of the majority of the population. This is particularly true because the states on either side of the border are coercively weak—limited in the degree to which they can engage in deterrence-based enforcement. Yet, some compliance with wood-gathering restrictions is happening, which suggests that not all individuals find compliance to be against their respective self-interests.

It seems reasonable to hypothesize, then, that many of those individuals who *can* afford to comply will do so. More specifically, among the relatively small segments of the population for whom the cost of compliance is low relative to their incomes, I expect compliance, so long as (a) this cost is lower than the perceived cost of non-compliance; and/or (b) so long as they believe that it is their duty to comply. Indeed, as mentioned briefly above, those who are relatively well-off in the area surrounding Chitwan and Valmiki tend to cook with gas and, thus, do not need the very resource—firewood—that they are prohibited from removing from these conservation areas. It is the poor, who cannot afford to cook with gas, who must choose between survival and compliance. As a result, my expectations regarding their behavior are quite different. These individuals face a very high cost of compliance and many of them would rather risk enforcement-related penalties than face the alternatives. Furthermore, even if these individuals believe they have a duty to comply, it is likely not powerful enough to overcome poverty-driven non-compliance.

Finally, among individuals who have the option to both comply and attend to their basic needs, fear and duty will kick in and this segment of the target population will comply in significantly higher numbers than those of their low-income counterparts who have no viable option other than non-compliance.

I expect to find higher rates of compliance among those for whom the cost of compliance is lower. To test this hypothesis, I first compare, in Chapter 6, the compliance behavior of those for whom the cost of compliance is relatively high to those for whom the cost of compliance is relatively low, using self-reported income as a means to determine relative cost of compliance.

More specifically, I look for significant differences in compliance between those living above and below the poverty line.[24] I then check to make sure that these two income groups do not report different levels of both fear and duty.

State Use of a Pragmatic Regulatory Strategy

Given the low coercive state capacity, inconsistent state action, and poverty present on both sides of the India-Nepal border, neither accurate legal knowledge nor poverty-driven non-compliance should vary as one moves across it. That is, unless regulatory pragmatism has been employed to alleviate principal-agent problems and to lower the cost of compliance with wood-taking prohibitions. In Nepal, the state has delegated enforcement of government-owned forest land just outside of Chitwan National Park to Community Forest User Groups.[25] In their management of these forest areas, User Groups can and do behave consistently, something that stands in stark contrast to the state's behavior in nearby Chitwan National Park; this contrast may be able to foster accurate legal knowledge among those who learn about the law via observation. Another way that individuals might acquire accurate legal knowledge is if local leaders are involved in information dissemination. Local leaders—who are trusted at the local level and often perceived to have connections to the state, even if informal—represent a possible pathway by which the state might disseminate accurate information about the law. Finally, the Nepali state's provision of Community Forests is also a pragmatic way to ameliorate poverty-driven non-compliance, in that those who live near them can both meet their basic needs and comply with wood collection prohibitions in Chitwan National Park.

I explore each of these strategies—delegated enforcement, information dissemination through local leaders, and amelioration of poverty-driven non-compliance—below.

Delegated Enforcement

States employing regulatory pragmatism may be able to circumvent principal-agent problems by delegating enforcement responsibility to *different* agents. If there are individuals, groups, and organizations at the local level that have the capacity to consistently carry out certain proscribed tasks, possibly under government oversight, and have reason to want to take over these tasks, a state that employs regulatory pragmatism may be able to take advantage of this resource and get help in carrying out its prerogatives by outsourcing specific functions to citizens and/or civil society. In this way, a state that has only minimal capacity can "punch above its weight" and reap the associated benefits without incurring tremendous costs. So long as the parties to whom responsibility is delegated benefit when they realize compliant behavior, more accurate legal knowledge and higher rates of compliance should result.

The psychology literature is helpful in terms of understanding how such an arrangement might foster accurate legal knowledge. Constructivist learning theory, which is based upon concepts first introduced by Dewey (1938) , Vygotsky (1962) , and Piaget (1967) , suggests that individuals, when learning or trying to learn, construct knowledge out of their experiences by continually making and remaking their sense of truth and reality. As individuals have new experiences, they update their knowledge accordingly. Piaget focused, at least initially, on children and argued that as children learn they use the processes of accommodation and assimilation to construct and then reconstruct their worldview and understanding of how particular aspects of the world work. Learning about the law may well follow a similar pattern. As individuals go about their daily business, my qualitative evidence indicates that they do focus on the state's behavior and their own when trying to determine what is legal and what is not. As they have new experiences, they update their understandings to reflect newly acquired information. In this way, consistent state action helps individuals to gain accurate information and inconsistent state action does the opposite. If the state were to delegate enforcement to an individual or group that could behave more consistently than itself, it follows that this increased consistency should help individuals to construct more accurate legal understandings.

Turning to the case at hand, those with Community Forest access have been able to observe, firsthand, the relatively consistent availability of penalty-free wood collection in Community Forests and the state's inconsistent enforcement of wood-taking prohibitions in Chitwan. This contrasting information should be helpful for the development of accurate legal understandings. Meanwhile, those without Community Forest access are forced to resolve discrepancies between observed or reported enforcement behaviors of individual bureaucrats over time, a situation that could just as easily resolve into inaccurate understandings as accurate ones. The former slate of contrasting information is easier to resolve into an accurate legal understanding of wood-taking restrictions than the latter.

In light of the above, I hypothesize that low coercive state capacity need not result in non-compliance, even when legal norms differ from social norms. States that use regulatory pragmatism to guide their regulatory design and implementation decisions can achieve high levels of compliance. However, in order for legal institutions to work under these circumstances, states must overcome the obstacle presented by their own principal-agent problems and the attendant widespread misunderstandings of the law. When a state cannot get its agents to behave consistently, it may still be able to deliver legal knowledge if it can design a system that circumvents principal-agent problems and the attendant information asymmetries.

More specifically, in the case at hand, the Nepali state has delegated management of and enforcement in Community Forests, wooded areas just outside of Chitwan, to User Groups from the community. Each of these groups is responsible for ensuring compliance with applicable regulations in its Community Forest and, if a group fails in this, the state may strip it of the land grant and all the benefits[26] that flow from it. Individuals who have access to a Community Forest are exposed to delegated enforcement and are able to observe the contrast between the norms in place in Community Forests and in Chitwan.

If delegation can solve the state's principal agent-problem and foster accurate legal knowledge, we should expect to see more accurate legal knowledge when the state delegates. I expect that delegated enforcement, in the form of Community Forests, is positively correlated with accurate legal knowledge. With higher rates of accurate legal knowledge, I also expect to find higher rates of compliance on the Nepal side of the border and, in particular, among those who have been exposed to delegated enforcement.

I measure exposure to regulatory pragmatism (via delegated enforcement) by asking respondents whether they have access to a Community Forest. I then conduct cross-border and within-country (for Nepal) analyses to determine whether exposure to regulatory pragmatism (via delegated enforcement) is associated with more accurate legal knowledge.

Information Dissemination through Local Leaders
Not all sources of information are treated equally when individuals are trying to gain accurate legal knowledge. Individuals can, of course, learn about the law themselves, so long as they have the requisite skills: education. But in most locations, this last statement should read "legal education," as determining what the law is has quite a bit to do with knowing where to look

for it and how to read statutes and, in common-law jurisdictions, case law. Possession of these skills is not common among average citizens and, as a result, many individuals must rely upon second-hand information.

Lawyers are thought to be a primary indirect source of legal knowledge. Muir (1973), writing about prayer in public schools, finds lawyers to be one of the agents responsible for distributing information about the law and key proponents of the attitude changes that some laws are designed to bring about. However, if lawyers are not present at the local level, or are either too costly or poorly educated, then they cannot serve as sources of accurate legal knowledge. This is the case in in rural South Asia, including in the areas surrounding Chitwan and Valmiki, as well as in many other places in which the state is largely weak.

Where lawyers fail to meet any one of the above conditions, there are other individuals who are situated in such a way that they might, at least partially, fill the role of lawyers in terms of distribution of reliable information about the law: local leaders. In rural South Asia, local leaders often act as information distribution agents and frequently achieve their positions, whether formal or informal, because of their perceived connections to the state. These are individuals who know the right person to talk to within the government or the right place to go when, for instance, an individual needs to procure a voter ID card. They are trusted and the information they provide is considered credible.

These leaders may be elected or unelected, but are considered leaders, at least in part, because of their recognized and reliable connection to the state, whether formal or informal. Thus, the information they provide about the law is considered more credible or trustworthy than information provided by laymen. As one respondent put it, as he was trying to explain why he believed his source of information regarding the law, "[t]he village headman is a savvy man and many in the government are known to him. We know his family." In situations in which front-line bureaucrats are often corrupt, as is the case in much of South Asia, the information local leaders provide may be privileged over that provided even by agents of the state. A state with limited coercive capacity that cannot behave consistently should nevertheless be able to foster accurate legal knowledge if it can circumvent its principal-agent problem (and the resulting information asymmetries). One way it may be able to do so is through local leaders.

This is consistent with the literature, which recognizes the importance of leaders. Wilson and Rhodes (1997) use a formal model to demonstrate that leaders play an important role in distributing information and coordinating followers. Along these same lines, Dixit (2003) and Banerjee et al. (2010) show that, when the state is weak, trusted contacts can facilitate information sharing; indeed, when they do so they can further informal institutions that are capable of providing law, order, and other services. Varshney (2003) and Bhavnani et al. (2009) also recognize the power of local leaders in information distribution and demonstrate that these individuals need *not* act as agents of the state. It follows that local leaders, if they can be persuaded to act on the state's behalf, may be able to at least partially fill the information distribution demand that remains unmet in the absence of an active, affordable, and well-educated legal profession at the local level.

In light of the above, I expect that even in areas of where the state is generally weak, legal institutions *can* generate compliance from a variety of different target populations. However, in order for legal institutions to work under these circumstances, state and/or non-state actors must use regulatory pragmatism to overcome the obstacle presented by widespread misunderstandings of the conduct required or prohibited by law. States may be able to do so in at least two ways: by delegating enforcement to interested parties or by communicating information about the law to target populations through local leaders.

To determine whether and how local leaders can foster accurate legal knowledge in a location in which legal knowledge has been shown to have a significant effect upon compliance, I randomly selected three villages from the set of villages included in my larger survey of Nepal.[27] I had baseline data for approximately twenty-five individuals in each of these villages. After randomly assigning treatments,[28] I returned to each village to conduct an intervention. In the first village, I simply visited and said that I was there to research the park. In the second village, I distributed fliers to forty individuals. These fliers accurately depicted Chitwan's wood-collection prohibitions, explained the logic behind them, and described the importance of the park to the local economy and ecology. In a third village, I had a local leader convey the information included in the flier, including an elucidation of the logic behind wood-collection prohibitions. He did so in an interactive session with forty-three individuals present; I accompanied him and participated in this session. I then returned two months later to measure post-treatment effects in all villages. I did so using a condensed form of the survey used for pre-treatment measures and with similar methodology: a survey of approximately fifty individuals in each location, but utilizing different starting points for right-hand rule randomization. This post-treatment survey also allowed me to partially replicate my findings from the larger survey.

Amelioration of Poverty-Driven Non-Compliance

Regulatory pragmatism suggests that those states that design implementation strategies around known obstacles to compliance can achieve high levels of compliance in spite of low coercive capacity. Nepal's Community Forests, which have the potential to foster accurate legal knowledge, also have the power to ameliorate another known compliance barrier along the India-Nepal border: poverty-driven non-compliance. As the population in this area is largely poor and reliant on fuelwood for cooking and keeping warm during the winter, many may be driven to non-compliance by their poverty alone and not by a lack of motivation to comply with law. If this is the case, providing these individuals with an alternative fuel source, one that does not involve wood taken from national park land, should facilitate their compliance.

Once individuals hold accurate legal understandings, fear and duty work as one would expect them to. The majority of my respondents are motivated by either fear or duty to comply with wood-taking restrictions, and there is no significant difference between the rates at which my respondents report these motivations when I subset them into those who hold accurate understandings of the law and those who do not.[29] Thus, we should expect large-scale compliance among the former. That is, unless there is poverty-driven non-compliance. Even if efforts by the state or other non-state actors have affected accurate understandings of the conduct required by law and brought about a threshold attitudinal change in the target population's consciousness, many individuals, businesses, and organizations in the developing world will still fail to comply. Why? Doing so is often so costly that it would undercut the abilities of these individuals, businesses, and organizations to meet their own basic needs.

Indeed, an individual might comply with a particular law or regulation because compliant action either aligns with or doesn't undercut that individual's pursuit of her/his self-interest (Pearce & Tombs 1990, 1997, 1998; Parker 2002; Molnar et al. 2004). For instance, at least in theory, an individual who has ample material resources is less likely to break a law that prohibits stealing than is an individual who has few resources and is desperate for, say, food. This means that while "in its majesty equality, the law forbids rich and poor alike to sleep under bridges, beg in the streets and steal loaves of bread,"[30] all individuals are not similarly situated to comply.

Throughout much of the developed world, poverty is fairly low and thus we can assume that non-compliance owing to poverty alone must also be relatively low. The fact that such a relatively small percentage of the population is poor means that deterring or motivating these individuals away from non-compliance is somewhat manageable[31] given the strength and resources that most developed-world states possess. In places like India or Nepal, where more than half of the population is poor, the effort required to coercively deter or otherwise motivate individuals away from poverty-driven non-compliance would be quite high. Such a high degree of effort/cost would be unmanageable for these states because it represents such a significant portion of GDP and state resources.

In contrast, states with ample resources have many options at their disposal to motivate compliance. Some choose to manipulate the incentives that individuals face so that individual pursuit of self-interest and compliant behavior are not mutually exclusive, thus aligning the self-interest of a larger swath of the population with compliant behavior. The financial capacity of regulated entities to comply with existing or proposed laws has been shown to affect the design of regulatory programs in the United States (Thornton et al. 2008; Huber 2011). Examples of such efforts include tax breaks or credits, subsidized government loans to cover the costs of compliance, certification regimes that help consumers identify compliant organizations (possibly generating higher revenues), payouts for compliant behavior, etc. (Huber 2011). Though somewhat diminished after the recent gutting of associated taxes/penalties, the US Affordable Care Act (aka "Obamacare") still includes many such components: all US citizens and legal residents are now required to carry health insurance, but this insurance is heavily subsidized for low-income individuals who would otherwise have difficulty covering this type of expense and, as a result, might not comply with the insurance mandate. Interestingly, states with the strength and resources to do so also use such approaches when the underlying behavior the state wants to change is not prohibited but remains, in the eyes of many, against the public interest or public health. In the United States, steep taxes on cigarettes and gun buyback programs would be examples of this type of approach to behavioral change. But all of these are programs and approaches that are far more easily carried off in a strongly institutionalized regulatory environments, by states with substantial coercive capacity, and when targeting a relatively small percentage of the population.

In the developing world, poverty is widespread and poverty-driven noncompliance can be endemic. Along the India-Nepal border, where most live at or below the poverty line and where many struggle to feed and clothe themselves, it is difficult to imagine compliance with regulations that run contrary to the basic needs of the majority of a population targeted by a given regulation. For instance, school attendance is mandatory and holidays do not always coincide with periods of intense agricultural activity. As a result, large numbers of students, whose families rely on subsistence agriculture, skip school during certain parts of the year to work on their parents' farmland. Compliance with regulations that run counter to basic needs is particularly problematic in this region because the governments in the area are weakly institutionalized and the states on either side of the border are limited in the degree to which they can engage in deterrence-based enforcement. Yet, some compliance with wood-gathering restrictions is happening: 66 percent of Nepali respondents and 29 percent of Indian respondents act in a manner that is compliant with wood-collection restrictions in place in both Chitwan and Valmiki National Parks. This suggests that not all individuals find compliance to be against their respective self-interests.

In areas where state capacity is generally low, individuals, businesses, and organizations often exist at the margins and it doesn't take much for a regulation to impose an unduly high cost of compliance on them. Therefore, large-scale compliance is only possible in places in which the state and/or non-state actors or other factors have ameliorated conditions to such a degree (for instance, by lowering the cost of compliance) that the targets of a particular regulation can both meet their basic needs *and* comply.

Given this information, I hypothesize that many of those individuals who *can* afford to comply will do so. More specifically, among the relatively small segments of the population for whom the cost of compliance is low relative to their incomes, we should expect compliance so long as (a) the cost of compliance is lower than the perceived cost of non-compliance; and/or (b) individuals believe that it is their duty to comply. Indeed, those who are relatively well-off in the area surrounding Chitwan and Valmiki cook with gas and, thus, do not need firewood. As one relatively well-off female business owner explained to me, "We use gas. It is easier and there is no facility for an open fire in a modern house."[32] The poor, however, do need firewood on a regular basis and must weigh this need against their motivation to comply. As a result, my expectations regarding their behavior are quite different. These latter individuals face a very high cost of compliance and, even if the cost of *non-compliance* were very high, many of them would rather risk enforcement-related penalties than face the alternatives. As one of my respondents explained, rationalizing her non-compliance, "They make us steal it. But even if we are thieves, we are alive."[33] Furthermore, even if these individuals believe they have a duty to comply, it is likely not powerful enough to overcome their poverty-driven non-compliance.

Finally, I hypothesize that among those individuals who have the option to both comply and attend to their basic needs, those motivated by either fear or duty will comply in significantly higher numbers than those of their low-income counterparts who have no viable option other than non-compliance.

External Validity: Shadow Cases

An example like the one I've been discussing, in which state regulations target ordinary individuals for compliance, could, on its own, be anomalous. An externally valid explanation of cross-border variation in compliance with wood-taking regulations in Chitwan and Valmiki National Parks should be able to withstand shifts to different regulatory contexts without generating contradictory findings. In order to probe the external validity of regulatory pragmatism, I include and examine two shadow cases. Through these shadow cases I explore the compliance-related behavior of two additional layers of Indian and Nepali society: businesses and organizations. More specifically, I examine: (1) the compliance of private school administrators/principals with regulations requiring particular, smaller-than-customary, teacher-student ratios in the classroom; and (2) the compliance of brick kiln owners/managers with child labor regulations. Doing so provides insight from two additional types of regulations in terms of subject matter and, perhaps more important, regulations aimed at two different target populations.

Overall, this book covers three different types of regulations, those related to conservation, education, and labor, because each regulatory context is, in many ways, unique and a good explanation of variation in compliance should retain its explanatory power as it travels among them. I did, however chose each of these regulatory contexts because they relate to major economic activities in the border region. In addition, regulations in both of these areas, as with the conservation regulations in the parks, attempt to bring about a public good, are of interest to most people, impose a cost on those who must comply, and have not been unduly influenced by India's colonial past.[34] In addition, in each of these cases, compliance requires behavior that is, at least to some degree, at odds with local cultural norms, while my key explanatory variable—state use of a strategy consistent with regulatory pragmatism— varies in the education case and not in the child labor/brick kilns case. Put differently, the shadow cases provide variation on both the independent variable and the subject area of regulation, while avoiding regulatory contexts in which confounding variables may limit hypothesis testability.

There is also variation amongst the three cases with respect to their target populations (i.e., the individuals or entities that are subject to regulation).[35] A good explanation of variation in compliance should continue to function even as the target population varies. Different target populations may prove more or less amenable to regulation for a number of reasons. For instance, target populations that are organizations or corporations may be more likely, because of their structure and purpose, to try to "game" a regulation that affects their financial interests by complying in only the most superficial manner. Such target populations, unlike individuals, may also feel less of a duty to comply with regulations because they do not "feel" in the traditional sense. Yet, this does not mean that corporate target populations do not respond to societal pressure. In fact, they may require what Gunningham, Kagan, and Thornton (2004) refer to as a "social license" to operate, something that individuals do not necessarily require and which can result in over-compliance. Thus, with the variation in compliance that can result from examining different target populations in mind, I examine whether ordinary individuals obey conservation regulations, whether private schools (organizations) follow teacher-student ratio regulations, and whether brick kilns (businesses) adhere to child labor regulations.

I chose these shadow cases as much for their similarity with my main conservation case as for the opportunity to observe the effects of varied state behavior that they offer. Education and brick manufacturing are major economic activities present on both sides of the border. Regulations governing these types of activities are commonly used by governments to try to change behaviors that are perceived to be harmful. Moreover, the behavior required by law in each of these cases stands in contrast to customary social practice and to self-interest. Yet, the efforts made by the governments on either side of the border vary distinctly in the schools case and not at all in the brick kilns case, allowing me to test the proposition that strategies consistent with regulatory pragmatism can foster accurate legal knowledge and compliance across multiple regulatory contexts. Collecting data on the compliance behavior of two additional commonly regulated target populations allows me to provide deeper analysis of the conditions under which coercively weak states are nevertheless able to generate compliance.

For these shadow cases I utilize the same variables present in the main conservation case: compliance, delegated enforcement, and accurate legal knowledge. I do, however, measure these variables differently. In the schools and brick kilns cases I measure compliance via observation, rating each school or kiln on the degree to which I observed it to be in compliance during my visit. In terms of delegated enforcement, I use this variable to distinguish between the two shadow cases, since none occurs in the brick kilns case, while the Indian government delegates to parents in the schools case via the 2009 Right to Education Act. Finally, I measure accurate legal knowledge in a manner that is quite similar to the method used in the conservation case. In the schools case, I ask principals/headmasters whether it is true that "[s]chools must provide at least one teacher for every 40 students (30 in India)"; I also ask, among other things, whether "[s]chools must ensure that all students have clean clothing to wear to school." In the brick kilns case, I ask managers/owners whether it is true that "[e]mployers must not hire workers under age 18" (the legal age of employment is actually fourteen); I also ask whether managers/owners "must provide workers with food and shelter in addition to pay." I discuss the methodology and measurement issues related to these two shadow cases more thoroughly when I discuss the cases themselves in Chapter 7.

Data Collection and Methodology

As few compliance-specific data have been collected throughout the world, never mind in India or Nepal, one of the primary purposes of my fieldwork and significant contributions of this book is the data itself. After briefly describing the units of analysis and units of observation, I will outline data sources for each of the cases below.

The empirical evidence used to support the argument in this book includes both survey data and interviews with relevant actors. I first collected[36] survey data from over 1,300 respondents, randomly sampling villages within walking distance of each park (10 km) and collecting randomized conven-ience samples[37] within each village. Each respondent was asked, in person, a series of questions that started with demographic information and proceeded to questions designed to help measure my variables of interest, including possible confounding variables. Both before and after survey data collection I conducted a series of thirty-five semi-structured, qualitative interviews.

In addition, to complement my survey data and to explore regulatory pragmatism further, I carried out an experiment designed to test the idea that local leaders can transmit legal knowledge. To do so, I first randomly selected three villages from the set of villages included in my larger survey and for which I had baseline data for approximately twenty-five individuals. I returned to each of these villages to conduct the series of interventions I described briefly above and then to measure post-treatment effects. As mentioned briefly above, this post-treatment survey also allowed me to par-tially replicate my findings from the larger survey.

Quantitative Data Collection

In order to avoid both reporting and response biases, I use indirect meas-ures to assess accuracy of legal understandings and compliance with na-tional park regulations.[38] For accuracy of legal understandings, I used a series of true-false questions about legal requirements to test the accuracy of respondent legal knowledge. For compliance, I asked respondents where they collected their firewood and then coded whether this was inside the na-tional park ("illegal") or outside of it ("legal"). Importantly, I asked this com-pliance question well before the accurate legal knowledge questions, so that respondents were not primed to answer in a compliant manner. I then coded responses based upon location-specific lists I developed for each country during preliminary fieldwork, as well as during the pilot for this survey. These lists roughly corresponded to the answers I received on either side of the border during the early phases of the project when I used a more open-ended question. The fact that the only substantial "other" response that I re-ceived during actual data collection was "purchase [firewood]" indicates that these categorizations are fairly accurate. Also, while concerns about the self-reported nature of this data are not unfounded, my experience has been that respondents on both sides of the border are quite forthcoming about where they collect wood, regardless of the legality of doing so. The fact that so many of my respondents on both sides of the border admit to collecting wood in the national parks is further evidence that self-reported compliance data are not problematic in this case. This is particularly true because I do not maintain that my data yield an accurate measure of compliance rates, only that relative rates should be accurate, as I have no reason to believe that respondents would be more or less likely to produce accurate responses on either side of the border.

In contrast to the measures for legal knowledge and compliance, I use direct measures, collected via survey, in order to assess Community Forest access, income levels, need for firewood, fear, duty, and a number of possible confounding variables, including dependence on eco-tourism, receipt of "goodwill program" benefits, and attitudes toward the national parks.[39] Relatedly, I construct a measure for amelioration of poverty-driven non-compliance by asking respondents whether they need fuelwood and whether they have access to a Community Forest. I then analyze this data by income level, comparing those below the poverty line and those above.

As questions related to Community Forest access, income levels, need for firewood, or any of my confounding variables are not likely to suffer from reporting or response bias in this context, direct assessment is not problematic. Direct questions related to fear and duty, however, may well suffer from either or both of these biases. In an effort to avoid same, I did test a number of indirect measures during the pilot phase of this project. In particular, I experimented with short, scenario-based questions to motivate and contextualize questions about fear and duty. Unfortunately, these stories merely confused respondents and many of them did not appear to have the patience to listen to them and make thoughtful decisions afterward. In fact, I got the impression that these measures were more likely to lead to bias than the direct measures I piloted. Respondents did not seem shy about reporting their fear of the state; they also didn't seem overeager to report that fear. The same was true for duty, though my subsequent qualitative interviews suggest that duty is the most complicated variable I measure. Many individuals seem to feel a genuine duty to obey the law, but they also feel other competing duties, like a duty to provide for their families. How they resolve these duties into action or inaction is not something I tackle in this book but, instead, is something I plan to examine in a subsequent project.

Qualitative Data Collection

In addition to the above-described large-N survey, I also personally conducted thirty-five follow-up interviews using snowball samples in three different locations and one focus group of forty-three women,[40] to better understand my survey data. I used semi-structured interviews during the first of these latter data collection endeavors in order to target particular information while still allowing respondents to communicate a wide range of answers. This technique allowed conversations to stray in sometimes unexpected directions and allowed me to gain quite a bit of insight into how and where respondents source information about the law. For the focus group, however, I used a slightly different technique. Here I chose to focus on women, as they are the members of a family who are typically responsible for wood collection and I believed they would speak more freely in a women-only environment. I introduced the topic by asking the group whether and why they needed wood, eventually steering the conversation toward regulations that govern wood collection. Group members started responding to one another, and many of the women seemed to feel more comfortable speaking freely among their friends and neighbors than they might in a one-on-one interview. This allowed me to sit back and observe not only the level of knowledge of wood-collection regulations, but who among the group was seen as authoritative on this particular subject and how information was passed between group members.

Units of Analysis and Units of Observation

Though this project is inherently local in focus and though I do not attempt to collect any generalizable, national-level data, I do analyze the data I collect at the inter-state level. In other words, I compare behavior on both sides of the India-Nepal border. As *intra*-state differences also exist and are illuminating, I conduct analysis at lower levels as well.

In order to avoid ecological inference problems, I make my units of observation correspond with my target populations. In the conservation case, individual behavior is regulated, so I collect individual-level data. In the case of private school and brick kiln regulation, I collect data at the school level and brick-kiln level, as individual schools and brick kilns are the units being regulated. In doing so, I was careful to collect data about the various higher-level units in which each target population is embedded to enable analysis at different levels of aggregation.

Data Sources

Ordinary Individuals (Conservation Regulation)

The survey data included in this book come from over 1,300 individuals living and/or working in proximity to Chitwan and Valmiki National Parks. These data facilitate measurement of compliance, accuracy of legal understandings, and poverty-driven non-compliance, all of which are detailed above. As the population of the districts surrounding these conservations areas is in excess of 1 million persons and no master list of these individuals is available, I sampled villages—a visual display of which can be found in Chapter 4—instead and then conducted convenience samples within these villages using a right-hand rule randomization technique. Sampling villages allowed me to collect data from individuals embedded in a variety of different geographic and administrative contexts.

In order to assess compliance, I asked respondents to state whether people "in this area" collect wood in the national park. Collecting data on compliance in this manner allowed individuals to freely report what they observe without forcing individuals—who are sometimes aware that this activity is illegal—into a situation in which they feel they should answer untruthfully in order to present themselves as law-abiding citizens or in order to avoid punishment.[41] In addition, I asked individual where they collect wood. I backed this approach up with observational data collected from two similarly situated sites, one at each of the park borders of Valmiki and Chitwan. At each site I collected data on twenty-five randomly sampled days, spread out over three months, observing and counting individuals exiting the forest with firewood.

As detailed above, I assess accuracy of legal understandings somewhat differently. Respondents were read a series of five "true-false" questions. I tailored these questions to assess respondents' understanding of both the law I was looking to investigate and closely related laws. So, for instance, respondents in this case, the conservation case, received questions about park regulations. After the fact, I was then able to compare respondents' answers, at different levels of aggregation, to the behavior required or prohibited by law, using the absolute value of the difference between average responses in a particular area—ones for true and zeros for false—and the "correct response." On the Nepal side of the border I also used a question regarding whether respondents have access to a Community Forest to assess whether individuals are privy to the legal understanding that wood collection in Community Forests is permissible under the law and preferable to wood collection in Chitwan National Park. While Joint Forest Management exists in India, and has been quite successful, no program is in place in the area surrounding Valmiki Tiger Reserve, so I did not ask this question in India.

Finally, I assess poverty-driven non-compliance by first examining individual's reported earnings, since low earnings mean that individuals will almost certainly be dependent upon wood for cooking and heating. I then cross-reference earnings with respondents' housing type, with poor housing being an indication that low reported earnings are indicative of meager resources and good housing being an indication that low reported earnings are inaccurate. Next I separate out those respondents who report having access to a Community Forest[42] and being motivated by fear or duty to comply with the law, from those who are motivated by either fear or duty, but lack access to a Community Forest. I then compare the locations that individuals in these two groups report that they get their wood, measuring poverty-driven non-compliance with the proportion of respondents, at a particular level of aggregation, who are poor, lack access to a community forest, are motivated by either fear or duty, and report wood collection in "the National Park."

I supplement the above-described survey data with qualitative data.[43] In total, I conducted thirty-five interviews with bureaucrats, local leaders, and ordinary individuals to explore different aspects of my data and to understand what attempts the states on either side of the border have made to bring about compliance with wood-collection regulations.

Organizations (Private School Regulation)

I examine compliance with teacher-student ratio regulations observationally, at least in part because this is the cleanest and most straightforward way to get accurate compliance data with respect to this more-sophisticated target population. I did do so under the premise of collecting survey data on the schools themselves and on how administrators perceive regulations, which I accomplished in much the same way as in the conservation case, asking respondents education law-related questions. This allowed me to collect data on the accuracy of legal understandings at the same time. I employ these data to measure the degree of overlap between legal understandings and behavior required by law in the same way I do in the conservation case above and the brick kilns case below. I do not assess poverty-driven non-compliance in this case because there is no "community forest option" that would allow me to compare the compliance of those of the poor who are who are given a low-cost compliance option to those who are not. I was able, however, to collect economic data, using revenue and fees, which allow me to evaluate whether compliance at the "poorest schools" is worse than that at the "wealthiest schools."

As the number of private schools in the region is manageable, I used lists acquired from the Ministries of Education in both India and Nepal to census rather than sample this "population" of entities—collecting survey data from senior administrators at each school. While there were three schools on the government lists that I was unable to locate in the field, I have no *a priori* reason to believe that these missing data limit the conclusions drawn from my census. Private schools regularly go out of business in both India and Nepal and my interviews indicate that it is not likely that these schools were driven "underground" by deterrence-based enforcement.

I also conducted fifteen interviews with bureaucrats and parents to add richness to the quantitative data and to explore interesting patterns in same.

Businesses (Child Labor Regulation)
As with the private school regulations above, I assess compliance with child labor regulations at brick kilns observationally. This strategy bypasses owners and managers and is the cleanest and most straightforward way to get accurate compliance data. Under the premise of collecting survey data on labor in brick kilns and on how brick kiln owners and managers perceive regulations, I was able to observe child labor, in much the same way I did for the private schools case, while assessing the accuracy of legal knowledge and asking respondents labor law–related questions. I employ these data to measure the degree of overlap between legal understandings and behavior required by law in the same way as in the conservation and private schools cases above. As with the private schools case, I do not attempt to assess poverty-driven non-compliance in brick kilns; in this case too there is no "community forest option" that would allow me to determine whether a low-cost route to compliance makes a difference in terms of demonstrated behavior. That said, I collected data on revenue and brick prices at each kiln and use this data to evaluate whether compliance is more common at the more profitable kilns than at the less profitable.

As the number of brick kilns in the region is manageable, as brick kilns are large and quite visible operations, and as no comprehensive list of them exists, I used satellite imagery to locate all brick kilns in the region surrounding Birgunj and Raxaul Bazaar, the twin border cities located in Nepal and India, respectively. I was then able to collect data on a census basis, from just over fifty brick kilns. I was also careful to look for brick kilns that had been built since Google Earth last updated its images of the region. These are easy to find since the region is completely flat and the chimney of a brick kiln can be seen from many miles away. While I found no new kilns, several of the kilns I found via satellite imagery were no longer in operation at the time of data collection. In addition, four kilns in my census refused to participate in the survey. Each of these is located quite close to Raxaul Bazaar and all were very concerned about their responses to child labor–related questions somehow getting into government hands. I will elaborate on this anomalous group later, but, for the moment, it is sufficient to state that observed use of child labor at these kilns was no more frequent than elsewhere in the region and I have no *a priori* reason to believe that these missing data undercut my census.

Though I had hoped to conduct a number of interviews with brick kiln workers to add richness to the quantitative data I collected and to explore interesting patterns in the data, I found that brick kiln owners and managers were unwilling, for somewhat obvious business reasons, to let me interview their workers.

4

Compliance in the Absence of Significant Coercive Capacity

Nepal and India share a border 1,770 km in length. Roughly in the middle of the long, southern stretch of that border is a largely forested region that is home to a variety of endangered species, of both the plant and animal variety. Living in proximity with this fragile natural landscape are millions of people who exist largely at the fringes of the larger societies they nominally belong to. Those living in Paschim and Purba Champaran, in Bihar, India, or in Chitwan, Parsa, Makwanpur, or Nawalparasi, in Nepal, would be considered to be relatively peripheral by government figures in Patna or in Kathmandu, respectively.

Despite their "peripheral" status, the Indians and Nepalis inhabiting this region live lives that are, in many ways, representative of those throughout the developing world. Small villages dot the landscape. These villages are surrounded by fields that are still plowed by hand or by water buffalo, not by large machinery. Most live by way of subsistence agriculture, the others from hand to mouth. Some of these villages are electrified, but many are not. The electricity coming to those villages that do have it is sporadic. Very few of the roads in the region are paved, and many are nearly impassible in the rainy season. Very little non-agricultural commerce occurs here. Hotels and restaurants are almost nonexistent, though the cities do have both. Your average village has a shop or two, but one could spend weeks or even months in the region without spending money at all. There simply aren't places to spend it.

Beyond the fields, but rarely out of view, lies the forest. For many living in this region, the forest supplies much of what they need on a day-to-day basis. It supplies wood for cooking and heating, a variety of building materials, edible plants and flowers, medicines, etc. If one has little income and few resources, living near the forest can be a good thing for those who are motivated. The forest is not an unqualified good, however. Living near

Capacity beyond Coercion. Susan L. Ostermann, Oxford University Press. © Oxford University Press 2023.
DOI: 10.1093/oso/9780197661116.003.0004

the forest and foraging in it can be quite dangerous. Every year people in this region are trampled and killed by rhinoceroses. Elephants also do damage and, in fact, while I was conducting the fieldwork for this book, there was a wild elephant that was terrorizing a group of villages in Madi, Nepal. Several people died while sleeping in their own homes at night. In another village I visited, a local man was killed by a tiger during the few days we were conducting interviews. I seriously considered throwing the data out until there was another incident in this village just a few months later. Those living in this region know better than I that the forest giveth and the forest taketh away.

One of the things that makes a tenuous existence worthwhile for those living along this stretch of the India-Nepal border is a very rich cultural life. On both sides of the border, the region is populated by people of the Tharu ethnic group, who have made it their home for as long as anyone can tell. They are considered indigenous to the area. Indeed, they have been living for so long in what was malarial jungle until recently that, as a people, they are resistant to malaria: it does not make them ill. And, despite an influx of "outsiders" after malaria was largely eradicated, Tharu customs and festivals continue to be mainstays of village life. The arrival of cell phones and other modern conveniences has not dented Jitiya and Maaghi celebrations, which go on and are celebrated regardless of ethnic group. The fabric of social life, at the local level, is quite strong.

The state, however, is quite weak. Signs of it are few and far between in the border region. For many, the state only comes to town during elections when politicians seek local votes, and the state facilitates the participation in public life of those who live in this region. In between elections, the most prominent examples of the state's presence are the existence of the national parks, the occasional border post, and the availability of public schools. It is also important to note the form the state took during this period. While India was federal and remained so after data collection was completed in 2013, Nepal was unitary. It was not, in fact, until Nepal's 2015 constitution that federalism was formalized and new province boundaries drawn up.

The three novel quantitative data sets collected for this project and the associated qualitative data represent a virtual treasure trove of information about this understudied part of the world. In this chapter I provide a snapshot into that world, looking largely at the conservation case, but also at the two shadow cases, namely the schools and brick kilns cases.

Conservation Case

Just outside of Chitwan and Valmiki National Parks lie many villages that fit the above description quite closely. Generally, the closer one lives to either of these parks, the poorer the population and the more limited the services that are available. A few of the homes are made of concrete and rebar, but most are more traditional, made of mud, bamboo, and thatch. Small garden patches exist outside of most homes and sometimes livestock as well. The sounds of the forest are never far away. The call of parrots and peacocks is nearly ever present. In the foreground, however, one often hears the sound of cooking and the friendly chatter of neighbors.

To gain great insight into the compliance behavior of people living in these villages, I conducted a survey of 1,344 respondents,[1] with 694 in Nepal and 650 in India. The location of the villages sampled for this data collection effort are depicted visually in Figure 4.1, and the number of respondents in each location can be found in Figure 4.2. Data were collected in January 2013.

As shown in Figure 4.3, there were 682 female and 662 male survey respondents. Gender was assessed by enumerators and not by respondents themselves, something that is relatively straightforward in this area due to the rigidity of gender roles and the style of dress associated with same.

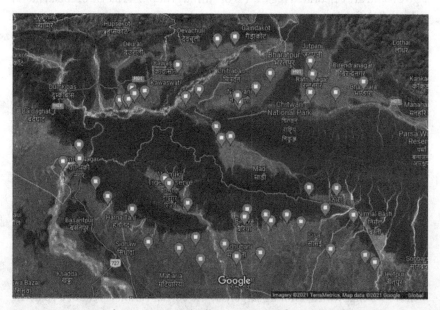

Figure 4.1 Respondent Locations (Villages Sampled for Data Collection)

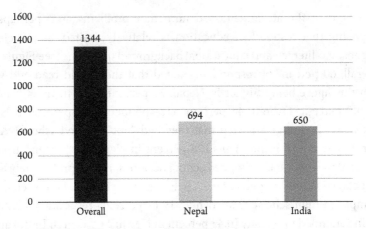

Figure 4.2 Number of Respondents by Location

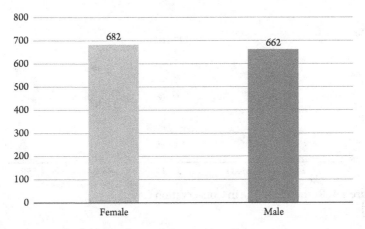

Figure 4.3 Respondent Gender in Conservation Case

As shown in Figure 4.4, the ages of these respondents covered the full spectrum from 18 to over 55. Approximately 10 percent of respondents stated that their age fell in the 18–24 category, while 21.21 percent claimed the 25–34 category, 27 percent the 35–44 category, 19 percent the 45–54 category, and 20 percent the over-55 category. Meanwhile, 3 percent of respondents stated that they did not know their age. The last category would, in my experience, be larger if I had asked for a precise answer to the age question rather than requesting that respondents pick a range of ages that was appropriate for them. Many individuals living in this area do not know their specific age, in part due to numeracy and record-keeping problems.

In light of the aforementioned numeracy problems, it is perhaps not surprising that respondent education is relatively limited, as reflected in responses to literacy and educational background questions (see Figure 4.5). Overall, 60 percent of respondents stated that they could read and write, with this figure being higher in Nepal, 71 percent, than in India, where it was 49 percent. Overall, 46 percent of respondents (49 percent in Nepal; 42 percent in India) reported that they had "not attended school." A further 35 percent of respondents (28 percent in Nepal; 43 percent in India) reported that they had "attended school occasionally." Approximately 6 percent of respondents (2 percent in Nepal; 11 percent in India) reported having "completed high school." Meanwhile, 19 (1 percent) respondents reported having attended university (0.43 percent in Nepal; 2 percent in India) and 47 (4 percent) respondents reported having "completed university" (6 percent

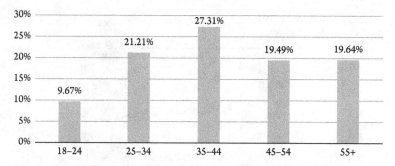

Figure 4.4 Respondent Age in Conservation Case

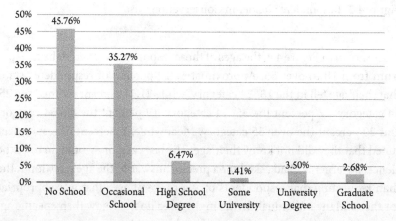

Figure 4.5 Respondent Education in Conservation Case

in Nepal; 0.46 percent in India). Finally, 36 (3 percent) respondents had "attended or completed graduate school" (5 percent in Nepal; 0.46 percent in India). These data suggest, among other things, that respondents would have great difficulty learning about the law by reading it themselves.

Respondents would likely be quite familiar with social norms, however, as respondents were not, on average, migrants to this area. Respondents were asked how long "you or your family have been living here?" As indicated in Figure 4.6, in Nepal, the average response was 33 years, with individuals giving responses that ranged from 1 year to 105 years. In India, the average response was 45 years, with responses from 1 to 405 years. These are, of course, estimates, and record-keeping is poor in this region. Thus, longer tenures should not be considered precise, while shorter tenures, those within recent memory, are more likely to be accurate. Most important for purposes of the argument advanced in this book, however, respondents were largely not recent transplants to the region who may have brought with them a different set of social norms or, potentially, familiarity with different laws.

Landownership has the potential to be an important correlate of need for firewood, as individuals who can source firewood on their own property are unlikely to need to enter a national park to collect same. Respondents, on both side of the border, were landowners, but few were business owners—facts that should not be surprising given the dominance of subsistence agriculture and poverty in the region. Overall, 71 percent of respondents stated that they owned land, with this number being 81 percent in Nepal and

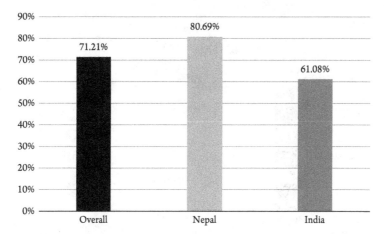

Figure 4.6 Respondent Land Ownership by Location in Conservation Case

61 percent in India. These statistics are not surprising in light of the fact that land reform is widely acknowledged to have been more complete in Nepal's Terai than just across the border in Bihar.

Business ownership, at least in theory, might indicate an ability to pay for firewood or different types of connections within the community that could plausibly related to compliance behavior. There was some cross-border variation in this regard, as shown in Figure 4.7. Only 24 percent of respondents stated that they or someone in their family owns a business. In Nepal, this figure was 32 percent of respondents, while in India, it was 15 percent. These figures, and in particular the cross-border variation in business ownership, are also not that surprising. Road quality in this area, at least at the time of research, was better in Nepal than in India and the time required to get to markets was somewhat shorter. That said, explaining this variation more thoroughly would be a fruitful area for future research.

Those who do not own a business are, for the most part, involved in subsistence agriculture. While the survey did not contain a measure for this, the vast majority in this region still feed and support themselves in this manner. A small minority are involved in ecotourism. Overall, when asked whether "you or your family members work in ecotourism," 5 percent of respondents answered in the affirmative. As might be expected, given that ecotourism is more developed and has a longer history in Chitwan than in Valmiki, far more of these individuals live in Nepal than in India: 91 percent of them. This puts the rates of involvement in ecotourism at 9 percent in Nepal and 1 percent in India. In addition to ecotourism, another small minority work for

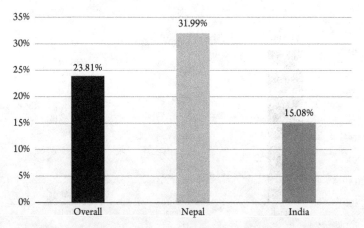

Figure 4.7 Respondent Business Ownership by Location in Conservation Case

the government. Overall, 15 percent of those surveyed responded positively to the question "do you or your family members work for the government?" In Nepal, this statistic was once again higher, with 27 percent having some familial employment connection to the government, while in India on 3 percent of respondents claimed the same.

Regardless of income source, poverty is rampant and few in this region are making significant sums of money. This is important because poverty has the potential to drive non-compliance when individuals cannot get their basic needs[2] met without breaking the law. Overall, as indicated in Figure 4.8, 72 percent reported earning less than 32,000 Nepali rupees or 20,000 Indian rupees per year (Category 1). This response was chosen by 71 percent of respondents in Nepal and 72 percent of respondents in India. A further 22 percent of respondents, overall, reported earning 32,000–100,000 Nepali rupees or 20,000–60,000 Indian rupees per year (Category 2). This response was chosen by 22 percent of respondents in Nepal and 23 percent of respondents in India. The next category, 100,000–500,000 Nepali rupees or 60,000–300,000 Indian rupees, was chosen by 4 percent of respondents, with this statistic being 5 percent in Nepal and 3 percent in India (Category 3). Finally, one individual in India and no individuals in Nepal reported earning more than 500,000 Nepali rupees or more than 300,000 Indian rupees (Category 4). The remaining 1 percent of respondents did not know the answer to this question or refused to say. Overall, the data suggest the potential for poverty-driven non-compliance on both sides of the border.

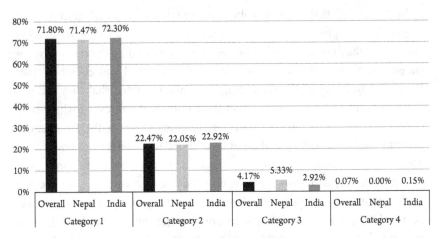

Figure 4.8 Respondent Income in Conservation Case

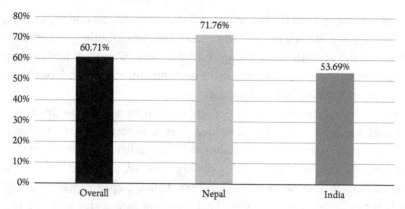

Figure 4.9 Respondent Fuelwood Need by Location

In light of the above-described poverty levels, it should not be surprising that 61 percent of respondents report needing fuelwood in order to cook or heat their homes, with 72 percent stating so in Nepal, and 54 percent in India (see Figure 4.9). Meanwhile, an additional 15 percent of respondents stated that they sometimes need fuelwood and 22 percent claimed that they do not use fuelwood. When asked what fuel they use to cook with and what they use to build their homes, responds gave a range of different responses. Those who do not use wood exclusively for cooking use fuels ranging from gas/ kerosene, to sugar cane leaves and corn cobs, to dung patties. Respondents also incorporate a variety of building materials into the construction of their homes. The most popular combination is mud, bamboo, and wood, but some more modern constructions use bricks and concrete.

In terms of their wood collection practices, a small minority of respondents, 7 percent, collect wood on their own land, while 61 percent stated that they collect wood elsewhere exclusively, and a further 7 percent stated that they collect wood both on their own land and elsewhere (see Figure 4.10). Many of the remaining respondents stated that they did not need wood in order to cook or heat their homes. When asked where they collected wood, respondents gave a variety of responses, with 53 percent of them providing answers that did not involve collection in the national parks. Their responses ranged from wood collection in the Community Forests and Buffer Zone to purchasing wood and collecting wood from other people's land. Interestingly, 65 percent of respondents (68 percent in Nepal; 62 percent in India) stated that "people around here go into the National Park to collect fallen wood." Meanwhile, only 28 percent of respondents had access

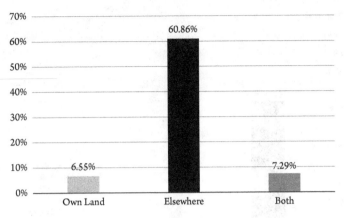

Figure 4.10 Fuelwood Collection Location Figure

to a Community Forest and all of them were surveyed in Nepal. Thus, the data indicate substantial demand for firewood on both sides of the border, with very few respondents able to meet this demand using private resources.

Importantly, in addition to substantial demand for firewood on both sides of the border, respondent beliefs and perceptions about firewood collection and related law vary in some ways, while remaining relatively consistent in others. Many respondents, as indicated in Figure 4.11, believe that some people are collecting wood in the national park in their area, with more doing so in Nepal than in India, while 24 percent of respondents (20 percent in Nepal; 28 percent in India) believe people have a right to collect wood in protected areas. Approximately 76 percent believe that they do not (80 percent in Nepal; 71 percent in India), as depicted in Figure 4.12.

Meanwhile, 82 percent believed that they *should* have a right to collect wood in protected areas and 2 percent believed they should not. These numbers suggest that there is strong support for wood-collection rights. What is unclear, however, is what respondents believe to be "protected areas." In Nepal, for instance, Community Forests are protected areas, but people do have a right to collect wood in them, whereas the opposite is true in the national park. In India, at least in this area, there is no Community Forest analogue.

In addition to needing firewood and other forest products and believing that they should have a right to them, respondents also believe they have responsibilities with respect to the forest, as shown in Figure 4.13. In terms of people's duties to the forest, 98 percent believe that people have a duty

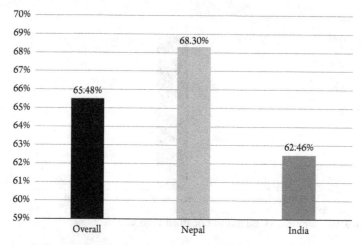

Figure 4.11 Percentage of Respondents Who Believe Others Collect Wood in the National Park by Location

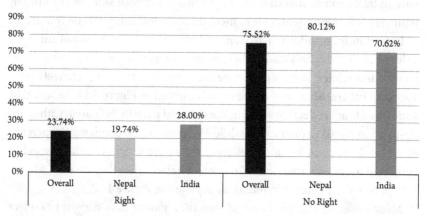

Figure 4.12 Perception of the Existence of a "Right" to Collect Wood in Protected Areas by Location

to protect the forest, while 1 percent believe that people do not. When asked whose duty protection should be, 10 percent believed the government alone should be responsible (2 percent in Nepal; 19 percent in India), while 12 percent believed the people alone should be responsible (12 percent in Nepal; 13 percent in India), and another 77 percent believe that both the government and the people should be responsible for protecting the forest (87 percent in Nepal; 66 percent in India). The fact that the overwhelming majority of respondents on both sides of the border believe they

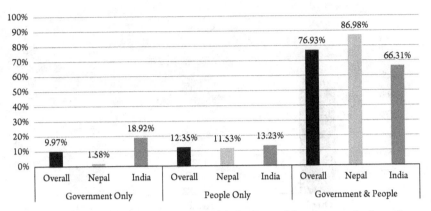

Figure 4.13 Perception of Party Responsible for Forest Management by Location

have a duty to project the forest, something that is ingrained in local culture, suggests that the background social norms, against which the Nepali and Indian states impose wood collection regulations, are quite similar on both sides of the border. It also suggests that legal norms are not actually at odds with social norms, even if they do differ regarding *how* to protect the forest.

In addition to legal norms not truly being at odds with social norms, respondents are largely not adverse to legal compliance more generally. In terms of how respondents view the law, 91 percent believe they always have a duty to obey it, with that number being 94 percent in Nepal and 89 percent in India (see Figure 4.14). In terms of the state's enforcement ability for wood-collection prohibitions, respondents perceive it to be high, at least relative to what the Nepali and Indian states claim to be capable of. When asked whether they believed someone would be caught by authorities if he or she went into the national park and collected wood, 66 percent believe that this person would be caught, while 33 percent believe that he or she would not be caught. If caught, 87 percent of respondents believe that a wood collector will be punished, while 8 percent of respondents believe that he or she will go unpunished. As indicated in Figure 4.15, only 15 percent of respondents believe that punishment to be "harsh," however, while 40 percent believe it to be "reasonable" and 35 percent believe it to be "not very harsh." These data suggest that variation in compliance along the India-Nepal border is likely not explained by variation in traditional deterrence-model factors like "fear" or "duty."

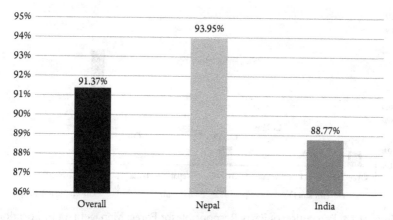

Figure 4.14 Perception of Duty to Obey the Law by Location in Conservation Case

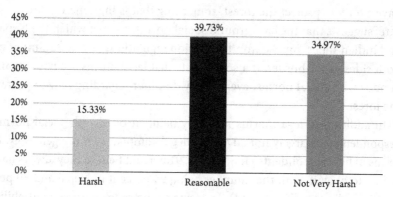

Figure 4.15 Perceived Harshness of Wood Collection Punishment

Finally, in addition to similar reported rates of fear and duty, respondents on either side of the border seemed to view the costs and benefits associated with leaving near the national parks quite similarly (see Figure 4.16). Indeed, 40 percent of respondents believed that they benefited from such a location (40 percent in Nepal; 39 percent in India). Meanwhile, 47 percent believed that living near the parks was harmful (46 percent in Nepal; 48 percent in India), and a further 12 percent believed that there were both benefits and costs to living near the parks (13 percent in Nepal; 11 percent in India). When asked to name these costs and benefits, many respondents stated that proximity to a grass and fuel collection areas was a benefit, while crop damage and loss of life due to wildlife incursions were costs. Approximately

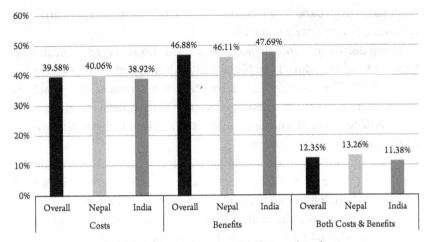

Figure 4.16 Perceived Value of Living near the National Park

38 percent of respondents reported that they had lost crops, livestock, or family members to wildlife (16 percent in Nepal; 62 percent in India), while only twelve individuals (1 percent of respondents) claimed they had received compensation for those losses, with all but one of those individuals being surveyed in Nepal. It is interesting, and an important sign of the times perhaps, that several respondents on both sides of the border stated that a benefit of being close to the parks was reduced pollution.

When taken together, the above-described and illustrated data suggest few major cross-border differences in terms of the demographic and other variables traditionally associated with compliance. Thus, the empirical puzzle that launched this research project remains unsolved after analysis of descriptive statistics alone.

Schools Case

Private schools in Birgunj, Nepal, and Raxaul Bazaar, India, take many different forms. Some are very simple one-room affairs with flimsy walls, a tin roof, a chalkboard, and benches for students to sit on. Others are remarkably sophisticated, with state-of-the-art classroom technology, good lab equipment, air conditioning, and other amenities. Many fall somewhere in the middle. Students arrive at these schools on foot, on bicycles, in share-ride vehicles, and in imported cars. The teaching and learning that goes on inside them range from barked orders and rote memorization to experiential education and Socratic-style dialogue.

To dig deeper into compliance in this context, I surveyed 53 principals/ headmasters,[3] including 17 in Nepal and 36 in India, in February 2013 (see Figure 4.17). The resulting data set represents a census of the principals/ headmasters at all private schools in operation at the time of the survey in the twin border cities of Birgunj and Raxaul Bazaar. Overall, there were 6 female and 47 male survey respondents.

Education levels, which are important for individual-level ability to learn about the law, were much higher among respondents in the schools case. Overall, all but one respondent (98 percent of respondents) stated that they could read and write, with the only non-"yes" response being from a respondent who refused to answer this question. Overall, as indicated in Figure 4.18, no respondents reported that they had "not attended school," "attended school occasionally," or only "completed high school." One respondent, representing 2 percent of the sample, reported having "attended university." This individual was surveyed in India. A further 55 percent of respondents (82 percent in Nepal; 412 percent in India) reported that they had "completed university." Meanwhile, a further 42 percent of respondents had "attended or completed graduate school" (18 percent in Nepal; 53 percent in India). One respondent refused to answer this question.

Unlike respondents in the conservation case, a minority of respondents, on both sides of the border, were land owners: only 38 percent, with that number being 24 percent in Nepal and 44 percent in India (see Figure 4.19). These relatively low land ownership numbers should not be surprising given

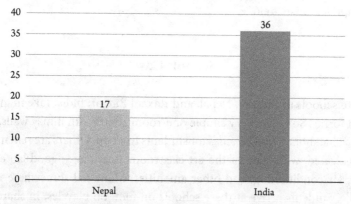

Figure 4.17 Respondent Location in Schools Case

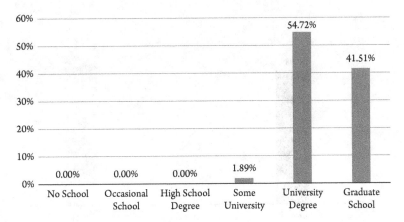

Figure 4.18 Respondent Education in Schools Case

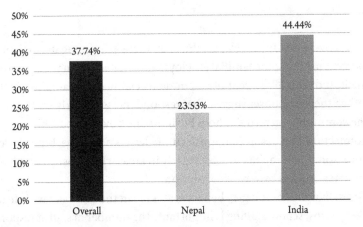

Figure 4.19 Land Ownership by Location in Schools Case

that this survey was conducted in an urban area. Meanwhile, as shown in Figure 4.20, a majority of respondents (or their families) were business owners: 60 percent of respondents stated that they or someone in their family owns a business. In Nepal, this figure was 59 percent of respondents, while in India, it was 61 percent. In all likelihood, the business many of these individuals (or their families) own is the school they are involved in running, as private education is a relatively lucrative source of income in this area. In addition, nearly half of respondents either work for the government themselves or have a family member who does. Overall, 49 percent of respondents responded positively to the question "do you or your family members work

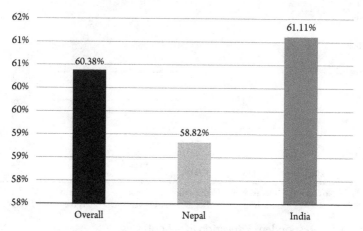

Figure 4.20 Business Ownership by Location in Schools Case

for the government?" In Nepal, this statistic was once again higher, with 71 percent having some familial employment connection to the government, while in India on 39 percent of respondents claimed the same. When taken together, these responses suggest that respondents were fairly well connected in the community in terms of both business and governance. This level of interconnection may result in more accurate legal knowledge, but this doesn't mean automatic compliance, particularly in areas where costly compliance is sometimes avoided by way of corruption.

Given that the compliance behavior at issue in the schools case is teacher-student ratios, school staffing is important. The number of staff at respondent schools ranged from 5 to 30. As depicted in Figure 4.21, the median number of staff at respondent schools was 12 (mean of 12.34), with this number being 11.88 in Nepal and 12.56 in India. Meanwhile, stated enrollment ranged from 50 to 1,000. The median in terms of enrollment was 250 (mean of 289), with these numbers being 225/237 in Nepal and 250/314 in India (see Figure 4.22). The ratio of students to staff ranged from 10:1 to 38.54:1, with the median ratio being 21.9:1 in Nepal and 23.1:1 in India). While these numbers sound relatively good, one should keep in mind that these are student-*staff* ratios, not student-teacher ratios. Still, the lack of cross-border variation is important.

Wealth or income, which can affect a target population's ability to comply, is an important factor to examine in this particular case, since hiring additional teachers may be more feasible for some than others. Regardless

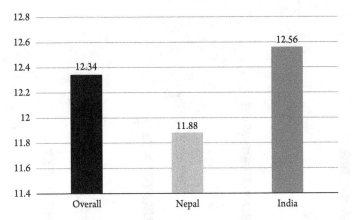

Figure 4.21 Mean Number of Staff by Location in Schools Case

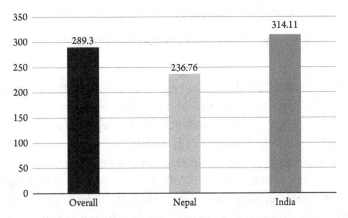

Figure 4.22 Mean Number of Students by Location in Schools Case

of income source, as indicated in Figure 4.23, few schools in this region are making significant sums of money. Overall, 9 percent reported earning less than 32,000 Nepali rupees or 20,000 Indian rupees per year (Category 1). All respondents who chose this category were located in India. A further 15 percent of respondents, overall, reported earning 32,000–100,000 Nepali rupees or 20,000–60,000 Indian rupees per year (Category 2). This response was chosen by 12 percent of respondents in Nepal and 17 percent of respondents in India. The next category, 100,000–500,000 Nepali rupees or 60,000–300,000 Indian rupees, was chosen by 11 percent of respondents, with this statistic being 6 percent in Nepal and 14 percent in India (Category 3). Finally, 9 percent of respondents reported earning

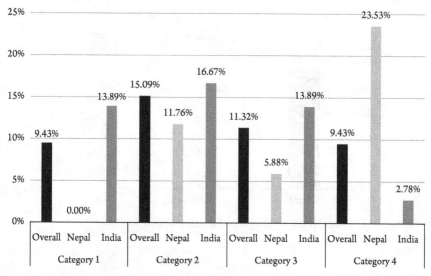

Figure 4.23 Percentage of Schools in Each Revenue Category by Location

more than 500,000 Nepali rupees or more than 300,000 Indian rupees (Category 4). Four out of the five who gave this response were in Nepal, meaning that 24 percent of respondents in Nepal reported earnings greater than 5 lakh, with only 3 percent of respondents in India chose this category. The remaining 49 percent of respondents did not know the answer to this question or refused to say. While the distribution of earnings does present differently on either side of the border, the data do not suggest that schools on either side are more or less capable of hiring additional teachers to comply with ratio regulations.

Another important constraint on schools' financial situation and ability to pay is how much they can collect in fees from students. Just as revenue varies tremendously from school to school in the Birgunj-Raxaul Bazaar area, school fees vary as well. To gain admission to school, students often pay admission fees. In Nepal, these ranged from no fees to 1,400 Nepali rupees, with a mean of 476 and a median of 400. In India, admission fees ranged from no fees to 5,000 Indian rupees, with a mean of 994 and a median of 500. Once admitted, students pay regular tuition fees to attend. In Nepal, these ranged from 5,400 to 9,600 Nepali rupees, with a mean of 7,311 and a median of 7,200. In India, regular tuition ranged much more widely, from 450 to 6,500 Indian rupees, with a mean of 2,456 and a median of 1,900. Here, again, the distribution on either side of the border is distinct, but schools on both sides take in reasonably similar fees overall, suggesting that this variable is not a significant constraint on compliance.

Finally, because the Birgunj-Raxaul Bazaar area has quite a bit of cross-border activity, I surveyed respondents regarding the citizenship of the students attending their schools. In Nepal, an average of 96 percent of students are Nepali, with a range from 90–100 percent at individual schools, at least according to administrators. In India, the same number for students holding Indian citizenship is 96 percent, with a range from 80 percent to 100 percent at individual schools. Thus, in general, students attend school on their own side of the border, but there is some cross-border enrollment.

Here, again, the above-described and illustrated schools suggest few major cross-border differences in terms of the demographic and other variables traditionally associated with compliance. Thus, descriptive statistics alone do not predict variation in compliance.

Brick Kilns Case

Brick kilns are dusty, hot places, especially in the month of May, which is when I completed the fieldwork for this portion of the project. The kiln itself is often oval-shaped (as seen from the air), with a single, tall smokestack that rises high above the flat plains, and can be seen from miles away. Bricks are typically made quite near the kiln and are constructed from the clay/mud in nearby fields. Some brick kiln workers form the bricks from this clay/mud, stamping each with a unique symbol associated with the kiln. Others transport the bricks to the kiln. Still others place these bricks in the kiln where they are fired until they reach the right color, removed, and then set aside to cool. Many kilns also have small encampments nearby, particularly if workers are migrant laborers. There is typically a tent or structure devoted to food preparation. There is often a sturdier structure or building as well. This is where the manager or owner stays while he oversees the operation. In the shade of this latter building, temperatures might be 45° C. In the sun, near the kiln, they are considerably higher. It must be nearly unbearable work.

To gain deeper insight into the child labor practices associated with these kilns, I surveyed 49 owners/managers,[4] 26 of whom were in Nepal and 23 of whom were in India (see Figure 4.24). I carried out the survey in May 2013. The resulting data represent a census of the owners/managers at all brick kilns in operation (at the time of the survey) within 10 km of

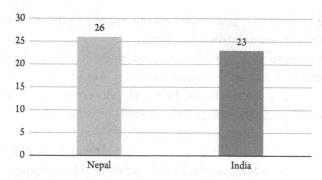

Figure 4.24 Respondent Location in Brick Kilns Case

the India-Nepal border as it runs from Chitwan and Valmiki in the west to Birgunj and Raxaul Bazaar in the east. Three brick kiln owners refused to participate in the survey, but I was still able to observe whether child labor was being used at each kiln. Overall, there were 6 female and 43 male survey respondents, with 4 out of 26 respondents in Nepal being female and 2 out of 23 in India.

Owners/manager of brick kilns were both literate and fairly well educated, which is important for their ability to learn about the law. Overall, all but 2, or 96 percent, of respondents stated that they could read and write. Meanwhile, no respondents reported that they had "not attended school." As indicated in Figure 4.25, two respondents, one in Nepal and one in India, stated that they had "attended school occasionally." A further 55 percent of respondents confirmed that they had "completed high school" (62 percent in Nepal and 48 percent in India). Approximately 12 percent of respondents had "attended university" (12 percent in Nepal and 13 percent in India), while a further single respondent surveyed in Nepal had "completed university." Finally, 8 percent of respondents, all of whom were surveyed in India, had "attended or completed graduate school." Another 9 respondents, or 18 percent of the sample (19 percent in Nepal and 17 percent in India), refused to answer this question. These data suggest that literacy, an important skill for learning about the law, will not prove predictive of cross-border variation in compliance with child labor law.

Unlike respondents in the conservation case, a majority of respondents, on both sides of the border, were land owners: 73 percent, with that number being 65 percent in Nepal and 78 percent in India (see Figure

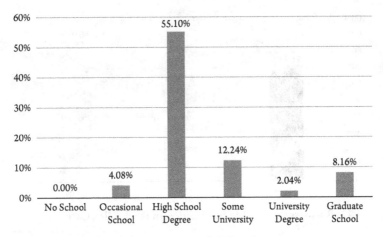

Figure 4.25 Respondent Education in Brick Kilns Case

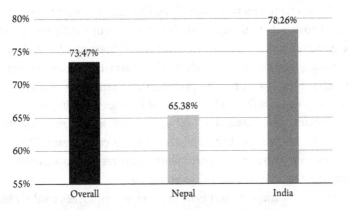

Figure 4.26 Land Ownership by Location in Brick Kilns Case

4.26). These relatively high land ownership numbers should not be surprising in light of the fact that respondents to this survey were business owners or managers.

Meanwhile, as depicted in Figure 4.27, a majority of respondents (or their families) were business owners: 71 percent of respondents stated that they or someone in their family owns a business. In Nepal, this figure was 58 percent of respondents, while in India, it was 87 percent. In all likelihood, the business many of these individuals (or their families) own is the brick kiln they are involved in running. In addition, unlike respondents in the schools

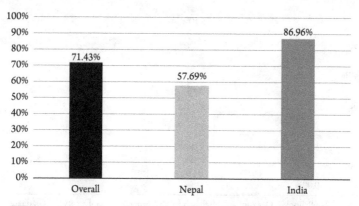

Figure 4.27 Business Ownership by Location in Brick Kilns Case

case, only a minority of respondents either work for the government themselves or have a family member who does. Overall, 20 percent of respondents responded positively to the question "do you or your family members work for the government?" Only one of these individuals was located in Nepal, representing 3 percent of respondents. In contrast, in India, 39 percent of respondents either work for the government themselves or have a family member who does. Still, landowning and business owning status does, as with the schools case, suggest a level of connection that may lead to more accurate legal knowledge, but not necessarily to compliance. The fact that cross-border variation exists, particularly with respect to business ownership, is worthy of note and further exploration.

The size of a business in terms of number of employees could, plausibly, affect compliance rates in terms of child labor, with it being more difficult for managers of the largest kilns to ensure that all staff are of a legal working age. The data indicate a very wide range in this case. The number of staff at respondent brick kilns ranged from 30 to 350. As shown in Figure 4.28, the median number of staff at respondent kilns was 125 (mean of 134), with this number being 100 in Nepal (mean of 111) and 150 in India (mean of 154). Figure 4.29 shows how far staff live from the kilns at which they work. Approximately half (51 percent) of the staff at respondents kilns (42 percent in Nepal and 61 percent in India) live less than five km from the kiln in which they are employed (Category 1), at least according to their employers. A further 35 percent of staff at respondent kilns live between 5 and 10 km away (35 percent in Nepal and 35 percent in India) (Category 2). Staff at another 6 percent of kilns live between 10 and 20 km away (8 percent in Nepal and

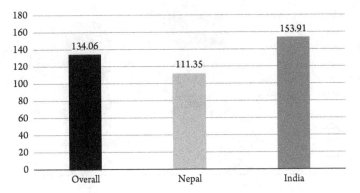

Figure 4.28 Mean Number of Staff by Location in Brick Kilns Case

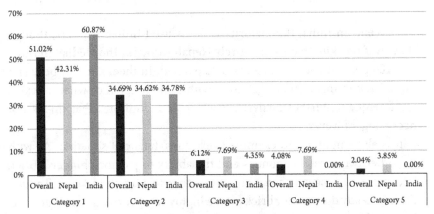

Figure 4.29 Mean Distance Traveled by Staff for Work in Brick Kilns Case

4 percent in India) (Category 3). Finally, 4 percent of kiln staff (all of which were in Nepal) live 20 to 50 km away (Category 4) and, at 2 percent of kilns (once again in Nepal), staff live more than 50 km away (Category 5), likely indicating that kilns in these latter two categories hire seasonal workers from elsewhere. In such cases, workers often set up temporary living quarters near the kiln during the brick-making season, which starts in November and lasts until May. Still, when looked at holistically, these data do not indicate significant cross-border variation in staffing patterns.

One large trend is evident, however. As Figure 4.30 indicates, the majority of brick kiln workers appear to be Indian. At kilns in Nepal, the percentage of Nepali workers, as estimated by their employers, ranged from 0 to 98 percent, with the median being 25 percent and the mean being

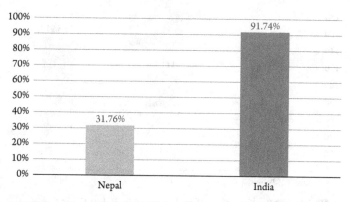

Figure 4.30 Mean Domestic Workers by Location in Brick Kilns Case

32 percent. In India, the majority of kilns used Indian workers, though there was one kiln that used entirely Nepali workers. The median in India was 100 percent and the mean was 92 percent. In theory, it may be easier for brick kiln managers to get away with non-compliance when workers are foreigners. Further analysis, in Chapter 7, indicates that this is not occurring, however.

It is also important to examine brick kilns' financial situation. As with the other two cases, economics and the ability to pay may hinder a brick kiln owner/manager's choice about whether to hire child labor. Though there is steady demand for bricks, it is a highly competitive industry and few kilns in this region are making significant sums of money (see Figure 4.31). Overall, 27 percent of surveyed kilns reported earning less than 100,000 Nepali rupees or 60,000 Indian rupees per year (Category 1). Approximately 12 percent of kilns in Nepal fell in this category, while the percentage of low-income kilns in India was much higher, at 43 percent. A further 31 percent of respondents, overall, reported earning 100,000–500,000 Nepali rupees or 60,000–300,000 Indian rupees per year (Category 2). This response was chosen by 27 percent of respondents in Nepal and 35 percent of respondents in India. The next category, 500,000–1,000,000 Nepali rupees or 300,000–600,000 Indian rupees, was chosen by 6 percent of respondents, with this statistic being 8 percent in Nepal and 4 percent in India (Category 3). Finally, one kiln, representing 2 percent of respondents, reported earning more than 1,000,000 Nepali rupees or more than 600,000 Indian rupees (Category 4). This kiln was located in Nepal and represented 4 percent of the sample. The remaining 31 percent of respondents did not know the answer

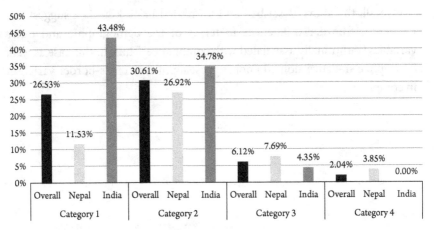

Figure 4.31 Brick Kiln Revenue by Location

to this question or refused to say. When taken together, these data suggest that kilns on the Indian side of the border may be in a better economic position to avoid hiring child labor.

Brick kiln revenues are underpinned by a host of other factors, however, and it is important to consider these as well. Just as revenue varies tremendously from kiln to kiln in the census area, brick prices and weekly production vary as well. Brick price is quite dependent on brick color. Redder bricks are perceived to be both more pleasing to the eye and stronger. As a result, they fetch higher prices on the market. The redness, however, is not something brick kiln owners/managers can readily change, as it is determined by the composition of the soil near the kiln. In Nepal, reported brick prices varied from 4 to 8.5 Nepali rupees per brick, with the median price being 7 and the mean price being 6.46. In India, brick prices varied more widely, ranging from 1.5 to 8 Indian rupees per brick, with the median price being 4 and the mean price being 4.20. Given that the price a brick kiln owner can get for his/her bricks is fairly locked in by the soil near his/her kiln, one of the only things a kiln owner can do to increase revenue is make more bricks. Reported weekly brick production in Nepal ranged from 6,000 bricks to 210,000, with median production being 50,000 and mean production being 64,800. In India, weekly brick production ranged from 15,000 to 200,000, with median production being 100,000 and mean production being 100,696. While these data do not indicate significant cross-border variation, they do suggest factors which may explain child labor use for the data set as a whole.

Overall, the above-described and illustrated brick kiln data suggest few major cross-border differences in terms of the demographic and other variables traditionally associated with compliance. Thus, in this case as well, descriptive statistics alone do not suggest significant cross-border variation in compliance.

5

Inconsistent State Action, Inaccurate Legal Knowledge, and Non-Compliance

Consistent with Aumann's (1976) "common knowledge assumption," the socio-legal compliance and rule of law literatures acknowledge that the law must be both widely known and understood to achieve high rates of compliance. The importance of this requirement cannot be overstated, however: knowledge of the law is essential for compliance in the many situations[1] in which legal requirements do not coincide with social or cultural norms. If individuals do not know what the law is, they cannot change their behavior to conform to its requirements.

For instance, as an undergraduate student, I regularly led hiking trips for my college's outdoor club and on one such trip, to Joshua Tree National Park, my group was awakened at our wilderness campsite—at approximately 7 AM on Easter Sunday, no less—by a park ranger who informed us that we were in violation of a regulation regarding backcountry camping. We were shocked. Having every desire to minimize our impact on the natural environment and comply with relevant regulations, we had examined all of the posted materials at the parking lot regarding backcountry camping the previous day and duly filled out a report on our proposed route, attached backcountry tags to our bags, etc. What's more, we had complied with all other backcountry norms, from refraining from cooking on open fires, cooking on tiny gas stoves instead, to disposing of human waste in the "proper" manner.

Since no one in the group had any idea what we had done to incur the ranger's early morning visit, we asked him and he indicated that we were sleeping less than a mile from human improvements (i.e., a road or building) and, thus, were not in the backcountry per se. We could not see the road from our location, but even if we could have, we would not have known that our location was problematic, as none of us had heard of this regulation before. We explained as much, apologized, and promised to leave immediately. The ranger, for his part, decided to give us two citations, one for every two members of our group. Though the citations, at $25 each, were not costly

Capacity beyond Coercion. Susan L. Ostermann, Oxford University Press. © Oxford University Press 2023.
DOI: 10.1093/oso/9780197661116.003.0005

enough to motivate future compliance on their own, we all had a healthy respect for the rules themselves and came away from the experience hoping to avoid such violations, and the associated hassle, in the future. Ever since, I have always carried up-to-date maps and checked at ranger stations prior to any backcountry excursion about where camping is and is not allowed.

The above anecdote and similar ones notwithstanding, it is true that in many parts of the world academics can generally get away with assuming that the law is widely known and understood and move on to exploring other explanatory variables. In the developing world, however, lack of education and state capacity—coercive and otherwise—often hinder the public's efforts to learn about the law. As many states here are limited in their ability to foster accurate legal knowledge, one should not assume that this precondition for both rule of law and compliance is met. With one's assumptions reoriented, individual behavior in the developing world begins to make more sense. For instance, if knowledge of the law is not common and an individual does not know that taking timber from public land is illegal, but needs or wants it, then he or she will likely take it. However, if that individual is told by a reliable source that such an action is illegal or observes someone being punished for doing so, his or her calculus changes; now he or she may consider other factors when choosing whether or not to comply, like the likelihood of being caught, the harshness of the penalty, reasons for voluntary compliance (i.e., desire to protect a natural resource), etc. Indeed, knowledge of the law matters so much for compliance that capable states often reach out to those they regulate to inform them about the rules or changes to them.

This isn't usually necessary for landmark legislation, which tends to generate its own press and a large national debate. For less well-known regulations, those governments which have the capacity to do so seem to go the "PR" or "awareness" routes before enforcement. For instance, in September 2013, the Scottish government started raising awareness, both among the general public and among business owners, regarding a "zero-waste" law, which would require the recycling of certain materials and go into effect on January 1, 2014. The awareness-related materials the Scottish government distributed, via multiple different media, included information on what the law required, penalties for non-compliance, the rationale behind the law, and information on the financial support the government would provide to blunt the financial impact of the legal change. Similar efforts have taken place in the subcontinent. Delhi has experienced a large-scale PR campaign to raise awareness of the importance of road safety. Materials connected to this campaign informed the masses of the scale of the problem and the impact of non-compliance, referred to existing regulations, and urged the public, seemingly "for their own sake," to comply. Another aspect of this campaign involved government officials—seemingly hoping to make an impact on impressionable young minds—going around to different Delhi schools to make presentations regarding road safety. Meanwhile, in Kathmandu, there have been large-scale campaigns, largely mediated by the NGO sector, to raise awareness of the existence and illegality of sex trafficking across the India-Nepal border. But campaigns such as these, at least in India and Nepal, are few and far between. Where they exist, they tend to focus—for arguably good, cost-effectiveness reasons—on urban areas.

In the case at hand, the Indian and Nepali states have not been involved, in a widespread and regular manner, in informing ordinary individuals living near Chitwan and Valmiki National Parks about wood-taking prohibitions. When I examined Chitwan National Park's annual reports, which do contain information about awareness-raising campaigns conducted to prevent rhino poaching, I found no evidence that such an effort had been made for wood-taking regulations. I also found little evidence that such a thing had taken place from my longer-form interview respondents. I was, however, told by frontline bureaucrats that they have occasionally gone to village headmen in locations in which wood collection was a problem (i.e., harming animal populations) and requested their assistance in preventing such widespread incursions. These efforts, however, per the accounts of the bureaucrats involved in them, were isolated rather than widespread and, perhaps more important, from the perspective of accurate *legal* knowledge, requests to move wood collection elsewhere, when mediated by village headmen, may not appear to villagers to be government regulations.

I found a similar lack of awareness-raising effort with respect to wood-taking regulations in the area just outside Valmiki. When I examined Valmiki Tiger Reserve's annual plans of operation, I did find that at least one recent budget included line items for awareness activities: "Brochure and handbills website of Valmiki TR" and "public awareness campaign in villages."[2] Subsequent budgets, however, including the one for 2014–2015,[3] do not include such allotments. Still, high-level park staff indicate that they have recently set up more than ninety eco-development committees in villages near the park boundary and use these committees to communicate park "do's and don'ts." My qualitative interviews with frontline staff indicate, however, that these activities largely focus on wildlife rather than wood collection. Interviews with villagers living just outside of Valmiki also failed to turn up any evidence of awareness-raising efforts related to wood collection, but this may have been because such efforts were conducted through intermediaries, as with efforts across the border near Chitwan.

Understanding Compliance with Law

The standard deterrence model suggests that individuals conduct a cost-benefit analysis when considering compliance and that fear (Gibbs 1968; Jensen 1969; Tittle 1977; Friedman 1975), a felt sense of duty (Braithwaite & Makkai 1994; Scholz & Pinney 1995; May 2004; Mazar, Amir & Ariely 2008; Pruckner & Sausgruber 2013), and social license pressure (Gunningham, Kagan & Thornton 2003) are the main factors that have the power to augment this analysis. Importantly, as Becker (1968) notes, this model remains the same, regardless of whether a so-called criminal is making the choices or an ordinary individual.

One can also glean from the rule-of-law, socio-legal compliance, and economic compliance literatures a list of the conditions under which fear, duty, and social license pressures are likely to impact compliance. Among them are likelihood of detection (of non-compliance) (Kleven et al. 2011; Blumenthal, Christian & Slemrod 2001; Klepper & Nagin 1989), severity of penalty (Becker 1968; Klepper & Nagin 1989; Scholz & Gray 1990), cost of compliance in both time and money (Becker 1968; Gerstenfeld & Roberts 2000; Yapp & Fairman 2004; Hillary 1995; Bowman, Heilman & Seetharaman 2004), knowledge of enforcement odds (Gerstenfeld & Roberts 2000; Hillary 1995; Hutchinson & Chaston 1995; Petts 1999 & 2000; Yapp & Fairman 2004; van der Wal et al. 2005), perception of regulators (Wilson & Kelling 1982; Braithwaite & Makkai 1994; Yapp & Fairman 2004), attitude toward regulation (Bardach & Kagan 1982; Gunningham, Kagan & Thornton 2003; Tyler 1990; Makkai & Braithwaite 1996; Kagan & Scholz 1984), formal management systems—in the case of businesses, organizations, or governments (Palmer & van der Vorst 1996), social pressure (Sandmo 2005; Kagan, Thornton & Gunningham 2003), the belief that others are complying (Gachter 2007; Elster 1989; Fellner et al. 2013; Coleman 1996; Kagan, Thornton & Gunningham 2003), the saliency of the need for compliance (Thaler & Sunstein 2008; Gray & Scholz 1991; Siskind 1980; Weil 1996; Ko et al. 2010; Bowman, Heilman & Seetharaman 2004), and formal allowances for self-regulation (Rees 1994).

Implicit in almost every single one of these articles is the fact that another factor—a factor so basic and integral that the literature rarely considers it a variable—is required in order to achieve compliance when law differs from social custom: legal knowledge. In fact, Thomas Carothers, one of the main proponents of the rule of law and development movement, defines rule of law as that stage at which laws have become widely known and understood. It follows that accurate legal knowledge should be predictive of compliance, but this has rarely been tested empirically. The socio-legal compliance literature also acknowledges the importance of what it calls "implicit general deterrence," the assumption that populations targeted by particular regulations are aware of those regulations and are, on average, deterred from non-compliance (Thornton, Gunningham & Kagan 2005). Though both the more normative rule of law literature and the socio-legal compliance literature acknowledge the importance of accurate legal knowledge, they rarely substantiate or problematize its absence (*contra* Winter & May 2000). This failure is particularly pronounced in light of the game theory literature's common knowledge assumption (Aumann 1976; Milgrom 1981), which suggests that people cannot agree to disagree and that divergent behavior results from divergent priors. Implicitly, if people are behaving differently, knowledge is not common or equal among different actors.

Though the literature lags on this issue, aid organizations seem to understand that legal knowledge is not common. Starting in 2001, the University of Maryland implemented a USAID Rule of Law program in Georgia designed to increase citizen awareness of laws. A 2006 evaluation of the program testifies to the efficacy of this approach. This empirical validation of the importance of legal knowledge suggests that this factor alone may explain a significant amount of the non-compliance we see in areas that are thought to suffer from low state capacity—as well as some of the remaining pockets of non-compliance that we see in places where the state is quite strong. Indeed, Fellner et al. (2013) find that, in Austria, where the state is strong and deterrence is a viable option, *information* about the law, when combined with a threat of enforcement, substantially increases compliance rates.

To explore whether knowledge of the law remains powerful in the absence of significant enforcement capacity (when the state is coercively weak), I conducted research in an area thought to be weighed down by low state capacity: the India-Nepal border. Up until recently, this border region has been plagued, both in India and Nepal, by Maoist insurgency. During this period, the state almost ceased to exist at the local level. Since the mid-to-late 2000s, the Nepali and Indian states have re-entered this region, but only minimally and signs of the state remain few and far between. This region is also one in which the *a priori* likelihood that members of a target population will have knowledge of laws that differ from customary norms and feel a strong duty to obey state-propounded regulations is low. Put differently, the research was conducted in a location in which legal norms' chances, vis-à-vis those of social norms, were quite unfavorable—a so-called hard case.

Forming Accurate Legal Understandings

How might people come to know that taking wood from park land is illegal, particularly when the social or cultural norm in the area is to do so? The simple answer, as I alluded to in the Introduction, is that many of them do not. The data indicate that, overall, 61.7 percent of those respondents who answered questions on both compliance and legal knowledge hold *inaccurate* understandings of the wood-taking prohibitions in place in Chitwan National Park and Valmiki National Park and Tiger Reserve. Yet, many individuals seem to want to avoid legal penalties—and the state more generally. This motivates them to try to determine the legal requirements that affect their lives in whatever way they can, using all resources available to them. This may be true even if they do not plan to comply. After all, even someone dealing illicit drugs may want to know what the law is so that he or she can better skirt it or defend him or herself if caught. Thus, it is safe to assume that most individuals will at least try to make educated guesses about the legality of the things they do on a regular basis.

But how do they go about doing so? Drawing on theories of knowledge acquisition, constructivism, and cognitive flexibility theory,[4] particularly as applied to "ill-structured domains,"[5] I suspect that individuals improve their guesses by constructing and iteratively reconstructing what the law "must be" based upon the information available to them at any particular moment. In the case at hand, in which ordinary individuals with little formal education are tasked with acquiring advanced knowledge of legal requirements, I suspect that these individuals draw information for updating from many different sources, ranging from prior interactions with the state, to their beliefs about what types of regulations the state might make, to rumors circulated by neighbors and friends regarding legal requirements. The result is an individually held understanding of what type of behavior is required or prohibited in a given situation that may or may not be accurate depending upon the pattern of observations and interactions that individual has witnessed.

Qualitative evidence suggests that individuals living just outside of Chitwan and Valmiki National Parks are doing just this. Having completed my first round of survey data collection, I found myself struggling to interpret responses to questions I had designed to measure legal knowledge, so I conducted a number of long-form, open-ended qualitative interviews in order to better understand how people came to their legal understandings. What I found was that much of my respondents' legal knowledge was based upon rumor: rumors about what other villagers said about the law, rumors about what the park employees said about the law, rumors about enforcement experiences, etc. But, it wasn't all rumor. People seemed to privilege both direct experiences, whether personal or observational, and information from what they viewed as a knowledgeable and/or trustworthy source. As one respondent put it, as he was trying to explain why he believed his source of legal information, "[t]he village headman is a savvy man and many in the government are known to him. We know his family." After considering evidence from various sources of varying trustworthiness, people then seem to form their legal understandings by trying to use all evidence available to them while also resolving inconsistencies between different pieces of evidence. For example, one respondent explained to me that wood collection is allowed in the park in some places and not in others and, when asked how she knew this to be true, she clarified that her neighbor got in trouble for wood collection, but that "[her] sister married and left for Thori and that everyone collects wood in the park there,"[6] seemingly privileging trustworthy information and resolving inconsistencies to form a generalization. And this is probably a useful generalization for her, in that enforcement near both Valmiki and Chitwan is inconsistent and does not necessarily reflect the law on the books. But all of this makes one wonder, in that the focus of this book is on compliance with the law on the books: under what circumstances do accurate understandings of formal institutions develop?

In a low-information environment, in which target populations have little means to read about the law on their own, I expect that principal-agent problems and the resulting inconsistent state behavior ensure that misunderstandings of legal requirements remain pervasive. When the state punishes or appears to punish a particular action some of the time, while

failing to punish the same behavior at other times, these mixed signals propagate through the legal understandings of a particular target population.
Those who have been punished or have seen others punished or heard about
others being punished receive information that suggests that the punished
behavior is illegal. Many of these same individuals will then receive conflicting information at some later point, which will likely cause them to
question whether their original assumptions regarding prohibited behavior
were correct and update them based upon new information. As one of my
respondents explained, "I have been fishing from this stream my whole life.
This must be allowed. The fish are God's, not the government's. But I hear that
if you stand on the bridge near the guard post and fish they will tell you it is
not allowed. It is their bridge." Of course, it is fishing itself, rather than fishing
from the bridge, that is not allowed in the park, but this respondent came to
a different—although not entirely illogical—legal understanding based upon
his experience, what he has heard and his understanding of the world and the
government. In this way, when the state behaves inconsistently with respect
to a particular rule or regulation, many individuals at any given point can
end up with inaccurate legal understandings.

It follows that consistent state action with respect to a particular law helps
to produce accurate legal understandings. The more regularly and visibly
the state either punishes or disallows behavior that is prohibited and refrains
from punishing behavior that is permitted, the more individuals observe this
to be the case and can, in turn, tell others what they have observed. When
the state behaves consistently, assuming it does so in a manner that is in line
with the law on the books, personal observations, beliefs about the state, and
rumors about what the state or its delegates have done are more likely to be
similar and individuals are more likely to form legal understandings that are
accurate. Under conditions of consistent state action, individuals will rarely
be presented with conflicting information about the law and, as a result, will
only occasionally have to resolve discrepancies into an updated legal understanding. Moreover, when they do resolve contradictions, they are more
likely to end up with accurate legal knowledge. In this way, knowledge about
the law can become common and behavior with respect to the law, at least
according to the game theory literature (Aumann 1976; Milgrom 1981), will
become more consistent.

It is important to note, however, that, as previously mentioned in the
Introduction, consistent state action is not always optimal for compliance. The literature on street-level bureaucrats (Tendler 1997; Pires 2008),

particularly in the developing world, indicates that state representatives sometimes achieve compliance through inconsistency. In particular, they modify their behavior—and in so doing, the behavior of the state—in order to meet the demands of unique circumstances. Doing so increases the compliance of some actors, but it can also appear "messy" from an outsider's perspective. While compliance-increasing behavior is commendable from the state's perspective, it is not without negative externalities. Inconsistency can simultaneously increase the compliance of particular actors and spread misinformation, making accurate legal knowledge less common and potentially decreasing the compliance of other actors. If the state does not simultaneously correct misinformation, compliance-inducing inconsistency can become problematic in terms of overall compliance.

A coercively strong state should have no problem delivering consistent punishment of illegal behavior and will be less likely have to resort to the type of compliance-inducing inconsistency that some street-level bureaucrats are forced to use. A coercively weak state, however, will struggle in this regard, that is, unless it takes additional steps to ensure that accurate legal knowledge is reaching relevant target populations.

Consistent State Action in South Asia

Despite the fact that South Asian countries are all still "developing," there are examples of displays of significant state capacity and consistent state action in the region, even if they are somewhat unusual. A good example of this is the Indian Election Commission, which does not appear to suffer from principal-agent problems and regularly achieves a high level of consistency. It behaves similarly from election to election and from place to place, so much so that Indians know that on election day they can go to the polls and vote freely and without interference. They also know that once they have voted, they will receive a deep purple mark on their right index finger. If they already have this mark, they will not be allowed to vote. Their own observations, their beliefs about the state, and the observations of their friends and family will almost certainly align with one another's in this regard. Because the Election Commission behaves so consistently, I would also venture a guess that the vast majority of voters have accurate legal understandings of the prohibition on double-voting. This accurate legal knowledge, in turn, is of fundamental importance to both individual-level compliance and to rule of law more generally. Few attempt to vote twice, and Indian elections are some of the most free and fair, not to mention institutionalized, in the world.

The problem, of course, is that the Indian Election Commission is unusual in its consistency. In the area surrounding Chitwan and Valmiki, consistent state action is rare, largely owing to meager state resources and large-scale corruption. Honest bureaucrats rarely have the resources or support to do their jobs properly and, perhaps more important, the behavior of dishonest bureaucrats, who are more numerous, undercuts the consistency of their efforts. Thus, consistent state action, while achievable in South Asia, is far from routine.

Hypotheses

I expect, first, that consistent state action is correlated with accurate understandings of the conduct required or prohibited by law in a particular situation and, second, that accurate legal understandings are predictive of compliance: the more widespread these accurate understandings are, the higher the rate of compliance and vice versa. I also anticipate that variation in the proportion of the population holding accurate legal knowledge explains, at least in part, observed cross-border variation in compliance with wood-taking restrictions around Valmiki and Chitwan. Finally, I hypothesize that accuracy of legal understandings at least partially explains variation in compliance among individuals on the same side of the border.

Data Collection

As described in greater detail in the preceding chapter, I measure the accuracy of legal understandings by asking members of each target population true-false questions regarding the conduct required or prohibited by law and then by aggregating their responses geographically. I ask ordinary individuals whether it is true that "[p]eople must not collect fallen wood." I also ask, among other things, whether it is true or false they "must stay on roadways at all times." By asking these questions of the target population for wood-taking prohibitions in Chitwan and Valmiki National Parks, questions that pertain to both regulated and unregulated conduct and require individuals to recognize both false statements about the law and true ones, I am able to get a fairly clear picture of what individuals believe is required or prohibited by law. Then, after aggregating responses geographically, I examine the proportion of people in a given location who hold an accurate understanding of the law and whether higher or lower proportions are associated with compliance.

Accurate Legal Knowledge and Compliance

The data suggest that, in the absence of accurate information, individuals and entities often do not make the shift from cultural norms to legal norms or from old legal norms to new ones, even if they are motivated to comply with government-propounded rules and regulations. Still, among individuals who possess accurate legal knowledge, compliance is significantly more common than among those whose legal knowledge is inaccurate. In the text that follows, I will substantiate these claims.

Consistent State Action and Accurate Legal Understandings

Given that legal understandings can be so consequential, it is important to understand how they are formed. Generally, my qualitative data suggest that those who take a particular action and are punished believe that behavior to be illegal, while those who take a particular action and are not punished believe that behavior to be legal. When I asked respondents how they determine whether something is illegal, the overwhelming sentiment was that something that you get in trouble for with the government is illegal. Many of my respondents focused on punishment as a source of information and elaborated with examples. One described the fact that she had ridden her scooter out to the main road and a policeman had stopped her; he told her she had to wear a helmet and made her pay a fine. As a result, this respondent believed that not wearing a helmet on a scooter was illegal.[7] Another respondent described the fact that the government had forced her to move her house during a road-widening campaign; she concluded that it was illegal to have your house too near to the road.[8] Interestingly, when I asked respondents how they can tell if something is legal, I received far fewer elaborations and many were unsure how to tell if something is legal other than to do it and see if punishment follows; if it does not, then that action is allowed. Some suggested that one can ask family and neighbors if something is legal. But few came up with a definitive answer, save for one older man who sagely observed that "everything is legal unless the government makes it illegal." In other words, for him, legal is the default and one doesn't need to find out if something is legal, one just needs to find out if it is illegal.

Along the same lines, those who know someone who took a particular action and was punished tend to believe that the punished behavior is illegal, while those who know someone who took the same action and was not punished believe the same behavior to be legal. If lacking personal experience with respect to the legality or illegality of a particular action, respondents seem to look first to the experiences of others. As one respondent put it, "Sometimes your friend gets in trouble for something and he tells you about it. My friend had too much alcohol when he tried to get on the bus. The driver would not let him on and said he would call the police. My friend had to stay the night at the bus stand. Now I know that you can't get on the bus if you are drunk." Another respondent stated that many of her neighbors had hired a local man to tap into the electric line for them and that she had thought this was legal, but that when the government came around to replace the electric poles, it removed all the lines that the local man had created and left only the ones with meters that the power company had put in place; as a result, she concluded the local man had been acting illegally. In her mind, something that seemed legal, due to its commonplace nature, transformed into something that seemed illegal because of the consistency with which her neighbors had lost their electrical connections (and the investment they made to set them up).

This last respondent's experience notwithstanding, the Indian and Nepali states, at least in the region covered by the research in this book, largely tend toward inconsistency, particularly with respect to enforcement of park regulations. When I spoke with high-level park staff in both Kathmandu and Chitwan, they explained that enforcement of wood-taking restrictions was not a priority, save for prevention of tree-felling by smugglers. Chitwan National Park's annual reports seem to reflect this fact. While the reports detail enforcement of anti-poaching laws, there is almost no mention of enforcement of regulations that prohibit wood collection in the park. And interviews with frontline bureaucrats confirm that this is a fairly accurate depiction of enforcement within the park; almost everyone I spoke with said that they had handed out fines for wood collection, but on a very infrequent basis. Across the border in Valmiki, I was told by high-level park staff that they do engage in enforcement of wood-taking restrictions, but when I visited the office of Bihar's Chief Wildlife Warden in Patna, I was told that enforcement of wood-taking prohibitions was impractical and that no major effort to do so had been made in Valmiki. When I spoke to frontline bureaucrats, forest guards in this case, they said that while they did occasionally enforce wood-taking regulations, they did not do so regularly. None of these individuals indicated that they were engaged in intentional, compliance-inducing inconsistency, however, suggesting that the behavior noted by Tendler (1997) and Pires (2008) is not at play in this particular case.

Inconsistency certainly is, though. Respondents' experiences suggest that while deterrence-based enforcement is not common, it is also not fully absent. For example, one respondent living approximately 100 yards from a Chitwan park boundary post described her experience as follows: "I go into the park sometimes. Many times I walk by the post and the guard is asleep or talking to another guard. I have not gotten into trouble, but my neighbor was bothered at the same post." When pressed on what she thought her neighbor might have been doing that got her into trouble she responded: "Who knows? She is just like me." In other words, to her, the system seemed unpredictable and her conclusion was that anything her neighbor, who is "just like [her]," may have been doing, could get her in trouble too. She was unable to resolve these contradictory experiences into a single principle that would keep her clear of legal problems. Another respondent, this one on the Indian side of the border, explained to me that he regularly collects wood in the forest, but has only once gotten into trouble: for taking a tree that had fallen during a storm out of the park. The forest guard threatened a fine, but, as my respondent put it, "he was a local man" and was swayed by the fact that the tree had fallen on its own and was not cut down. My respondent did not end up paying a fine, but the legal understanding he took from this encounter is both interesting and *in*accurate: "It is okay to take small wood, but not big wood." In fact, neither is allowed, but it would be difficult for my respondent to be able to determine that based upon his behavior and interactions with park staff.

If one generalizes from these experiences, and the many others I collected via open-ended interviews, it should hardly be surprising that respondents' legal understandings were often inaccurate. Indeed, only 38.5 percent of respondents displayed accurate knowledge of wood-taking prohibitions. Individuals living in this region struggle to gain accurate information about the law. They generally do not have the resources to contact a lawyer and, even if they did, the lawyers in the region are poorly educated and not exactly plentiful. Moreover, the states in this border region rarely communicate with citizens regarding legal norms and behave too inconsistently with respect to those norms for accurate understandings to develop.

Accurate Legal Knowledge and Compliance

The understandings of the law that target populations hold are important because they relate to another significant relationship: the one between accurate legal knowledge and compliance. I test the proposition that those who hold accurate legal understandings are more likely to be in compliance than those who do not by first aggregating the data at different levels of geographic analysis: (1) the entire study region; (2) individual countries; and (3) replication villages in Nepal.[9] Within each of these geographic areas I then subset the data into two groups: those who hold an accurate understanding of prohibitions on wood-taking from nearby national parks and those who do not. When I subset by accurate legal knowledge in this manner, I find significant differences in compliance at all levels of geographic aggregation. Looking at the entire study region, I find that those who hold accurate legal understandings, regardless of where they are located, report behavior consistent with compliance 70.2 percent of the time. Meanwhile, those of their counterparts who hold inaccurate legal understandings comply 39.1 percent of the time. As indicated in Table 5.1, a t-test run on these two groups reveals a significant difference ($p < 0.000$). And, importantly, this trend holds on both sides of the border when I look at intra-country variation. In Nepal, the numbers are 70.9 percent and 56.6 percent, whereas in India, they are 55.0 percent and 28.0 percent; in the replication villages in Nepal, the numbers are 63.4 percent and 43.9 percent. Each of these differences is significant as well (Nepal, $p < 0.000$; India, $p = 0.011$; replication villages, $p = 0.019$).

Table 5.1 Compliance Rates among Those Who Hold Accurate vs. Inaccurate Legal Knowledge at Different Levels of Geographic Aggregation

Variable of Interest	Accurate	Inaccurate	p-value	SE
Entire Study Region	0.702	0.391	0.000	0.016
Nepal	0.709	0.566	0.000	0.019
India	0.550	0.280	0.011	0.016
Replication Villages	0.634	0.439	0.019	0.042

Importantly, this analysis, which relies on self-reported data, is supported by two other measures. The first is an observational study. It involves data collected by two individuals who sat in similar locations—a main road leading directly into the national park—on twenty-five randomly selected days over the course of three months. These individuals simultaneously spent four hours recording the number of individuals exiting the park with wood. The data in Figure 5.1 reveal that the number of individuals exiting Valmiki with wood was higher than the number exiting Chitwan, despite greater population density on the Nepal side of the border.

The second source of support for the above analysis comes from a Forest Canopy Density (FCD) estimate. Figure 5.2 shows the western region of both Chitwan and Valmiki National Parks, overlain with local roads and borders. The India-Nepal border is in bold and park boundaries are marked in thinner lines. (A complete description of this measure and how the below figure was created is included in Appendix 3.) While FCD analysis does not allow for inferences to be made about individual-level motivations and behavior and likely captures the behavior of criminal gangs involved in illegal logging, it does provide a snapshot of how a population is behaving as a whole. Figure 5.2 reveals that FCD is greater on the Nepal side of the border. It also allows one to see, via the density of road networks on either side of the border, how

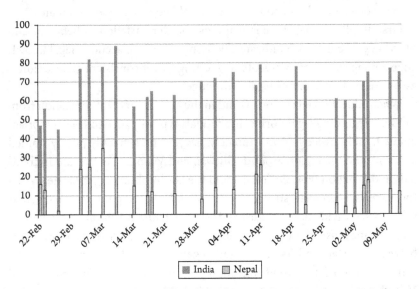

Figure 5.1 Observationally Collected Incidents of Non-Compliance in India and Nepal

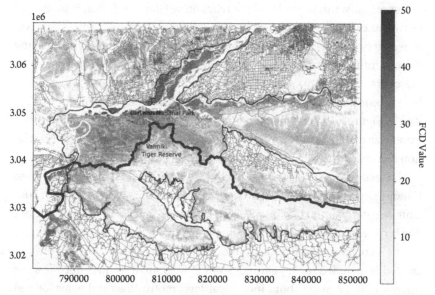

Figure 5.2 Modeled Forest Canopy Density in India and Nepal

much more populated the regions right outside of the park are in Nepal. And, overall, the FCD analysis suggests that we can be reasonably confident that self-reporting on compliance was not wholly inaccurate.

What does this tell us about accurate legal knowledge and compliance?

First, it tells us that there is real cross-border variation in behavior and outcomes. The data also indicate a widespread lack of accurate legal knowledge among survey respondents, suggesting that inconsistent state action is associated with inaccurate legal knowledge.

When education levels are low and in the absence of communication from the state regarding legal norms, individuals typically turn to lawyers for accurate legal knowledge. Unfortunately, lawyers are generally poorly trained and scarce in the region around Chitwan and Valmiki. As a result, individuals in this region typically learn about the law by observing the state. When the state is coercively strong, regularly and visibly punishing particular behaviors, individuals conclude that these behaviors are illegal. When behavior goes unpunished, they conclude the opposite. Principal-agent problems between the state and its bureaucratic agents have led to inconsistent state action with respect to wood collection prohibitions near both Chitwan and Valmiki. This inconsistency means that individuals struggle to discern what the law is and, in particular, whether wood collection in these two national parks is illegal.

I also find, as I will discuss in Chapter 6, that implementation strategies that are consistent with regulatory pragmatism and design around principal-agent problems, are associated with accurate legal knowledge in spite of inconsistent state action. This is important because accurate legal knowledge is associated with significantly higher compliance rates, regardless of geographic unit of aggregation.

My findings with respect to the relationship between accurate legal understandings and compliance also broadly indicate that many of those who are not in compliance are not intentionally flouting the law. In fact, many likely believe that they are in compliance, and this implies that if those with *inaccurate* legal understandings were provided with accurate information, quite a few of them would be motivated to alter their behavior to meet legal mandates. Finally, the fact that compliance is only 70.2 percent among those who possess accurate information about the law suggests that legal knowledge alone will not result in high levels of compliance. In Chapter 6, I will explain the relatively low compliance rates among those who do possess accurate legal knowledge by taking a close look at another piece of the puzzle: poverty-driven non-compliance.

6

Accurate Legal Knowledge under Adverse Conditions

Accurate information about the law need not be scarce, even when the state is coercively weak and incapable of consistent action, when education levels and communication of legal norms are both low, and when poverty is pervasive. States that recognize legal knowledge to be a compliance barrier and pragmatically design their regulatory implementation strategies might choose to foster accurate legal knowledge in untraditional ways. States can do the same for poverty.

This chapter examines two pragmatic strategies for increasing the accuracy of legal knowledge: delegated enforcement and information dissemination through local leaders. Delegated enforcement mimics consistent state action and allows target populations to gain knowledge that they wouldn't have been able to achieve in an environment dominated by inconsistency. Individuals exposed to delegated enforcement by way of Community Forest access often hold more accurate legal understandings than their similarly situated counterparts without such access. Local leaders also play an important role in fostering accurate legal knowledge, likely because they make information about the law seem trustworthy and credible. Those who have received accurate information about the law via a local leader are more likely to update their legal understandings to reflect that information.

After exploring the relationship between legal knowledge and compliance, the chapter turns to poverty, which remains a compliance barrier, even after accurate legal knowledge is widespread. In the developing world, where many exist at the margins, regulations that impose a cost on poor target populations are, *a priori*, problematic. Many individuals who possess accurate legal knowledge and feel motivated to comply are not likely to be able to do so because compliance would undermine their basic survival. But does this mean that widespread poverty and regulatory compliance cannot coexist, particularly when the regulations in question require behavior that differs from those dictated by social norms? The data presented

Capacity beyond Coercion. Susan L. Ostermann, Oxford University Press. © Oxford University Press 2023.
DOI: 10.1093/oso/9780197661116.003.0006

in this chapter suggest that regulatory pragmatism can guide states toward policies that lower the cost of compliance for a significant proportion of the population and that such efforts can make widespread regulatory compliance achievable, even when poverty and the coercive weakness of the state act as significant constraints.

Sources of Legal Knowledge

Legal knowledge remains undertheorized in the rule of law and socio-legal compliance literatures. As a result, hypotheses regarding sources of legal knowledge must be drawn, for the most part, from other bodies of scholarly work.

Individuals can, of course, learn about the law themselves, so long as they have the requisite skills: primarily education. But in most locations, this last statement should read "legal education," as determining what the law is has quite a bit to do with knowing where to look for it and how to read statutes and, in common law jurisdictions, case law. Possession of these skills is not common among average citizens. As a result, and as mentioned previously, lawyers are thought to be an important, though indirect, source of legal knowledge. Muir (1973), writing about prayer in public schools, finds lawyers to be one of the agents responsible for distributing information about the law and key proponents of the attitude changes that some laws are designed to bring about. However, if lawyers are not present at the local level, or are either too costly or poorly educated, then they are only a supplementary rather than a primary source of accurate legal knowledge. This is the case in in rural South Asia, as well as in many other places in which the state is weak, coercively or otherwise.

There are, however, individuals who are situated in such a way that they might, at least partially, fill lawyers' legal knowledge dissemination role: local leaders. In rural South Asia, local leaders often act as information distribution agents and frequently achieve their positions, whether formal or informal, because of their perceived connections to the state. These are individuals who know the right person to talk to within the government or the right place to go when, for instance, an individual needs to procure a voter ID card. They are trusted and the information they provide is considered credible. Wilson and Rhodes (1997) use a formal model to demonstrate that leaders play an important role in distributing information and coordinating followers. Along these same lines, Dixit (2003) and Banerjee et al. (2010) show that, when the state is weak, trusted contacts can facilitate information-sharing; indeed, when they do so they can further rich informal institutions that are capable of providing law, order, and other services. Varshney (2003) and Bhavnani et al. (2009) also recognize the power of local leaders in information distribution and demonstrate that these individuals need *not* act as agents of the state. It follows that local leaders, if they can be persuaded to act on the state's behalf, may be able, at least partially, to fill the information distribution demand that remains unmet in the absence of a communicative state or an active, affordable and well-educated legal profession.

But what happens if neither lawyers nor local leaders take part in legal knowledge distribution at the local level? Individuals will, as argued in Chapter 5, still infer what the law is from their observation of how the state behaves. If the state behaves inconsistently, these observational inferences are likely to be inaccurate, at least on average. However, if a system existed at the local level either to make the state's behavior more consistent or to provide contrast and put the state's inconsistency into perspective, such a system might assist individuals as they strive to accurately update their legal understandings. Even a coercively weak state can, for instance, delegate regulatory responsibility to individuals or groups at the local level. So long as those individuals or groups have an incentive to get involved and to comply with the law, such a state might achieve better results, in terms of consistent state action, than if it had acted on its own.

As noted in Chapter 3, the psychology literature is helpful in terms of understanding how such an arrangement might foster accurate legal knowledge. Constructivist learning theory in particular suggests that individuals construct knowledge from experience by continually making and remaking their sense of truth and reality. Learning about the law seems to follow a similar pattern. My qualitative evidence indicates that individuals do focus on the state's behavior and their own when trying to determine what is legal and what is not. They update their understandings to reflect newly acquired information. When the state behaves consistently, they can more easily gain accurate information. When the state is inconsistent, inaccuracy results. That said, if a coercively weak state—consistent with regulatory pragmatism— delegates regulatory responsibility to an individual or group that can and does behave more consistently than the state, this should facilitate the construction of accurate legal understandings at the individual level.

Legal Knowledge through Delegated Enforcement

Even if a state is coercively weak, suffers from principal-agent problems, and behaves inconsistently, many individuals can resolve inconsistencies and come to an accurate understanding of the conduct required or prohibited by law if the state delegates enforcement. When the state delegates enforcement to interested parties, these parties can create or mimic consistent state action in places in which the state itself struggles to do so. Consistency from delegates, particularly when set against large-scale inconsistency from the state, provides information to those seeking it regarding the conduct permitted or prohibited by law.

While consistency is not a hallmark of state action in the border region near Chitwan and Valmiki, the Nepali state has delegated regulatory responsibility for sustainably managing tracts of government-owned forest land just outside of Chitwan to local "User Groups." These local groups have petitioned the government to take over a portion of government land and are required to maintain certain forest cover standards, among other regulations. Once granted a Community Forest, however, they are free to remove a number of forest products, including wood, from the area.

Anecdotal and observational evidence suggests that the Nepali state and its delegates do behave consistently with respect to Community Forests in this area. Most User Groups consistently allow locals to collect wood in their Community Forests, sometimes for a small fee, but certainly without punishment. The government, for its part, has consistently abstained from interference in Community Forest governance. The absence of adverse government action in Community Forests sets up a situation in which it should appear to those living near Community Forests as if the state and its delegates are allowing (rather than punishing) a permitted behavior. This is particularly true when this consistent state action is set in contrast to the infrequent-but-unpredictable enforcement the state carries out in nearby Chitwan National Park. The contrast between how wood collection is treated in Community Forests versus Chitwan National Park, according to constructivist learning theory, should help individuals who are able to observe both, either directly or indirectly, to come to more accurate legal understandings as they seek to accommodate the contrasting information they have assimilated. The consistency of the Nepali state's non-interference[1] in Community Forests, combined with the fact that Community Forest management is fairly consistent in allowing access for wood collection or purchase, should foster the accurate legal understanding that wood collection is *legal* in Community Forests. Moreover, consistency with respect to this seemingly orthogonal law should also help foster the accurate understanding that wood collection is *not* legal in Chitwan National Park, at least among individuals who have access to both are able to observe some enforcement in Chitwan and no enforcement in nearby Community Forests.

The data confirm this. As indicated in Figure 6.1, consistency of delegated enforcement in Community Forest areas, when contrasted with occasional enforcement in Chitwan National Park, is associated with more widespread accurate legal knowledge. As shown in Figure 6.2, those with access to areas of delegated self-regulation are more likely to develop the accurate legal understanding that taking wood from Community Forests is legal, while taking wood from the Chitwan National Park is not. Of those who reported having access to a Community Forest and, thus, exposure to delegated enforcement, 75 percent hold an accurate understanding of the wood-taking prohibitions in place in Chitwan National Park; the same number among those who do not have access to a Community Forest, and, thus, no exposure to delegated enforcement, is 53 percent. When I subset by access to a Community Forest, which acts as a proxy for exposure to delegated enforcement, a t-test on accuracy of legal understandings indicates that there is a significant difference between these groups ($p = 0.000$; SE $= 0.019$). The same is true when I subset geographically, with Nepal being a proxy for exposure to delegated enforcement ($p = 0.000$; SE $= 0.014$).

Moreover, when I check for demographic differences between the latter two groups, those have been exposed to delegated enforcement through Community Forest access and those who have not, I find few significant differences across all eight demographic indicators, suggesting that delegated enforcement (by way of Community Forest access) is itself related to accurate legal understandings and is more than just a proxy for other variables (see Table 6.1). There are no significant differences between my two subsets on business ownership, involvement in ecotourism,[2] government employment, literacy, or age.

There are, however, significant differences on land ownership, education, and income. In particular, those who do own land are more educated, have higher incomes, and are less likely to report that they have access to a Community Forest than those who do not own land, are less educated, and have less income. And, if one thinks about the on-the-ground realities of why one might want to gain Community Forest access, this makes sense. Land

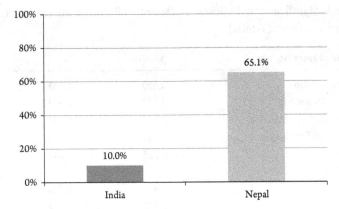

Figure 6.1 Percentage of Respondents Possessing Accurate Legal Knowledge by Country (Exposure to Delegated Enforcement) (N = 1,264; 669 in Nepal and 595 in India). Significantly more respondents in Nepal reported accurate legal knowledge, namely, that collecting wood in the national park is illegal, than in India.

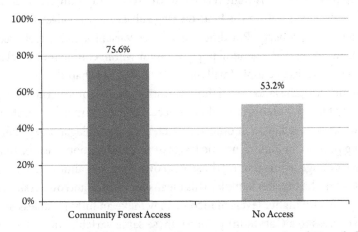

Figure 6.2 Percentage of Respondents Possessing Accurate Legal Knowledge by Community Forest Access (Exposure to Delegated Enforcement) (N = 366; 273 with accurate knowledge and 93 with inaccurate). Accurate knowledge of wood-taking prohibitions was much more widespread among those who had community forest access.

ownership, education, and income are highly correlated with one another and those who own land and have higher income levels are less likely to need to collect wood in either Chitwan National Park or a Community Forest in the first place. Each of these variables is, to some degree, a proxy for the

Table 6.1 Significance of Exposure to Delegated Enforcement for Different Population Subsets (T-tests)

Variable of Interest	p-value	N
Land Ownership	0.050	1,343
Business Ownership	0.148	1,344
Involvement in Ecotourism	0.478	1,342
Government Employment	0.431	1,344
Literacy	0.253	1,341
Education	0.000	1,278
Age	0.392	1,340
Income	0.002	1,324

others, as well as for a general lack of need to gain access to a Community Forest, as verified by the fact that the rate at which the use of gas is reported among these subsets is high relative to the rest of my sample. In addition, many individuals within the land-owning subset report collecting firewood on their own property. Put differently, these variables collectively seem to capture a subset of the general population for whom compliance is relatively inexpensive or easy, a topic I will return to later in the chapter.

Importantly, the land ownership, education, and income variables capture subsets of the population that do not necessarily have more accurate information about the law than others. In fact, accuracy of legal understandings among those with higher income levels or more education is lower than the sample average, while among those who own land it is almost exactly as accurate as in the broader sample. This means that while land ownership, more education, and higher levels of income may make an individual less likely to report access to a Community Forest, these same variables do not automatically make that individual more likely to possess an accurate legal understanding. When taken together, these data suggest that exposure to delegated enforcement, by way of Community Forest access, is an important correlate of accurate legal understandings, but they do not explain how.

As alluded to above, there are theoretical reasons, grounded in the psychology literature, why this might be the case. Those exposed to delegated enforcement, via Community Forest access, have had the opportunity to observe, firsthand, the contrast between the state's consistent non-interference in Community Forests, Community Forest management's relatively consistent provision of penalty-free wood collection, and the state's inconsistent enforcement of wood-taking prohibitions in Chitwan National Park. According to constructivist learning theory, observation of this contrast sets up a situation of cognitive conflict or tension. Individuals deal with this tension by resolving observed discrepancies into a new understanding of the world. While those without Community Forest access are forced to resolve discrepancies between the observed or reported enforcement behavior of individual bureaucrats over time, a situation that could just as easily resolve into inaccurate understandings as accurate ones, those who have Community Forest access are presented with a slightly different opportunity. Indeed, those who have been able to observe or have had access to information regarding enforcement in Community Forest areas have had more, and more directly contrasting, information to work with when forming their legal understandings. These individuals have had information regarding inconsistent enforcement in Chitwan National Park *and* information regarding consistent access to penalty-free wood collection in Community Forest areas.

This latter slate of contrasting information is easier to resolve into an accurate legal understanding of wood-taking restrictions than the former. As one respondent put it, "There is no trouble collecting wood [in the nearby Community Forest], but in the park there can be trouble, so I go to the Community Forest." The fact that those who have been exposed to delegated enforcement, via Community Forest access, hold more accurate legal understandings than those of their counterparts who lack Community Forest access suggests that the contrast between delegated enforcement in Community Forest areas and inconsistent state action in the national park is helping individuals with access to construct the accurate legal understandings that I find disproportionately present on the Nepal side of the border. In other words, in a sea of mixed signals and the attendant misinformation, the Nepali state's pragmatic delegation of enforcement in Community Forests, when set in contrast to its occasional enforcement inside Chitwan National Park, provides important information to those with Community Forest access that seems to help many of them modify or reconstruct their legal understandings to be more accurate over time.

Legal Knowledge through Local Leaders

In rural areas of South Asia the state often fails to adequately communicate legal norms, people generally struggle to read about the law themselves, and well-trained, affordable lawyers are a rarity. As a result, those who want to learn about the law, even if only to keep out of trouble, are forced to do so by way of nontraditional sources and methods. Many acquire or construct this information by observing the state and its behavior, as described extensively in Chapter 5 and above, or by seeking out trustworthy sources of legal knowledge.

The state and its actions are important sources of information regarding the law. Generally, my open-ended interviews reveal, as described more fully in Chapter 5, that those who take a particular action and receive government punishment believe that behavior to be illegal, while those who take a particular action and are not punished by the government believe the opposite. Respondents often focused on punishment as a source of information and elaborated with the examples detailed in Chapter 5. But respondents were less sure of how to tell if something is legal other. Their main strategy for acquiring legal knowledge was experimental. To take action and see if punishment follows; if it does not, then that action is legal. One other legal knowledge acquisition strategy that they suggested was that one can ask family and neighbors if something is legal. Given these approaches, inconsistent state enforcement of existing laws and regulations can operate to prevent even careful state observers from developing accurate legal understandings.

It is perhaps for this reason that individuals seem to privilege information that comes from a trustworthy—and often non-print—source. My experimental findings indicate that local leaders, who sometimes act as a conduit for communication from the state and/or local bureaucrats, are an important vector for legal knowledge. As a reminder, conducting this experiment involved a return to three randomly selected villages that had previously been surveyed for the large-N survey component of this project. For a full description of the metholodology used in the latter portion of this experiment, see Chapter 3.

As shown in Table 6.2, I found no significant differences in terms of the pre- and post-treatment accuracy of legal understanding in either Village 1 or Village 2. However, in Village 3 there was a significant difference ($p = 0.017$). Before my intervention, about 58.8 percent of my semi-random sample of villagers knew that collecting wood in Chitwan National Park is illegal. After my intervention, this number stood at 78.7 percent, suggesting that local leaders can be effective conduits for accurate legal knowledge. Local leaders are widely believed to be an accurate source of information about the state. Thus, what they say matters—it is trustworthy—and villagers will

Table 6.2 Percentage of Respondents with Accurate Legal Knowledge by "Source of Knowledge" Treatment (N = 297, 150 pre-treatment and 147 post-treatment). Analysis indicates that the only significant difference between the pre- and post-treatment survey was in Village 3, where a local leader presented accurate information about the law.

Variable	Pre-Treatment	Post-Treatment	p-value	SE
Village 1	0.625	0.681	0.286	0.049
Village 2	0.642	0.667	0.392	0.045
Village 3	0.588	0.787	0.017	0.047

update their understandings of the law accordingly, with many seemingly privileging this information over both firsthand observation and information received from secondhand sources.

While more research on legal knowledge acquisition is certainly required before we can understand exactly how this process occurs among a largely uneducated population faced with an often inconsistent state, my data suggest that delegated enforcement and information dissemination through local leaders are two means by which a coercively weak state can use regulatory pragmatism to foster accurate legal knowledge.

The consistent state action that a coercively strong state can readily muster is not the only way to foster accurate legal knowledge. My findings indicate that local leaders can act as a conduit for this information and that they can distribute information about the law to target populations more effectively than printed media, particularly when literacy and education levels are low. Delegated enforcement can also fill this role. The data suggest that more widespread accurate legal knowledge present on the Nepal side of the border is driven at least in part by exposure to delegated enforcement (via Community Forest access) and that this variable has significant explanatory power in terms of cross-border variation in compliance. Those who have the ability to observe consistent state action in Community Forests and gain accurate legal understandings from doing so are better situated to make a conscious choice to comply with the law. Those on the Indian side of the border, who do not have this opportunity, are at a significant disadvantage. When taken together, these findings demonstrate those states that are coercively weak and cannot manage consistent action are not without options in terms of attempting to foster both accurate legal knowledge and compliance. Such states can allow regulatory pragmatism to guide their legal design and implementation strategies—for instance, by choosing delegated enforcement or information dissemination through local leaders rather than deterrence—and realize legal knowledge and compliance improvements.

Poverty and the Limits of Legal Knowledge

Legal knowledge is not a panacea, however. It too has its limits. Legal knowledge merely opens up the possibility of a cost-benefit analysis type calculation regarding compliance with a particular regulation. If the costs still outweigh the benefits, continued non-compliance is likely. In the developing world, poverty is endemic and makes many individuals functionally incapable of complying with regulations that are costly and impact their basic survival. In this way, poverty can severely limit the efficacy of a legal knowledge-based strategy to secure compliance.

Chitwan National Park, Valmiki National Park and Tiger Reserve, and the area surrounding them represent an ideal scenario in which to explore the degree to which widespread poverty can undermine the ability of accurate legal knowledge to foster compliance. As mentioned previously, collecting timber is prohibited by law in both parks in spite of the fact that individuals living in this area have been collecting wood—from what is now park area—for centuries, if not millennia. Refraining from doing so means that they have great difficulty keeping warm and cooking. In other words, conservation law creates a situation in which the poverty of the population in this area comes into direct conflict with compliance.

Such a conflict carries with it the potential to create a politics that pits wood collection for personal use and basic survival against the state and its prerogatives. Such conflicts are not without precedent. In India, for instance, as detailed by Ramachandra Guha (1989) in *The Unquiet Woods*, such a politics has developed in a number of different places—though seemingly not in the area outside of Valmiki—around the total prohibitions on resource use in protected areas. Guha's account details the Chipko movement in Uttarakhand. There, local protest against commercialized forestry took the form of contravention of forest laws and the embrace of the forest at the risk of bodily harm. Guha argues that this movement did not emerge in a vacuum and that it arose in reaction to the 1878 Forest Act, which broke the bond between communities and the nearby forests on which their lives depended.

Eventually the Forest Act was amended, in 1927, to allow local communities to resume some limited aspects of their relationship with the forest. But it was not until the 2006 Forest Rights Act that the rights of tribal groups, and other forest-dwelling communities, to forest products was recognized. Of course, this has not halted the politics surrounding forest use, but it has, through law, brought state prerogatives more into line with community needs.

Now, in places where the state is coercively strong and well resourced, political conflict regarding forest rights is often overcome by the state's use of force or persuasion (by instilling a felt sense of duty to comply) to secure compliance. But the states on either side of the border near Chitwan and Valmiki have little to offer in terms of traditional, deterrence-based enforcement capacity (i.e., policing), particularly in this context: thousands of square kilometers of jungle augmented with only minimal infrastructure. The states on either side of the border also struggle to foster a widespread sense of duty to obey conservation regulations. Given these constraints, the standard deterrence model of compliance suggests that we should expect similar rates of compliance with wood-taking restrictions on both sides of the border—which is to say, similarly low. This is particularly true because, as previously mentioned, the human populations that live near these parks are nearly identical, both culturally and demographically, and have been permitted to pass at will, unimpeded by legal restrictions, across the India-Nepal border for as long as this border has existed. We would also not expect to see much in the way of formal or informal protests against limitations on forest rights, simply because the state has not been able to muster enough enforcement capacity to generate this politics.

The data presented in Chapter 4 and above suggest that the Indian and Nepali states have managed to motivate their respective target populations to comply with law, at least in a generalized way, but that variation in the degree to which individuals report these motivations does not explain cross-border variation in compliance. Variation in the cost of compliance, however, may be able to do so. Indeed, even if accurate legal knowledge is in place, poverty can limit the effectiveness of the standard deterrence model factors—fear and duty—when the cost of compliance is so high that individuals believe their material existence is threatened. Even if individuals know that wood collection is prohibited in the nearby national park, fear and duty work to alter their behavior only when high compliance costs have been lowered enough that individuals are no longer choosing between complying with applicable regulations and feeding themselves or keeping themselves warm.

Survey respondents in Nepal and India do not report significantly different levels of fear or duty, nor do they report a need for firewood at significantly different rates—in fact, the reported need for firewood is lower on the Indian side of the border, where compliance is worse. However, survey respondents in Nepal have access to a cost-of-compliance-lowering resource that is not available near Valmiki: Community Forests.

Nepal's Community Forests are numerous and there are over fifty located just outside of Chitwan National Park (and contiguous with park land). As explained in Chapter 3, these Community Forests, once government-owned and managed forest land, were handed over to local management after groups of individuals who reside in the region successfully petitioned the Department of Forests with sustainable management plans. Wood collection is permitted in Community Forests, so long as it conforms to an approved sustainable management plan, which typically mandates stable forest cover. As a result, Community Forests represent an excellent source of firewood for those living near Chitwan National Park ,and in many (though not all) cases, locals can meet their firewood needs, both cheaply and easily, within them. Among those of my respondents who reported having access to a Community Forest, the majority also reported collecting wood there instead of within Chitwan National Park.[3] Relatedly, the existence of Community Forests in Nepal should, in theory, put a damper on large-scale forest-use politics.

In contrast, in India, though the government does engage in Joint Forest Management in other areas, no such policy was in place in the area around Valmiki at the time of research. Thus, many locals who could not afford to cook or heat with gas had no meaningful option, other than Valmiki, for the fuel necessary to cook and keep warm during the winter. Under these circumstances, it would not be wrong to say that many are forced into non-compliance despite being otherwise motivated to protect the forests, obey the law, and avoid legal penalties. If the state were to engage in a significant enforcement campaign against wood collection, such circumstances could provide fuel for forest-use politics to develop. To date, however, enforcement has not been an issue; the state has not truly attempted this. And it follows that forest use remains relatively apolitical in the area outside of Valmiki.

Compliance in the Context of Poverty

The socio-legal compliance literature includes a whole host of variables that correlate with compliance. However, the evidence for many of these factors is often drawn from places where the state is coercively strong and poverty is limited—places where traditional legal enforcement, even if largely not used in practice, retains its deterrent value.[4] In light of this fact, what should we expect to find in the developing world where poverty is widespread and where, for many types of regulations, effective and predictable enforcement is simply not a realistic option?

Some research has examined compliance in developing world contexts. As detailed fully in the Introduction to this book, context matters for compliance and the developing world is contextually distinct. Meanwhile, deterrence-based enforcement sometimes works when state capacity is relatively limited, but the assumption that it works similarly for all individuals and regulated entities is untenable. This is particularly true when those targeted by a particular regulation regularly confront their own mortality and desperately need the very resource they are prohibited from taking from a nearby source they will not always be deterred. It also begs the following questions: 1) what happens when enforcement is nearly nonexistent and target populations have little to lose and quite a bit to gain from non-compliance? 2) are there ways to overcome the poverty problem?

A number of papers suggest that compliance is possible when poverty is widespread and the state is coercively weak (Barr 2000; Contreras-Hermosilla 1997, 2000, 2007; Goncalves et al. 2012). But this literature provides limited empirical evidence for the claims it makes and instead relies largely on "best practices" derived from years of policy-promotion work. The hard case examined in this book, however, allows us to get a better handle on whether weak states can generate compliance in spite of widespread poverty. This is because the states involved have relatively weak deterrence-based enforcement capacity[5] and in which the *a priori* likelihood that members of the target population will feel a strong duty to obey state-propounded regulations is low.

Poverty-Driven Non-Compliance

As described more fully in Chapter 3, self interest drives many individual-level decisions regarding whether or not to comply with a particular law or regulation (Pearce & Tombs 1990, 1997, 1998; Parker 2002; Molnar et al. 2004).

Recognizing this, many states manipulate the incentives that individuals face so that individual pursuit of self-interest and compliant behavior are not mutually exclusive.[6] In so doing, states act to align the self-interest of a larger swath of the population with compliant behavior. In the developing world, poverty is widespread, poverty-driven non-compliance can be endemic, and states often lack the capacity or the resources to create a system of incentives that align the self-interest of much of the populace with compliant behavior. Along the India-Nepal border, where most live at or below the poverty line and where many struggle to feed and clothe themselves, it is difficult to im-agine compliance with regulations that run contrary to the needs of the ma-jority of a population targeted by a given regulation. This is particularly true because the states on either side of the border are coercively weak and limited in the degree to which they can engage in deterrence-based enforcement. Yet, some compliance with wood-gathering restrictions is happening. This suggests that not all individuals find compliance to be against their respective self-interests.

As detailed more fully in in Chapter 3, I expect those for whom the cost of compliance is low relative to their incomes to comply, so long as (a) the cost of compliance is lower than the perceived cost of non-compliance; and/ or (b) they believe that it is their duty to comply. As described above, it is the poor who need firewood on a regular basis and must weigh this need against their motivation to comply. As a result, my expectations regarding their behavior are quite different. These latter individuals face a very high cost of compliance and, even if the cost of *non*-compliance were very high, many of them would rather risk enforcement-related penalties than face the alternatives. Furthermore, even if these individuals believe they have a duty to comply, it is likely not powerful enough to overcome their need to survive. The result is poverty-driven non-compliance.

Finally, I expect that among those individuals who have the option to both comply and attend to their basic needs, those motivated by either fear or duty will comply in significantly higher numbers than those of their low-income counterparts who have no viable option other than non-compliance.

Community Forests as a Pragmatic Regulatory Strategy

The high cost of compliance associated with wood-taking prohibitions represents a major barrier to compliance; at the same time, regulatory prag-matism suggests that a state that lowers this cost will be rewarded with higher compliance rates. Thus, I focus on a compliance cost-lowering strategy used by the Nepali state: community forestry. Nepal's 1993 Forest Act, which followed at least fifteen years of high-level and grass-roots efforts to de-centralize forest management, brought the Community Forestry Program into existence. As described briefly elsewhere in this book, the landmark Community Forest program allows citizens to come forward as a "User Group" and petition to take over and sustainably manage government-owned forest land, with government oversight.

The most important feature of community forestry in Nepal, particularly for the purposes of this chapter, is the fact that, while "User Groups" are re-sponsible for sustainable management, this does not preclude the harvesting of fallen wood. Indeed, sustainable wood collection is allowed within Nepal's community forests, so long as forest cover is maintained and the ecosystem is not made unsuitable for particular wildlife species. For those living near Community Forests in Nepal, this means that they are a source of fuelwood that carries little to no risk of legal penalty. As there are many Community Forests just outside of and often contiguous with Chitwan National Park, individuals who have access to a Community Forest can legally use it for fuel-wood rather than illegally removing wood from the national park. Put differ-ently, Community Forest access, a strategy that is consistent with regulatory pragmatism, lowers the cost of compliance for those who have secured it and, thus, has the power to reduce poverty-driven non-compliance.

Poverty, Community Forests, and Compliance

The data indicate that 78 percent of more than 1,300 respondents live on less than a dollar per day. Moreover, 85 percent of these respondents in Nepal and 66 percent of these respondents in India indicate that they use firewood on a regular basis to either cook food or heat their homes. These data suggest that there is both a great need for firewood and, given the percentage of the pop-ulation living below the poverty line, few cost-effective alternatives (i.e., gas) to this important resource. Below I present relevant sub-sets of the sample and then use t-tests to test hypotheses, a type of analysis made possible by this study's design.

I begin to test the first hypothesis—that regulatory pragmatism can guide weak states to strategies that reduce poverty-driven non-compliance—by sub-setting the data by income level and location. As indicated in Table 6.3, when I run t-tests on these subsets, I find a significant inter-class difference

Table 6.3 Compliance Rates by Location and Income Level

Location	Above Poverty Line	Below Poverty Line	p-value
Nepal	0.75	0.63	0.001
India	0.42	0.25	0.002

between rates of compliance: for Nepal, p = 0.001, and for India, p = 0.002.[7] Importantly, rates of compliance for both income groups are lower on the Indian side of the border, a fact to which I will return later on.[8]

Next I check to make sure that differing levels of fear are not driving these numbers. Here I find that 95 percent in Nepal and 88 percent in India believe they will be caught and punished if they remove firewood from the national park.[9] These numbers are similar when I subset by income level, indicating that those above and below the poverty line are not differentially motivated by fear (Nepal: p = 0.222; India: p = 0.163). These basic findings with respect to fear are buttressed by the fact that individuals do not perceive the penalties for non-compliance differently on either side of the border. Respondents' average "harshness of the penalty" response was 2.36 in Nepal and 2.37 in India, with 2 being "Reasonable" and 3 "Not Very Harsh." Then, taken together, these data suggest that fear is not driving cross-border variation in compliance.

I also check to make sure that variation in the felt sense of duty to obey the law is not behind the income-wise disparity in compliance rates. Reporting rates for relevant duties—"duty to obey the law" and "duty to protect the forest"—are available in Figure 6.3. When I subset by income level, I find no significant difference in the rate at which my respondents who live above the poverty line and below the poverty line report either of these duties. With respect to the duty to protect the forest, in Nepal, p = 0.241 and in India, p = 0.831. With respect to the duty to obey the law, in Nepal, p = 0.605, and in India, p = 0.337.

Finally, I test whether pragmatic regulatory strategies that lower the cost of compliance—access to a Community Forest, in particular—have an effect on compliance rates. Community Forests—which lower the cost compliance for those who have access to them—are only available on the Nepal side of the border. This low-cost compliance option allows individuals who live near a Community Forest and are allowed to remove wood from it to choose compliance more freely than can individuals whose only source of wood is the national park. Individuals who have Community Forest access are able to meet their own firewood needs and comply with Chitwan National Park's wood-taking prohibitions. As indicated in Table 6.4, when examining those who *have* Community Forest access, approximately 56 percent of respondents in Nepal, I find no significant difference when I look across income-levels: p = .406. However, I do find a significant difference across income levels when I look at those who do *not* have access to a community forest: p = 0.000. This finding supports my hypothesis—that those who can afford to comply generally do so and that strategies consistent with regulatory pragmatism, like community forestry, can reduce poverty-driven non-compliance. This finding also indicates that cross-border differences in compliance are at least partially explained by the fact that the extremely high cost of compliance for the poor has been lowered to some degree in Nepal through relatively widespread access to Community Forests, while in India the cost of compliance for the poor remains unmitigated.

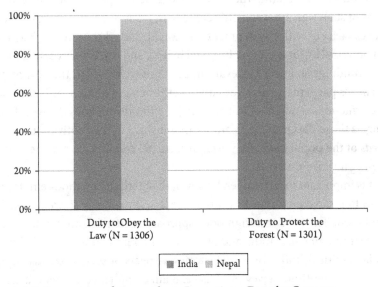

Figure 6.3 Percentage of Respondents Reporting a Duty by Country

Table 6.4 Compliance Rates by Community Forest Access and Income-Level

Location	Above Poverty Line	Below Poverty Line	p-value
Community Forest Access	0.80	0.79	0.406
No Access	0.71	0.39	0.000

Thus, strategies that reduce the cost of compliance for the poor are associated with increased compliance. The data generally confirm that policies that lower compliance costs for the poor—consistent with regulatory pragmatism—can achieve widespread compliance. Nepal's Community Forestry Act does just that. It works around a known barrier to compliance and explains, at least in part, the unexpected success the Nepali state has had in securing the compliance of local populations with conservation regulations that seemingly run counter to self-interest.

These findings suggest that developing world conditions are problematic for regulatory compliance not only because the state in such areas is often coercively weak, but also because weak states must contend with poor target populations for whom compliance is often prohibitively costly. The data also show that in some cases, particularly when the state uses regulatory pragmatism to guide its choices, there are inexpensive policies that states can adopt to lower the cost of compliance for the poor and foster compliant behavior. In addition to correcting the widely held misconception that compliance in areas of state weakness will only come with either increases in a state's coercive capacity or with development (i.e., wealth and education), such a finding is a powerful lesson for those involved in legal and regulatory design. Indeed, these findings should be relevant in any context in which the cost of compliance is particularly high for large swaths of a population, as is the case in poor, ghettoized neighborhoods of major cities throughout the world. As so long as those designing regulations are sensitive to the motivations and the *needs* of the populations they seek to regulate, compliance may be possible, even against the odds.

It is important to remember, however, that both the methods employed in collecting the data utilized in this analysis and the analysis are not without limitation. The border design does approach as-if-random conditions, but the fact remains that India and Nepal are different countries, with different social, political, and economic histories. Aspects of secular trends not captured in a one-time survey may also explain compliance behavior along the border. Not only that, but the border is also unique. It is an area of exchange, of cross-over, of melding. It may be the case that similar research conducted elsewhere in Nepal or elsewhere in India would look very different and might well lead to divergent conclusions, which is to say that these results are not necessarily generalizable. The generalizability issue is particularly acute for the field experiment. Designed to test whether legal knowledge could be diffused into a population by written materials or by a local leader, it is still an experiment and subject to the limitations of experiments in the social sciences. Its findings are not generalizable. They simply hold true for this one situation at a particular time and place. Still, the data and analysis included above, as well as elsewhere in this volume, go a long way toward helping us question and rethink compliance in the absence of strong coercive capacity. Future research may be able to answer the generalizability question.

Regulatory Pragmatism and Its Implications

The data presented in this chapter suggest that pragmatic regulatory strategies can both foster legal knowledge and reduce poverty-driven non-compliance. Those who possess accurate legal knowledge are more likely to comply with wood-taking prohibitions, but this is less true among the poor, whose material survival is threatened by such regulations. Moreover, income-level variation in compliance is not being driven by differing reported rates of fear or duty in the populations targeted by regulations that prohibit wood-taking from nearby national parks. Instead, those who live above the poverty line are more likely to comply with regulations that impose a high cost of compliance than their counterparts living below the poverty line. There is also evidence that, when a low-cost compliance option is available, there is no income-wise variation in compliance. Taken together, these findings suggest that, even in developing world conditions, characterized by an often coercively weak state and endemic poverty, conditions that many have assumed to be incompatible with rule of law, regulatory compliance can be achieved under the right parameters. There are four important implications of these findings for both the socio-legal compliance literature and for those who try to use law to change customary norms and social practice in similar environments throughout the world, be they in inner-city Detroit, the coastal waters of Somalia, or along the India-Nepal border.

First, even coercively weak states with meager resources can bring about both fear of legal sanctions and a felt sense of duty to comply, but they must first ensure that accurate legal knowledge is relatively widespread among target populations. This suggests that across the developing world, increased compliance with key regulations is not as challenging as once thought. If coercively weak states had to become coercively strong in order to secure compliance, dedicating resources to this task would make for challenging policy, particularly when resources could be spent on health or education. This is particularly true in light of the fact that many developing world states have weak democratic traditions or none at all and coercive capability might not be welcomed by or good for populations that might be repressed by it, no matter how noble the secondary goal, be it environmental improvement, better education, or the eradication of child labor. But if, instead, reliable information was the tool of choice, this would leave the choice to comply in the hands of the people, with little risk of increased repression, but would likely still result in increased compliance.

Second, fear and duty are sometimes not enough to bring about compliance. This is particularly true when prohibited behavior is necessary to the material existence of a large percentage of the population targeted by a particular regulation, thus driving the cost of compliance to extraordinary heights for many of those regulated. I spoke with many people on both sides of the India-Nepal border who were quite motivated to comply with government regulations and quite eager to protect the parks they live near, but who also willingly admitted to "stealing" wood from those parks to cook and to heat their homes. The fact that many of them chose the word "steal" in this context is telling: they feel that even though they are otherwise upstanding citizens, they have been forced into a position in which the very resource on which they are dependent—one that was once theirs—is no longer available to them without risk of sanction. The non-compliance of these individuals does not result from an absence of fear or sense of duty, as many have assumed. Instead, it results, at least in part, from a dearth of low-cost compliance alternatives. My findings show that many people will comply with the law if given a low-cost opportunity to do so.

Relatedly, pragmatic regulations that lower the cost of compliance can serve a secondary function for both state and society: aligning the interests of both. As Guha's (1989) work indicates, a regulation that essentially outlaws the lifestyle of a segment of the population, even a marginalized one, can create its own politics. In this case, Nepal and India both outlawed an activity that certain populations rely upon for survival. Had either state had significant coercive capacity, it may have faced a sizable political backlash. Lack of coercive capacity, thus, prevented this politics from developing. But, in the case of India, it also resulted in large-scale non-compliance. Nepal, however, managed relatively widespread compliance without facing the kind of political headwinds that Guha writes about in Uttarakand. Here, a pragmatic regulatory strategy that made compliance less costly for the poor seems to have had the added benefit of making it possible for those living outside of Chitwan National Park to be supportive of, or at least not averse to, the state's wood-taking prohibitions.

The third important implication of these findings is that pragmatically designed regulations and policies, ones that take into account the various motivations and needs of those targeted by them, can be used to change social practices, even in places previously thought to be challenging rule of law environments. The ancestors of many living just outside both Chitwan National Park and Valmiki National Park and Tiger Reserve used and managed the forest now inside park boundaries for centuries, depending upon it for basic building materials, food, medicines, and firewood. Some of them even lived inside what are now park boundaries. Despite the limited capacity of government authorities to exercise control over such a large tract of heavily forested land, many of these individuals, armed with legal knowledge and motivated by either fear or duty or both, are willing to alter their customs and source these materials outside of the park—so long as they can source them *somewhere*. Nepal's Community Forests have become this somewhere and meet the needs of those who have access to them. Compliance is particularly high among this subset of the general population, regardless of income level. Across the border in India, and in some locations in Nepal, similar conditions prevail, yet, with this key resource missing, compliance with wood-taking regulations is low. When forced to choose between compliance and meeting basic needs, many choose the latter. Taken together, these results suggest that high levels of compliance are possible, even in areas where the state is coercively weak, but the burden of turning possibility into reality lies with those crafting regulations. Regulations that fail to account for legal knowledge dissemination or pose an extremely high cost of compliance for populations that can ill afford it will likely be met with non-compliance, whereas those that are pragmatic, foster legal knowledge dissemination, and lower the cost of compliance stand a much greater chance of success.

Interestingly, after data collection for this project was complete, the Indian state implemented a pragmatic regulation that, at least in theory, should reduce poverty-driven non-compliance with wood-taking regulations in the area around Valmiki National Park, as well as elsewhere in India. This program, the Pradhan Mantri Ujjwala Yojana, is emblematic of regulatory pragmatism. With the goal of improving women's health and reducing the negative environmental effects of firewood collection, it provides free LPG (cooking gas) connections to rural and "deprived" households. The idea here is that if collecting wood in protected areas is illegal, but these areas an important source of firewood for local populations, the only way to realistically expect compliance is to provide alternative means of cooking. Though it was put into place in 2016, after data collection was complete, my strong suspicion is that the Ujjwala Yojana is reducing poverty-driven non-compliance in the area around Valmiki National Park as this book goes to press.

The fourth implication of these findings is that the regulations and policies that ultimately drive compliance may be different from and, at first glance, seem orthogonal to the initial regulation against which compliance is measured. In the case at hand, the original regulation is a prohibition on removing wood from a protected government forest, but the regulation that appears to be driving compliance actually allows for wood collection on government-owned forest land, just in a slightly different location—importantly, a location which the government does not consider crucial for the survival of the big game species living in the nearby national park. If we only look at the original regulation and then at the means available to secure compliance, we might come away wondering how the state has fostered such high rates of compliance under adverse conditions. But the fact of the matter is that regulations and policies, like the people they regulate, do not exist in isolation. Instead, they form a complex system of incentives, threats, and obligations that people navigate to the best of their ability, while also trying to live their lives in the ways that they see fit. Those involved in regulatory and policy design should be mindful of the fact that regulations and policies that create opportunities for individuals to comply with other regulations while also allowing those individuals to continue living in the ways that they are accustomed to living may provide a viable path to compliance, not only in areas where the state is coercively weak, but in any context in which legal norms contrast with cultural ones.

Though many assume that coercively weak states lack the capacity to generate fear or instill a sense of duty in target populations and that this is why we find rule of law to be limited in such areas, my data suggest otherwise. It does not take much to instill at least a generalized sense of both fear and duty in the population targeted by a particular regulation. Instead, the problem in such places may lie with doctrinaire regulatory design. The data suggest that when legal knowledge is inaccurate and when a regulation imposes a high cost of compliance on a poor target population, compliance will be low, but that if the same or related legislation can foster accurate legal knowledge and lower the cost of compliance for a substantial percentage of this same target population, compliance will be significantly higher. States guided by regulatory pragmatism can make these choices and secure compliance even if they struggle to project force and behave consistently.

7

Regulatory Pragmatism outside of the Forest

In the preceding chapters I presented data and arguments that suggest that the cross-border variation in compliance observed just outside of Chitwan and Valmiki National Parks can be explained primarily by variation in the degree to which the states involved have employed strategies consistent with regulatory pragmatism when designing and/or implementing their laws. In the preceding argument I also suggest that one of the most significant compliance barriers when the state is weak, coercively or otherwise, is inaccurate legal knowledge. Yet, the data indicate that states that pragmatically design for legal knowledge dissemination can achieve higher rates of compliance. In particular, I tested two different paths to more accurate legal knowledge: (1) delegated enforcement, which can provide contrast between enforcement environments and allow individuals exposed to it to update their legal understandings more accurately than those who have not been exposed; and (2) local leaders, who can foster accurate legal knowledge if they are involved in information dissemination. I then examined a second barrier to compliance, poverty-driven non-compliance, which explains why some fail to comply despite widespread accurate legal knowledge and the presence of fear and/or duty. Use of regulatory pragmatism is predictive here as well. In Nepal, where poverty-driven non-compliance has been reduced by a state-fostered program, compliance is significantly higher than in other nearby places where the cost of compliance remains high.

But, as suggested at the beginning of this book, the conservation case that is its primary focus could be anomalous. I, therefore, introduce two additional cases in this chapter that are drawn from different layers of Indian and Nepali society: businesses and organizations. The first, as previously noted in the introductory chapter, involves compliance with teacher-student ratio regulations in private schools. The second, as also noted in the Introduction, involves compliance with child labor regulations in brick kilns. I use these

Capacity beyond Coercion. Susan L. Ostermann, Oxford University Press. © Oxford University Press 2023.
DOI: 10.1093/oso/9780197661116.003.0007

cases not only to confirm many of my findings in the main conservation case, but also to explore variation among the cases. Analysis of this variation allows for a deeper understanding of compliance in areas where the state is coercively weak.

When I examine compliance behavior in private schools I find that, unlike the conservation case, compliance is better in India than in Nepal. Yet, accuracy of legal knowledge remains an important predictor of compliance. Poverty-driven non-compliance also remains predictive of compliance behavior, though not among the wealthiest or most expensive private schools. It just so happens that in this case the state in which the first factor, legal knowledge, is higher and second factor, poverty-driven non-compliance, is lower, is India. When I examine compliance with child labor regulations in brick kilns, the picture gets more complicated. Managers and owners of brick kilns who possess more accurate legal knowledge are more likely to be in compliance and those kilns that are economically strapped are least likely to be in compliance, but there is no cross-border variation in compliance, or in either of these other variables.

In this chapter I build upon the concept of regulatory pragmatism, which I first explored in the Introduction and Chapter 2. Here I use it to explain how the Indian state has managed to foster more compliance in private schools in Raxaul Bazaar than the Nepali state has in Birgunj, while neither state has secured much compliance with child labor regulations in brick kilns in this same area. Delegated enforcement, a strategy consistent with regulatory pragmatism which was effective near Chitwan and Valmiki, involves the outsourcing of some aspects of governance. Delegation should be important in these latter regulatory contexts because principal-agent problems are significant here as well and the state has proven helpless to solve them. Delegation is, thus, a way to design around that problem.

In the conservation case, Nepal delegated enforcement authority over government-owned park land just outside of Chitwan National Park to citizen "User Groups" through its Community Forestry Program. User Groups are responsible for regulating themselves, with minimal government oversight. India, though it engages in "Joint Forest Management" elsewhere, did not have a similar program in place outside Valmiki. In the private schools case, the roles are reversed. The Indian government has delegated enforcement to parents via the 2009 Right to Education Act, which allows parents to take government funding with them from school to school, regardless of whether the school is government-run or private. Parents' increased ability to remove students from poorly performing schools means that threats to private school administrators to remove students from schools with high teacher-student ratios are believable. Nepal has no analogous program and does not appear to have delegated enforcement capacity through any other channel; in fact, it doesn't seem to have behaved pragmatically at all in this regulatory arena. Finally, in the brick kilns case, neither India nor Nepal has delegated enforcement or, seemingly, employed any other strategy that is consistent with regulatory pragmatism.

If regulatory pragmatism is generalizable beyond the conservation case, we should see variation in compliance that is consistent with variation in the employment of regulatory pragmatism across all three cases. This is, in fact, what I find. Compliance with teacher-student ratios is more common on the Indian side of the border than it is in Nepal, and compliance in the brick kilns case, in which neither employed a pragmatic regulatory strategy, is similar on both sides of the border.

This pattern of findings suggests that regulatory pragmatism can be used by coercively weak states to choose strategies, like delegated enforcement, that will foster both accurate legal knowledge and compliance. I further explore both regulatory pragmatism and delegated enforcement, and the implications of each, toward the end of this chapter. Before then, I explain my choice of cases, briefly discuss hypotheses, variables and methodology, and relate my findings.

Why Private Schools and Brick Kilns?

In order to further test the efficacy of regulatory pragmatism and the power of accurate legal knowledge to foster compliance, I examine two important, additional layers of Indian and Nepali society: businesses and organizations. The decision to examine the compliance of private schools and brick kilns is admittedly not an obvious one. In order to understand this decision, one must first remember that the border itself is arguably the most formidable constraint of this project. The border lends my analysis methodological traction and yet can also be problematic because of the nature of life and society in the border region. As mentioned previously, the people living in this area are quite poor. It follows that economic activity is somewhat limited, which severely narrows one's choices when it comes to types of businesses and organizations, and the attendant regulations, to examine. In addition, I wanted to examine regulations that affect large swaths of the population, not just small niches. Finally, I needed to examine compliance with regulations that required or prohibited behavior that was inconsistent with local cultural norms and that was easily observable. This left me with relatively few viable choices.

Private schools and brick kilns are two of a very small number of businesses and organizations that are ubiquitous along this section of the India-Nepal border and subject to regulations that run counter to cultural norms. While neither private schools nor brick kilns affect everyone's lives, they do affect many lives in the region. Private schools are considered to be almost "necessary" for those parents who want their children to lead different lives from their own and even poor parents try to scrape together the funds necessary to enroll their children in one. Meanwhile, brick kilns are virtually the only source of non-agricultural employment for the largely uneducated, unskilled labor force living in this area. Finally, government regulation of both of these entities involves regulations that, when violated, are easily observable. One can tell just by walking through a school if many or most of the classrooms exceed the legal maximum. Similarly, one can tell just by entering the premises of a brick kiln if the kiln employs child labor. Thus, in many ways, the choice of private schools and brick kilns was not a choice, it was the only way forward given the other constraints of the project.

Hypotheses and Variables

I broadly hypothesize that widespread compliance is possible, even in areas where the state is coercively weak. However, in order for legal institutions to work in this context, state or non-state actors must overcome applicable compliance barriers. In these latter cases, as in the conservation case, the most formidable obstacles were those presented by both inaccurate legal understandings and poverty-driven non-compliance. Regulatory pragmatism suggests that, as with the conservation case, one way to foster more accurate legal understandings when the state is plagued by principal-agent problems and not well positioned to handle this task itself, is to delegate enforcement to interested parties.

Dependent Variable

The major dependent variable remains compliance. As has been discussed more thoroughly in other chapters, I will merely remind of its definition here: compliance occurs when an individual acts or refrains from acting in such a way that his or her behavior is consistent with that required by law. This involves private schools maintaining teacher-student ratios that are at or below the legally mandated maximum, which in this case is 1:30 in India[1] and 1:40 in Nepal. Brick kiln compliance involves refraining from hiring those who are below the age at which individuals are legally allowed to work in a hazardous industry, which in the cases of both India and Nepal is fourteen.

In both the private schools and brick kilns cases, I measured compliance by observation in order to avoid respondent biases that might lead to inaccurate self-reporting of non-compliance. I did so in the schools by requesting a tour of the premises during my interviews and observing the classrooms. I then rated the compliance of each school on a scale of 1 to 5, with 1 indicating that no classrooms were compliant and 5 indicating that all classrooms were compliant. In the brick kilns, observing compliance with child labor regulations was even easier. A brick kiln is open to the elements and the manager's/owner's office typically sits in a location where he/she can observe all workers. I was, therefore, generally able to observe compliance while conducting my interviews with managers/owners. But *accurately* observing compliance with child labor regulations is not as straightforward as observing compliance with teacher-student ratio regulations. As I could not speak to the workers themselves, I had to guess their ages and accurately guessing whether a worker is over fourteen is not easy, particularly for children whose ages are close to the limit itself. Thus, I measure non-compliance in the brick kilns case by observing whether a kiln employs workers who appear to be under age ten, an age that is more easily discernible from a distance and that still provides a relatively accurate measure of which kilns are employing child labor. As with the private schools, I rated brick kiln compliance on a scale of 1 to 5, with 1 indicating that none of the workers appear to be under age ten and 5 indicating that all of the workers appear to be under age ten.

Independent Variables

I examine, as noted above, a region that is characterized by the same basic rules, the same culture, and, seemingly, the same basic incentives to comply with or break the law. Within that context I examine how accurate legal understandings, poverty, and compliance vary when strategies consistent with regulatory pragmatism are present or absent. I discuss each at length below.

Delegated Enforcement

When the state is coercively weak, it sometimes suffers from principal-agent problems and struggles to carry out basic tasks. In such cases, the state is often *functionally*, even if not intentionally, inconsistent in the way that it enforces the law. This is true even if no corruption is involved. A state may well be corruption-free, but its agents may lack the resources or competency to consistently enforce the law. As a result, for reasons discussed at length in Chapter 3 and in the next section, the populations targeted by particular regulations tend to end up with inaccurate understandings of the very laws with which the state would like them to comply. If we consider that states need the capacity to, for instance, collect taxes in order to provide the resources necessary to bring about further state capacity, lack of same seems to be a trap from which few states will ever emerge, especially as there is little academic consensus on how to foster state capacity. This leaves one wondering: if a state lacks resources and/or coercive capacity, does this mean that increasing both is the only means by which to bring about regulatory compliance?

I have argued in this book that increasing the state's enforcement capacity is not the only means by which a coercively weak state can bring about regulatory compliance. Indeed, a state need not have tremendous coercive capacity if it employs regulatory pragmatism and designs around known compliance barriers. In the cases at hand, principal-agent problems are pervasive and delegation of enforcement to interested parties is a pragmatic regulatory solution. If there are individuals, groups, and organizations at the local level that have the capacity to consistently carry out certain proscribed tasks, possibly under government oversight, and have reason to want to take over these tasks, a state can take advantage of this resource and get help in carrying out its prerogatives by outsourcing specific functions to citizens and/or civil society. In this way, a state that has only minimal enforcement capacity can behave as if it is coercively strong, reaping the associated benefits without incurring tremendous costs. So long as the parties to whom enforcement is delegated benefit when they realize compliant behavior, more accurate legal understandings and higher rates of compliance should result.

In the three cases I examine, there is considerable variation on the use of regulatory pragmatism, generally, and delegated enforcement, in particular: two involve delegated enforcement, one by Nepal and the other by India, while in the third, neither state has delegated. In the conservation case, the Nepali state has delegated enforcement power over large swaths of government-owned forest land just outside of Chitwan National Park to over fifty different Community Forest "User Groups." As described earlier, in Chapter 3, each of these groups is responsible for ensuring compliance with applicable regulations in its Community Forest and, if a group fails in this, the state may strip it of the land grant and all of the benefits that flow from same. Further, as I discuss in Chapter 3 and will discuss further below, there is reason to believe that the contrast between regulatory consistency in the Community Forest and a lack thereof in Chitwan National Park fosters more accurate legal understandings of *national park laws* among those who have access to a Community Forest. In the schools case, the Indian state has delegated enforcement of some education regulations to parents via the Right to Education Act (RTE). As discussed briefly above and further below, the RTE allows parents to remove their children from schools with high teacher-student ratios and to take their state funding with them to schools with lower ratios. This flexibility is a benefit to parents, allowing them to demand compliance with legally mandated teacher-student ratio maximums from school administrators. When they do so, they foster more accurate understandings of this particular education regulation. Finally, in the brick kilns case, neither the Nepali nor the Indian state has delegated child labor enforcement to interested parties.

With the above in mind, I expect that a pragmatic regulatory strategy, delegated enforcement, allows states to create consistency of enforcement in the absence of tremendous coercive capacity and that we should see both more accurate legal understandings and higher levels of compliance in those places and cases in which the state has done so. We have already seen this in Nepal, in the conservation case. We will see this in India, in the schools case. In all other places and cases we should and do find relatively fewer accurate legal understandings and lower levels of compliance.

Accuracy of Legal Understandings

The target population in the conservation case existed in a low-information environment, in which members had little knowledge of the law and little means to find out about it. The target populations in the private schools and brick kilns cases are situated somewhat differently. All headmasters/principals and almost all brick kiln managers/owners I surveyed are educated/literate; many of them also have the financial means and connections to get competent legal advice. This means that they are more capable of finding out about the law on the books if they want to.

But, realistically, many do not take the time to do this kind of research, nor does education/literacy mean that one will be able to definitively determine whether a given action is legal or illegal. In addition, few seek out legal advice. Instead, headmasters/principals and brick kiln managers/owners seem to often learn about the law just like their less-educated counterparts, through observation.

In both the private schools and brick kilns cases, as with the conservation case, inconsistent state behavior fosters widespread misunderstandings of legal requirements. When the state punishes or appears to punish a particular action some of the time, while failing to punish the same behavior at other times, these mixed signals propagate through the legal understandings of the relevant target population. Nearly all principals/headmasters, as well as those brick kiln managers/owners located close to the main highway, have seen inspections before (and other have heard about them), but I found that the interpretations of the law that flowed from these experiences were often at odds with one another. Those who were punished, or saw others punished, or heard about others being punished, received information that suggests that the punished behavior is illegal. Many of these same individuals then received conflicting information at some later point in time and this caused them to question whether their original assumptions regarding prohibited behavior were correct; they then updated their legal understandings to reflect this new information. In this way, the Indian and Nepali states' inconsistent actions with respect to a variety of regulations mean that, at any given moment, many individuals, even relatively wealthy and well-educated ones, hold inaccurate legal understandings.

Given this, I expect that, as in the conservation case, consistent enforcement of a particular law, either by the state or via delegation, will be associated with accurate legal understandings. The more regularly and visibly the state and/or its delegates punish schools that exceed the maximum teacher-student ratio allowed by law or brick kilns that employ child labor, the more target populations observe this to be the case and can, in turn, tell others what they have observed. Under these conditions, target populations will rarely be presented with conflicting information about the law and, as a result, will only occasionally have to resolve discrepancies and update their legal understandings. Moreover, when they do resolve contradictions, they are more likely to end up with accurate legal knowledge.

But the state, as mentioned briefly above, does not behave consistently with respect to either teacher-student ratio regulations or child labor regulations in this particular area. I was never, despite spending many months in the region, able to locate the district education officer (DEO) for either Purba Champaran (India) or Parsa (Nepal). The headmasters/principals I spoke with verified that the applicable DEOs were rarely present and many stated that, while enforcement of teacher-student ratio regulations was rare, they viewed it as potentially costly. The situation with respect to child labor regulation was even less consistent. I was also never able to find out who precisely at the local level was responsible for enforcing such restrictions, but several brick kiln owners/managers stated that enforcement of labor regulation has happened at kilns. It has typically been politically motivated and precisely targeted. In their experience, enforcement followed scandal and scapegoats were made, but all other violators were left alone. This level of inconsistency, if the conservation case is any guide, should result in widespread misinformation about the law, particularly if it's not clear which aspect of child labor regulation was violated.

That is, unless consistency is achieved via delegation. While neither state has delegated enforcement of child labor law and, thus, we should not expect to find cross-border variation in same, India has, as briefly detailed above, delegated education regulation to parents via the 2009 RTE. This act, which is essentially a voucher system, allows parents to take a child's state funding with him or her, whether he or she attends a government school or a private school. As parents can supplement this funding with their own resources, this program effectively means that poor parents have additional choices when it comes to where to send their children to school. Before the RTE, many parents were stuck with only the cheapest schools, but now most can consider slightly more expensive ones. It also means that even poor parents should be more believable when they tell school administrators who are not complying with applicable regulations that they will take their children to another school unless they hire additional teachers.[2] In other words, the RTE allows parents to become enforcers and if they act as such, they should be able, through delegation, to create the consistency needed to bring about accurate legal understandings—and compliance—despite the fact that the state has not succeeded in doing so directly. As Nepal has no analogous program, accurate legal understandings should be more widespread in India than in Nepal in this case. In contrast, in the brick kilns case, in which state action is inconsistent and neither state has delegated, accurate legal understandings should be similarly low in both India and Nepal.

Poverty-Driven Non-Compliance

As discussed in greater detail in Chapters 3 and 6, individual level compliance is often driven by self interest (Pearce & Tombs 1990, 1997, 1998; Parker 2002; Molnar et al. 2004). Individuals with more resources are less likely to break certain laws than those with fewer resources, simply because of the relatively low cost of compliance. The poor, on the other hand, may engage in non-compliance simply because they are poor. In the developed world, low poverty rates and typically well developed state coercive apparatus combine to make deterrence a reasonable strategy. In the developing world, the opposite is true, states that often have limited coercive capacity end up targeting much larger swaths of the population.

It should not be surprising, then, that poverty-driven non-compliance can be endemic in the developing world. Along the India-Nepal border, businesses and organizations often run on extremely low margins or at a loss. This has important implications for compliance behavior. Many schools struggle to raise tuition for students whose parents can barely afford to pay even low school fees, so hiring an additional teacher at a private school to bring that school into compliance with teacher-student ratio regulations may mean that that school either runs at a loss or must cut other important programs. Brick kilns face similar constraints. A brick kiln that is located far from a market on poor clay soil can only fetch so much for its bricks and incurs heavy costs to get those bricks to market. The manager of such a kiln is forced to choose between compliance, with accompanying losses and possible business closure, and hiring child labor to handle some tasks. This same manager is also seen as a pillar of the community and employer of last resort. If he/she closes his/her kilns, the local economic effects on a very poor population are tremendous and the reputation effects for the owner/manager are similarly bad. Thus, any government regulating in this arena faces very stiff headwinds in terms of securing compliance that is costly.

When legal knowledge is accurate, I expect that many businesses and organization that *can* afford to comply to do so. More specifically, among the relatively small number of businesses and organization for which the cost of compliance is low relative to their revenues, I expect compliance, so long as (a) this cost is lower than the perceived cost of non-compliance and/or (b) they believe that it is their duty to comply. For those organizations and businesses that face a very high cost of compliance, my expectations are different, even if they are well aware of the law. Indeed, even if the cost of *non*-compliance were very high, many of these businesses and organizations would rather risk enforcement-related penalties than face the alternatives. Furthermore, even if the individuals in charge of these business and organizations believe they have a duty to comply, it is likely not powerful enough to overcome their poverty-driven non-compliance. Thus, I hypothesize that, among those business and organizations that have the option to both comply and continue functioning, those motivated by either fear or duty will comply in significantly higher numbers than those of their low-income counterparts who have no viable alternative to non-compliance.

To test these hypotheses, I first compare the observed compliance behavior of those for whom the cost of compliance is relatively high to those for whom the cost of compliance is relatively low, using school fees and brick prices as a proxy for the relative cost of compliance. These are approximate measures of revenue, as labor prices do not vary much in this area. Then, using methods described below, I check to make sure that these two income groups do not report different levels of both fear and duty.

Methodology

I utilize both survey data and interviews with relevant actors to explain variation in compliance. In the schools case, I collected survey data from the headmaster/principal of every[3] private primary school in Birgunj, Nepal, and in Raxaul Bazaar, India, twin border cities located a short drive from both Chitwan and Valmiki. Each respondent was asked, in person, a series of questions that started with demographic information and proceeded to inquiries designed to help measure my variables of interest. A complete list of these questions and an explanation of how I coded responses is located in Appendix 1. I did not ask respondents about their compliance with teacher-student ratio regulations. Instead, as described briefly above, I observed same while touring the premises.

In the brick kilns case, I collected survey data from the manager/owner of every[4] brick kiln located within 10 km of the India-Nepal border as it runs from Chitwan and Valmiki National Parks in the west to just past Birgunj and Raxaul Bazaar in the east. As no government list of brick kilns exists for this area in either Nepal or India, I located these kilns using satellite imagery. Kilns are large operations that are quite distinctive and easily located via satellite. Though several of the kilns I found by way of this methodology had subsequently closed, I found no kilns in operation that were not on my satellite maps as I traveled around this area conducting interviews. As with the schools case, I asked each brick kiln owner/manager, in person, a series of questions that started with demographic information and proceeded to inquiries designed to help measure my variables of interest. A complete list of these questions and an explanation of how I coded responses is located in Appendix 1. As with the schools case, I once again did not ask respondents about their compliance with child labor regulations and, instead, observed same while touring the premises.

Evidence of Regulatory Pragmatism in Schools and at Kilns

To determine whether consistent enforcement, even if achieved through delegation, is associated with accurate legal understandings, I compare the number of school administrators who have accurate legal understandings in India to that number for Nepal. I also conduct a cross-border comparison of the number of brick kiln managers/owners who possess accurate understandings of the law. In the first case, my hypothesis predicts that accuracy should be more widespread in India than in Nepal. In the second case, my hypothesis predicts that, since state action remains inconsistent on both sides of the border and has not been augmented by delegated enforcement on either side, there should be no statistical difference between the numbers of managers who have accurate understandings on each side of the border. As indicated in Table 7.1, when I run t-tests on these subsets, I find a significant cross-border difference in the schools case, p = 0.044, but not in the brick kilns case, p = 0.364.

Next I check to make sure that, consistent with my findings in the conservation case, accurate legal knowledge is in fact associated with higher levels of compliance in both the schools and brick kilns cases. On the whole, 69 percent of the schools in India and 47 percent in Nepal were in substantial compliance with teacher-student ratio regulations, which I consider to be having fewer than the maximum number of students allowed in all or most of their classrooms. When I subset by accurate legal knowledge, these numbers change to 77 percent in India and 60 percent in Nepal. While this change may not seem significant, when compared to the compliance rates among those with inaccurate legal knowledge, the differences are fairly pronounced, as shown in Table 7.2.

Table 7.1 Accurate Legal Understandings by Regulatory Context and Location

Regulatory Context	India	Nepal	p-value
Private Schools	0.83	0.59	0.044
Brick Kilns	0.35	0.27	0.364

Table 7.2 Private School Compliance Rates by Accuracy of Legal Knowledge and Location

Location	Accurate Legal Knowledge	Inaccurate Legal Knowledge
India	0.77	0.33
Nepal	0.60	0.29

The data are similar in the brick kilns case. On the whole, 52 percent of brick kilns in India and 54 percent in Nepal were in compliance with child labor regulations, which I consider to be having no children observed to be working on the premises at the time of the survey. Though the difference between these country-wise rates of compliance is not significant, the differences when I subset by accuracy of legal knowledge are, once again, substantial,[5] as reported in Table 7.3.

Finally, I check to see whether poverty-driven non-compliance is a factor. If it is, those who can afford to comply and are motivated to do so will comply in higher numbers than those who are motivated to comply but cannot afford to meet legal requirements. When I look at private schools, those schools in Nepal with median or greater tuition (most schools' only source of funds) complied at higher rates than their lower-tuition counterparts. However, in India, the same was not true. Here I found, as depicted in Table 7.4, that while overall compliance was higher in India, schools that charged the least tuition were *more* likely to be in compliance than their higher-tuition counterparts, a fact that makes sense if you consider that it is parents at less expensive schools who are more likely to use the RTE to threaten administrators with a transfer away to a different—possibly more expensive—school. Schools with high tuition rates tend to be the elite schools with better exam-passing rates and parents who are unhappy with these schools have little RTE-based recourse. There is no better school that they can transfer their students to, save for an even more expensive boarding school. As a result, we should not expect administrators at these schools to feel threatened by parents and we

Table 7.3 Brick Kiln Compliance Rates by Accuracy of Legal Knowledge and Location

Location	Accurate Legal Knowledge	Inaccurate Legal Knowledge
India	0.75	0.40
Nepal	0.67	0.47

Table 7.4 Private School Compliance Rates by Income and Location

Location	> Median Earnings	=< Median Earnings
India	0.64	0.78
Nepal	0.55	0.38

should only expect them to comply for other reasons. Interestingly, if I look at the most elite schools in Nepal, I find the same pattern: only 33 percent of the truly high tuition schools in Nepal are in compliance.

When I turn to the brick kilns, I find, as reported in Table 7.5, that few of the kilns making below the median earnings in my sample were in compliance. By comparison, those making median earnings or greater were much more likely to comply. In Nepal, these kilns were in compliance 64 percent of the time. In India, higher-income kilns were in compliance 71 percent of the time.

I then check to make sure that differing levels of fear or duty are not behind wealth-based disparities in compliance rates. In private schools in India, 57 percent of headmasters/principals at high-tuition schools and 64 percent at low-tuition schools fear being caught and punished if they fail to maintain teacher-student ratios below the legal maximum. The same statistic for private schools in Nepal was 55 percent in high-income schools and 57 percent in low-income schools. Neither of these differences is significant (India, $p = 0.340$; Nepal, $p = 0.477$). In terms of duty, 100 percent of principals/headmasters at high-tuition schools in India felt a duty to comply with teacher-student ratio regulations; this number was 95 percent at low-tuition schools. Meanwhile, in Nepal, 88 percent of high-income and 75 percent of low-income headmasters/principals felt a duty to comply with ratio regulations. Neither the difference in India nor the difference in Nepal is significant (India, $p = 0.165$; Nepal, $p = 0.247$).

Table 7.5 Brick Kiln Compliance Rates by Income and Location

Location	> Median Earnings	=< Median Earnings
India	0.71	0.40
Nepal	0.64	0.40

The data for the brick kilns are similar. In India, 73 percent of owners/ managers at high-income kilns feared being caught and punished if they hired child labor, whereas this statistic was 83 percent at low-income kilns. The difference between these rates is not significant (p = 0.318). In Nepal, the statistics are not terribly different: 66 percent of high-income kiln managers/owners reported this fear, whereas 50 percent of low-income managers/owners reported the same. Here, again, the difference is not significant (p = 0.238). In Indian brick kilns, 95 percent of respondents reported a duty to obey the law, while in Nepali brick kilns, 100 percent of respondents reported this duty. It should not be surprising then that the income-wise differences here are not significant (India, p = 0.167; Nepal, p = 1.0).

Finally, it is important to consider the interrelatedness of the schools and brick kilns cases and whether one of India's premier social programs, its Madhyahan Bhojan Yojana or Midday Meal Program, confounds these results. The Madhyahan Bhojan Yojana, which began in 1995, allows all students who attend school to receive a free and relatively nutritious meal at the state's expense. As originally conceived, one of the goals of this program was to reduce child labor and increase school attendance. The mechanism by which the program does so is by lowering the opportunity cost associated with school attendance, so that children from poor families who need to work just to eat can instead both eat and receive education.

As the Madhyahan Bhojan Yojana is present in India and not in Nepal, we would expect it to confound results by raising the number of children attending school in India and, potentially, raising teacher-student ratios; we would also expect the program to reduce child labor in India. The data suggest, however, that the Midday Meal Program is not dramatically skewing my results. In the schools case, teacher-student ratios are lower in India than in Nepal, so the presence of the Midday Meal Program does not appear to be driving more children into schools and, as a consequence, raising teacher-student ratios in classrooms. Meanwhile, in the brick kilns case, the presence of the Midday Meal Program in India (and not in Nepal) has not resulted in observed cross-border variation in child labor rates. Indeed, no cross-border variation was observed. Thus, while the Madhyahan Bhojan Yojana is undoubtedly an important social program, it does not appear to be driving the results presented in either shadow case.

Regulatory Pragmatism Travels

The above-detailed data and analysis suggest that, in places in which the state generally behaves inconsistently, delegated enforcement can help foster accurate understandings of the law. In the private schools case, India delegated enforcement to parents via the RTE and accurate legal knowledge was more widespread among principals/headmasters in India than in Nepal. In the brick kilns case, neither state delegated to interested parties and knowledge of child labor regulations was similarly low on both sides of the border. The data also suggest that my general findings from the conservation case hold up in these shadow cases as well. Accurate legal understandings are associated with higher rates of compliance in both the private schools and the brick kilns cases, and there is evidence of poverty-driven non-compliance in both. All this suggests that even in developing world conditions, characterized by coercively weak states and endemic poverty, conditions that many have assumed to be incompatible with rule of law, regulatory compliance can be achieved if states allow regulatory pragmatism to guide their choices regarding legal design and implementation strategy. These findings have three important implications for both the socio-legal compliance literature and practitioners—be they bureaucrats, politicians, or aid workers—trying to use law to change behavior throughout the world.

First, even coercively weak states with meager resources can achieve higher levels of compliance, if only they can foster more accurate legal knowledge. I argue that the main way in which states do this is by behaving consistently. Through the consistent action of state representatives, populations receive information regarding what is allowed and what is not allowed under law. This is particularly true when literacy and education levels are low. But achieving consistency is no small feat for weak and/or underfunded states. The literature would have us believe that increased state capacity alone will allow states to meet these ends. My findings suggest, however, that there is another way to achieve consistency, at least in some regulatory scenarios: states can delegate enforcement to interested parties. These parties, by definition, must have an incentive to get involved and to pursue the state's agenda, but so long as these parameters are in place, interested parties can do the work necessary to mimic consistent state action. When interested parties are present and enforcement has been delegated, understandings of regulatory requirements at the local level become more accurate. With more accurate legal understandings, compliance is also higher.

But delegation to interested parties is not always possible, particularly when interested parties cannot be found. If there aren't individuals, groups, or organizations present in civil society whose interests align with those of the state on a particular regulatory issue, delegated enforcement is not likely to work. For instance, while one might enlist citizens in a city to help with parking enforcement, since there are groups and individuals who stand to gain from turnover of cars in a particular location or from the removal of cars parked illegally across driveways, such individuals and groups are not always readily available. In the brick kilns case, it is hard to know who the interested parties might be. Brick kiln owners facing tight margins can benefit from lowering costs by hiring child labor. Parents in rural areas in India and Nepal, most of whom are quite poor, benefit from their children's labor in terms of realizing short-term monetary gains, even though they might benefit more in the long term from children who have attended school. Yet, many of the brick kiln owners with whom I spoke stated that poor parents will literally beg to have their children hired. Their material existence is that tenuous. And I suspect that any program that was able to align parents' long-term interests with the state's anti-child labor prerogatives would be quite expensive, thus putting this type of program out of reach for most developing world states trying to curb the use of child labor. It follows that delegated enforcement is not a panacea for inducing regulatory compliance in weak and/or underfunded states. Instead it should be seen as one possible way to do so if the regulatory scenario permits. Regulatory pragmatism can guide states to other options.

It's also true that delegation of criminal law enforcement to civil society is problematic. While the state can engage with communities and get their assistance in criminal enforcement, via programs like "Neighborhood Watch" or the "Amber Alert" system in the United States, enlisting individuals and/or groups within society who have not been professionalized to actually wield the state's monopoly over force in *criminal* cases is fraught with problems. Members of one group within civil society might use this power to treat other groups, groups that they do not like for one reason or another, poorly. Along the India-Nepal border, one can easily imagine high-caste groups wielding this power against lower-caste groups, or vice versa. Now, of course, the same could happen with delegation of civil regulatory power, but in the case of the latter the consequences are often both less dire and more avoidable with government oversight. In addition, there is the problem that criminal law enforcement typically involves *criminals* and dealing with individuals or groups engaged in criminal activity requires sophistication and, often, weaponry. It is difficult to imagine how the state might delegate this type of authority to civil society in a way that is less costly or problematic than hiring additional police.

The other important implication of my findings is that states that employ regulatory pragmatism to carefully design regulations and policies to take into account the various motivations and needs of those targeted by them, can use law to change social practices, even in places previously thought to be challenging rule of law environments. Accurate legal knowledge, when combined with the fear and duty generated by even a minimally capable state, is often enough to bring about compliance—but not always. This is particularly true when prohibited behavior is necessary to the material existence of the population or types of entities targeted by a particular regulation, thus driving the cost of compliance to extraordinary heights for many of those regulated. I spoke with numerous principals/headmasters on both sides of the India-Nepal border who were quite motivated to comply with government regulations and eager to reduce their teacher-student ratios below the legal maximum, but who could not do so due to financial constraints. My respondents explained that there was demand for private school education, even from the poor, but that the ability of these parents to pay was extremely limited. Several principals/headmasters explained that they felt a responsibility to provide private education at a low cost and that private schooling with too many students in a classroom was better for students than education in government schools in which the teachers fail to even show up at work. The non-compliance of these individuals does not result from an absence of fear or felt sense of duty, as many have assumed. Instead, it results from a dearth of low-cost compliance alternatives. My findings from the conservation case show that many people will comply with the law if given a low-cost opportunity to do so.

While there is no directly analogous program in place in either of the private schools or brick kilns cases, one aspect of the RTE has the ability to lower the cost of compliance and, therefore, bears further discussion. The

RTE makes the same public education funds that the state would spend on a child's education in a government school available to that student if his/her parents choose to enroll him/her in a private school. What this means is that parents effectively have more to spend on private school education. For example, those parents who might only have been able to contribute 1,500 rupees to their daughter's education for the year would, with the government RTE subsidy, have at least an additional 4,700 rupees to spend in Bihar. This means that they could send their daughter to a school that costs more and may provide better education. It also, as I have argued, means that they can threaten administrators of their daughter's current school and demand that the school hire additional teachers. This school, for its part, is now in a better position to afford to raise prices to pay for additional teachers as all parents can spend at least 4,700 rupees per year on private school education. This may well be part of the reason that compliance rates amongst low-tuition schools in Raxaul Bazaar were higher than those found in high-tuition schools. Not only could parents of children in low-tuition schools demand more teachers and have their threats to transfer student seem credible, the very program that facilitated those demands made it possible for schools to charge more in order to meet legal/parental expectations. In contrast, administrators at high-tuition schools were largely unmotivated to hire additional teachers. As one administrator explained, "hiring more teachers is expensive and we already have one of the highest pass-rates in the area. Parents are only concerned with teachers if the pass-rate is low." And to some degree this rationale makes sense—in that the goal of the legal mandate is to achieve better learning outcomes—even if it involves non-compliance.

In private schools in Nepal, principals/headmasters have not experienced the same cost-of-compliance lowering effects. The same is true of brick kiln owners/managers on both sides of the border. Yet, one can imagine programs that might lower the cost of compliance for cash-strapped private schools and brick kilns. In the schools, the Nepali state could attempt to mimic India's RTE or it could provide loans to low-tuition schools in order to allow them to hire enough staff to comply with legal mandates. If, on inspection, they are found in compliance, the state could forgive all or part of that loan. Just having additional staff might, in the end, result in higher-quality education and that might help attract parents of students who can afford to pay more, thus creating a virtuous cycle. In the brick kilns, the state might allow brick kilns to draw workers from the Mahatma Gandhi National

Rural Employment Guarantee Act (MGNREGA), which promises workers at least 100 paid days of labor every year. These workers typically work on state projects, but if reducing child labor is considered a state project, using state funds to employ adults in place of children might be an effective use of government funds. Many of the owners/managers I spoke to stated that they vastly preferred hiring adult workers because they are more productive, but that even the low, unskilled-labor wages in Bihar and Nepal's Terai are sometimes beyond their reach given the overhead at their particular kilns. While these statements indicate that a drop in wages would help reduce child labor, a decrease in already low wages would not be beneficial to the rural poor, nor to the politicians who represent them; thus, use of MGNREGA workers at kilns might better achieve both ends.

The assumptions implicit in the standard deterrence model of compliance remain appropriate in areas where the state is coercively weak and across varied regulatory contexts. Low compliance in such areas is, at least in part, driven by inaccurate legal knowledge and widespread poverty. Though the compliance and rule of law literatures largely assume that these latter factors will only be ameliorated by either economic development or increased coercive capacity, two variables that are often correlated, I have presented evidence that neither of these is necessary to achieve higher levels of compliance in places where state enforcement capacity and incomes are low. Regulatory pragmatism can, in places where non-compliance is associated with inaccurate legal knowledge and poverty, guide states to implementation strategies that account for these problems. Inaccurate legal knowledge can be ameliorated if a state behaves consistently (a tall order for many weak and/or underfunded states) or, if it cannot, if it: (1) delegates regulatory responsibility to interested parties who are capable of consistent action; or (2) utilizes local leaders to convey accurate legal knowledge to target populations. Moreover, these are likely not the only ways to foster accurate legal knowledge. Once knowledge is in place, fear and duty work in the ways that we understand them to, even when coercive capacity is minimal. Still, among those whose compliance costs are high and, seemingly, for those businesses that are quite profitable, challenges remain. Here I have shown, particularly in Chapter 6, but also with evidence in this chapter from the private schools case, that thoughtful regulatory design can sometimes be used to lower the cost of compliance for a substantial percentage of a target population. When states are able to do so, compliance rates are significantly higher.

8
Putting Regulatory Pragmatism
into Practice

The research contained in this book started, oddly enough, while investigating another possible project related to the politics of Madhesis, people thought to be of Indian origin living in the South of Nepal. It was pure happenstance that I walked by the auxiliary park headquarters of Chitwan National Park and saw a map that depicted Chitwan National Park on one side and Valmiki National Park on the other. All of my subsequent efforts, however, have been quite intentional and, in the preceding chapters, I have attempted to leave no stone unturned in trying to understand why those living on the Nepal side of the India-Nepal border comply with Chitwan National Park's wood-taking prohibitions in greater numbers than those living in India comply with Valmiki National Park and Tiger Reserve's nearly identical regulations. These efforts involved explaining the seemingly inexplicable: in a region that is dominated by the same ethnic group and language, in which people are largely poor and uneducated, in which people have a real need for firewood, and in which the state has little power to stop them from taking it from nearby conservation areas despite wood-taking being prohibited, why some people refrain from doing so. The literature suggests that with all of these factors held relatively constant, we should not see cross-border variation in compliance.

Methodologically, I start from the premise of a least-favorable case design: in places where the state is coercively weak, particularly when the behavior required by a legal institution is different from that required by local customary norms and self-interest, we should not expect to see compliance. Then, with the open India-Nepal border as a backdrop, I use both qualitative and quantitative evidence to demonstrate that one thing varies at the border and makes the inexplicable seem more plausible: regulatory pragmatism.

In the conservation case, the Nepali state adopted a strategy, Community Forestry, that was consistent with regulatory pragmatism and fostered compliance in two different ways: (1) by fostering accurate legal knowledge via

Capacity beyond Coercion. Susan L. Ostermann, Oxford University Press. © Oxford University Press 2023.
DOI: 10.1093/oso/9780197661116.003.0008

delegated enforcement; and (2) by lowering the cost of compliance for the poor and ameliorating poverty-driven non-compliance. In the schools case, the Indian state adopted a strategy, incorporated into the 2009 RTE Act, that was consistent with regulatory pragmatism. Here the state fostered compliance by delegating enforcement to parents. Finally, in the brick kilns case, neither India nor Nepal utilized regulatory pragmatism to guide their legal design and implementation strategies for child labor regulations, and compliance was poor on both sides of the border. But regulatory pragmatism is just an approach and, as a result, I spent much of the book exploring two key intervening variables that are pervasive in areas where the state is coercively weak. These variables are intimately connected to compliance and, therefore, essential to any effort to foster higher rates of it.

The first is legal knowledge. Understandings of wood-taking prohibitions are more accurate in Nepal than they are in India. And, importantly, accurate knowledge of a specific regulation is a strong predictor of compliance with same, at least in this context. I find this to be true on both sides of the border, with a disproportionate number of those possessing accurate legal knowledge being located in Nepal. What's more, my measurements of standard explanations for compliance, particularly fear and duty, do not seem to vary with accurate legal knowledge. In other words, fearing legal sanctions or feeling a sense of duty to obey the law does not seem to be driving individuals to acquire more accurate legal knowledge. I argue that, before these standard deterrence model factors can come into play, consistent state action drives accurate legal knowledge, allowing target populations, particularly when education levels are low,[1] to observe those behaviors that the state punishes and those that it does not and to come to relatively correct understandings of the law. If the state cannot behave consistently, it is not without options. It can delegate regulation to groups capable of consistency or engage with local leaders and secure their assistance in disseminating accurate information about the law.

At the time of data collection, neither the Nepali state nor the Indian state was behaving consistently—at least with respect to enforcing wood-taking prohibitions—in and around Chitwan or Valmiki. Indeed, those in charge of enforcement seemed to do so one day and not the next. But, in Nepal, a collection of state delegates *were* behaving consistently: those running the many Community Forests just outside of Chitwan regularly allow sanction-free access to their forests for wood collection. When locals are able to collect wood in Community Forests without penalty, they are better able to observe that, in contrast, there are sometimes penalties in the park. They can then update their legal understandings more accurately by inferring that wood collection in Community Forests must be legal, while wood collection in the park is *illegal*. But this is likely one of several methods by which target populations in Nepal acquire more accurate legal understandings. I also present evidence that local leaders, like the lawyers in Muir (1973), have the power to transmit accurate legal knowledge and that, relative to printed transmission, this method seems to be both credible and durable.

This finding is particularly interesting because of the historical context in which it is embedded. Especially in Nepal, but also in India, as Bihar had also experienced a protracted period of law-and-order problems, law was ambiguous to many. Though the hierarchy- and status quo–challenging conflict in Nepal had officially ended, without truly decimating the caste and landowning hierarchy it sought to break down, the form that the new regime would take and the associated institutions were far from clear. Though officially, all administrative regulations remained in place and the bureaucracy was more functional than during the conflict, even a trained lawyer might have struggled to determine what the rules really were during this period, from the local level up to the constitution. In India, the regime was never truly in question. In addition, while the rules were less ambiguous and the bureaucracy, at least at the state and national level, was far more robust, all of these were tested in practice by hierarchy-challenging Maoist violence. All of which is to remind the reader that this was truly a hard-case scenario. Any pragmatic regulatory approach under these constraints would have to clarify legal requirements if it was to be efficacious, with any other effort being ancillary.

The second intervening variable that helps to explain variation in compliance with wood-taking prohibitions across the India-Nepal border is poverty-driven non-compliance. Even if most individuals hold accurate understandings of the law, they are not all equally situated to comply with it. Individuals who have disposable income, who can afford to buy wood or cook with gas, need not risk non-compliance. Meanwhile, those who rely on wood for cooking and heating their homes and have few assets to expend on alternative sources of fuel, are forced into a position in which they are aware of the law, are motivated by either fear or duty to comply with it, and yet cannot reasonably do so while also furthering their own survival. On both sides of the border, I find that those who live below the poverty line comply in significantly fewer numbers than their only slightly wealthier counterparts.

And, yet, they report similar levels of fear and duty. I also find that, in Nepal, some of the poor have an alternative source of fuelwood, whereas, elsewhere in Nepal and in India, they do not. Indeed, the same Community Forests that help foster accurate legal understandings in Nepal also provide those living near them with an affordable compliance option. In other words, those who live near Community Forests—which are typically located right outside of park boundaries—can make a meaningful choice between compliance and non-compliance, one that is not driven by a need for resources necessary to basic survival. Elsewhere in Nepal, for those not living near enough to a Community Forest to make use of it, and across the border, in India, where Joint Forest Management has not been used outside of Valmiki, individuals face a much more difficult choice. As a result, it is not surprising that many of these individuals, even though they report a sense of fear or duty to comply, still enter Chitwan and Valmiki on a regular basis to collect fuelwood.

Having explained some of the cross-border variation in compliance with wood-taking prohibitions in the region just outside of Chitwan and Valmiki National Parks, I turned, in order to determine whether my findings were generalizable, to two additional cases drawn from different layers of Indian and Nepal society: businesses and organizations. More specifically, I examined the compliance of: (1) private school administrators/principals with regulations requiring particular, smaller-than-customary teacher-student ratios in the classroom; and (2) the compliance of brick kiln owners/managers with child labor regulations. I chose these latter cases as much for their similarity with my main conservation case as for the opportunity to observe the effects of varied state behavior they offer. Education and brick manufacturing are important economic activities present on both sides of the border, and regulations governing these types of activities are commonly used by governments to try to change behaviors that are perceived, at least by those writing and supporting these laws, to be against the public interest. Moreover, the behavior required by law in each of these cases stands in contrast to customary social practice and to what appears to be the self-interest of regulated entities. The efforts made by the governments on either side of the border, however, vary distinctly in the schools case and not at all in the brick kilns case. This variation allowed me to further test the proposition that while consistent state action *is* necessary for accurate legal understandings to develop and accurate legal knowledge facilitates compliance, both can be achieved through delegation. These shadow cases also allowed me to confirm that implementation strategies consistent with regulatory pragmatism, like delegation, are associated with higher compliance rates across multiple regulatory contexts.

In the twin border cities of Raxaul Bazaar, India, and Birgunj, Nepal, I conducted a census of school administrators at all private schools in the metropolitan area. As part of this exercise, I collected data on school demographics and administrators' legal knowledge and perceptions of the state; I was able to observe compliance with teacher-student ratio regulations as I toured each school. Here I find that, unlike in the main conservation case, compliance is more common in India than in Nepal. Yet, accuracy of legal knowledge remains an important predictor of compliance. Poverty-driven non-compliance also remains predictive of compliance behavior, though not for those private schools with the most resources. These elite schools were, in fact, less likely than their resource-poor counterparts to be found in compliance with teacher-student ratio regulations. Here, again, my findings largely mirror the conservation case, it's just that this time the state in which legal knowledge is more accurate and poverty-driven non-compliance is less prevalent is India. It is also India that adopted an implementation strategy consistent with regulatory pragmatism: India delegated enforcement to parents via the 2009 RTE Act.

Meanwhile, when I examine compliance with child labor regulations in brick kilns, the results are once again consistent. In this case, I surveyed the managers and owners of all brick kilns lying within 10 km of the border between Chtiwan and Valmiki to the west and Raxaul Bazaar and Birgunj in the east. I find that those of my respondents who possess more accurate legal knowledge are more likely to be in compliance and those whose kilns are economically strapped are least likely to be in compliance, but I find no significant cross-border variation in compliance. Put differently, compliance on each side of the border is similarly low, which is to be expected given that neither state has adopted a pragmatic strategy in the design or implementation of its child labor regulations.

In the end, the variation I examine across all three cases helps to confirm one of the more interesting findings of this book: that states that are coercively weak, but behave pragmatically in the regulatory arena, enjoy higher rates of compliance than those that adopt legally doctrinaire approaches. I was able to observe this across multiple cases and with multiple implementation strategies.

Perhaps the most important pragmatic regulatory strategy I looked at was delegated enforcement. When the state is coercively weak, but the social fabric at the local level is strong, states can delegate enforcement to interested parties,[2] those who have an incentive to get involved and act according to law, and achieve significantly higher rates of compliance. In the conservation case, the Nepali government adopted a policy that fosters accurate legal knowledge and compliance by delegating enforcement to the User Groups that manage Community Forests. User Group members had reason to get involved because they are able to secure access to an important resource and are continually incentivized to comply with law and encourage others to do so by the threat that the state could reassert its right to the land on which the Community Forest is located. In the schools case, it is the Indian government that adopted a law that facilitates accurate legal knowledge via delegation. The 2009 RTE in India allows individuals (parents) to take an active role in enforcing teacher-student ratio regulations by removing or threatening to remove their students from schools with high ratios and send them to better schools with lower ratios. Meanwhile, in the brick kilns case, neither state has taken significant action to enforce child labor regulations, through delegation or otherwise. It is, therefore, not surprising to find a lack of cross-border variation in both consistency of enforcement and rates of compliance.

Two other pragmatic strategies seem to be effective in terms of fostering compliance, at least in the conservation case. I conducted a field experiment in which I explored whether local leaders might effectively transmit information about the law to target populations. My results suggest that this strategy, if adopted by the state, would be more effective than written communication. My conservation case survey data also indicate that Community Forests, which lower the cost of compliance for the poor, can effectively ameliorate poverty-driven non-compliance. Relatedly, and as mentioned in Chapter 6, India's Ujjwala Yojana is emblematic of regulatory pragmatism. The program provides free LPG (cooking gas) connections to rural and "deprived" households with the goal of improving women's health and reducing the negative environmental effects of firewood collection. Though it was put into place in 2016, after data collection was complete, and, as a result, I have no data indicating its effects, it is my strong suspicion that the program is reducing poverty-driven non-compliance in the area around Valmiki National Park as this book goes to press. Finally, data collected for the schools and brick kilns cases suggest that implementation strategies designed to lower the cost of compliance for target populations in these regulatory contexts would also be effective in terms of raising compliance rates.

Exploring these shadow cases allowed me to confirm my findings regarding accurate legal understandings from the conservation case, while also shedding further light on three mechanisms—delegated enforcement, information transmission through local leaders, and amelioration of poverty-driven non-compliance—by which enforcement can be regularized and targets of regulation—be they individuals, businesses, or organizations—encouraged to shift from customary norms to legal norms. When looked at together, my findings indicate that coercively weak states *can* generate compliant behavior so long as they let regulatory pragmatism guide their actions: *smart* states can be almost as effective as strong states. These findings not only add to the standard deterrence model of compliance by exploring the circumstances under which compliance can be brought about when the state is coercively weak, they go a long way toward providing information to governments and non-state actors in developing and/or weak states about strategies they can adopt to foster compliance, even if the states in question cannot muster the capacity necessary to do so by force.

How far can regulatory pragmatism be extended? One way to address this issue is to ask: what regulatory arenas might benefit from regulatory pragmatism? There are many, but, for the moment, let's consider problems with power regulation (and here I mean electricity, not something more abstract), which are germane to the South Asian experience. Today, nearly all South Asian countries struggle to produce enough electricity to meet demand. In India, the problem is less about overall demand and more about delivering adequate power in the locations in which demand is greatest. Across the border in Nepal, both overall demand and the location of that demand are problematic. Complicating matters is the fact that, in both India and Nepal, many individuals illegally tap transmission lines, making the grid less reliable and making the costs of running the system more expensive for the states involved. The states, in both India and Nepal, have proved incapable of enforcing regulations that require only permitted and metered electrical connections. Without this consistent enforcement, I have found, at least anecdotally, that individuals see that their neighbors get electricity by hiring a local line-tapper and then do the same themselves. What's more, even if they know that getting an electrical connection requires a permit from the state and a meter, many would still be driven by their relative poverty towards non-compliance. How might the state use regulatory pragmatism to increase accuracy of legal knowledge and reduce poverty-driven non-compliance in this particular scenario?

While there are almost certainly a variety of ways to do so, my findings seem to point to a combination of local leaders and/or delegated enforcement and cost reduction through the use of renewable-energy based micro-grids. Running new lines to far-flung villages where state agencies will likely struggle to collect revenue from electricity delivery is problematic on a number of different levels. The opportunities for fostering accurate legal knowledge are low and the likelihood that power will be stolen is high. Further, this scenario yields many opportunities for principal-agent problems to develop, during both the line extension and public goods delivery processes. After installation, the politicization of power delivery (Min & Golden 2014) is likely to be a problem as well. In contrast, micro-grids, whether fueled by solar, wind, micro-hydro, or any other locally abundant power supply, but particularly when adopted by local leaders, have the potential to foster accurate legal knowledge, lower the cost of compliance, and circumvent some of the principal-agent problems involved in power delivery across South Asia.

Micro-grids are, like they sound, small electricity grids. One can be set up to run a single village or collection of villages. They require less in the way of infrastructure than traditional grids, though their start-up costs are high. Importantly, micro-grid installation in South Asia would necessarily decentralize power over electricity supply in much the same way that Community Forests decentralize control over forest resources. I can imagine a system in which the state agrees to set up a micro-grid in response to an interested party petition and that the state could generate interest in micro-grids by communicating with locals leaders. As with Community Forests, these interested parties would have to show how they plan to sustainably manage this resource: answering questions in advance about who, what, when, and where. After a successful petition, the state would deliver the micro-grid hardware, perhaps on a cost-sharing basis, relying on locals to set and collect fees for using the system and delivering those fees to the state.[3] By placing control in the hands of locals, and particularly local leaders, the state would gain the advantage of tapping local power networks (of the non-electrical variety) for some of its responsibilities, instead of attempting to get its own employees to do this work. By cutting out the middlemen—and the often attendant corruption—in this process, revenue would likely be higher than under a traditional system and costs to consumers would likely be lower, thus reducing poverty-driven non-compliance.

Would interested parties still try to take advantage of their position of authority over power delivery? Possibly. And those who are currently experimenting with micro-grids in India suggest that elite capture and inter-group conflict over the power supply can be problems. As discussed in Chapter 3, local hierarchies in South Asia, which are often caste- or religious community–based, dominate local politics and compliance patterns. Those individuals without grid connections in India are not stochastically distributed. They are often poor, uneducated, of lower-caste background, or from minority religious groups. Thus, even if power was produced and distributed locally in India or Nepal, wealthier, more educated, higher-caste Hindus would most likely end up in positions of authority over local distribution.

Though such a situation would, *ex ante*, tend toward reifying local hierarchies, there are two related reasons to believe local control would still be superior to state-level control. First, the number of bureaucratic layers that locals would have to deal with would be minimized and made proximal to their location, thus lowering transaction and travel costs. Second, many locals have ways of influencing those in their community that they lack over members of the bureaucracy. In other words, if those in charge of a hypothetical micro-grid deny power to a particular individual, that individual can exert whatever local influence he or she may have in order to gain access. Is this a perfect system or a perfect solution? No. Local hierarchies would likely feature prominently in the politics of access to micro-grid power. But it's important to remember that hierarchies and abilities to pay dominate the current system, they are just different in character and, arguably, more costly.

It's also important to keep in mind the information that flows from a locally managed system. Local leaders have the power to distribute accurate information about the law and about micro-grid power. In Nepal's Community Forests, local control, via delegated enforcement, plays an important role in facilitating accuracy of legal knowledge. As it currently stands, many do not know that tapping an electric line without the state's permission is illegal. Individuals see many others engaging in this behavior and often infer that it is legal. This is particularly true in those rural areas in which grid power is available. If a micro-grid were installed, local leaders or other interested parties would be able to distribute accurate information about it and entice people to connect to it with the promise of lower overall costs and the promise of a legal connection that is more reliable than a grid connection. As individuals start signing up to this locally controlled public good, others will see them doing so and learn from their experiences. This is particularly true in light of the fact that local leaders and interested parties are, by definition, locals. As such, they are better situated to both spread accurate information and enforce against those who might illegally tap the micro-grid. This positive feedback loop currently does not exist in most places with respect to the formal process involved in acquiring an electrical connection. Pervasive principal-agent problems mean that those who attempt to secure a grid connection legally often come back poorer for their efforts and without having achieved their goal. Others who hear about these failed efforts may infer that getting power in this way is either illegal or unfeasible. In other words, micro-grids have the potential to create a smaller and more local feedback loop, a mechanism that furthers both accurate legal understandings and compliance.

Further, my findings, while definitively based upon circumstances in South Asia, are not regionally specific and their implications need not be either. For instance, I expect that consistent state action would lead to more accurate legal knowledge regarding problematic building code regulations in, say, San Francisco. The code that the city has adopted for all new construction and modification of existing structures is very stringent, but not widely known or understood. The city government, for its part, only sometimes enforces the code against those engaged in non-permitted construction. It should not be surprising then, based upon my findings, that knowledge of the building code and what constitutes a building code violation is quite low. There are many rumors and things people say and assume are violations, but my experience, having lived in the city for many years, was that little of it matched up to the law on the books. What's more, even when individuals do go through the permitting process, some inspectors will go after every little detail, while others will eyeball a project and sign off without spending more than a minute looking for possible violations. If the city were to enforce more regularly and more consistently, something that it *is* capable of doing (if its enforcement of parking violations is any guide), my findings suggest that violations would go down.

But they would not disappear altogether. My research also suggests that if compliance is expensive and people are forced to choose between obeying the law and their basic, material existence, even those who have accurate knowledge will often end up engaging in non-compliant behavior. Now, in a city in which the median house sells for well over $1 million, it's hard to envision there being what I call "poverty-driven non-compliance" in terms of building code violations. But reality is more complicated. The median house does sell for quite a lot in San Francisco, but the city is also home to myriad longtime, older residents who have owned their homes for fifty years or more, who can't imagine living anywhere else in terms of both community and the practicality of getting around without a car, and who live on very limited budgets. When these individuals have a problem with their plumbing, they call a plumber and the plumber tells them that he can do the job for $4,000. Shocked by the cost of modern home mainte-nance and knowing that their Social Security checks won't cover this type of expense, many older residents will then ask the plumber if there is any way to cut costs. Many plumbers then tell their customers that they can do the job without a permit for, say, $2,700. Why such a big difference? The permit itself probably costs $300 to $400. But the real discount is available because the plumber may be able to cut a few corners and, more impor-tant, won't have to deal with the hassle of inspections, which often require a plumber to be onsite, waiting for the city inspector, for hours at a time. Given these options, the homeowner, who is cash-strapped and doesn't be-lieve that selling his/her home and moving elsewhere is a possibility given his/her constraints, will probably end up engaging in poverty-driven non-compliance, even in wealthy San Francisco.

So, how could San Francisco reduce building code violations, which are currently rampant? My research suggests that, as detailed briefly above, more consistent enforcement would probably lead to more accurate knowledge and fewer violations, but that poverty-driven non-compliance may still pre-sent itself, even in a wealthy city, in the so-called developed world. This latter hurdle can be removed, however, if the city is willing to put in some effort and invest some resources in doing so. One can easily imagine a program that allows residents who live below a certain income level to pay reduced permit fees. One could also imagine the city using technology to be more accurate in its estimates of building inspector arrivals. This would allow contractors to waste less time waiting for inspectors. Contractors, who could then spend this time on other construction work, would not have to charge residents as much for the permitting portion of a construction project. Would a per-mitted plumbing project for a low-income resident like the one I mentioned above cost $2,700 (the price of an un-permitted repair) under this scenario? Almost certainly not. But it might cost $3,000. And when the difference be-tween legality and illegality is reduced to such a great degree, my research suggests that those who have accurate legal knowledge will often be motivated by either fear or duty to choose compliance.

Having said all that, it makes sense to return to one of the central questions of this book, one that various literatures have grappled with for a long time now: can law be used to change norms? The answer that this book provides is a qualified yes. Though Sumner (1907) argued otherwise, law can change social norms, but only when context is carefully considered and implementation strategies are designed to fit that context. But Sumner was also not wrong. It bears mentioning that, if non-compliance were to become politicized, something that was not true in any of my cases, law would likely have very little power vis-à-vis social norms. Thus, the evidence contained in this book should not be read to suggest that law can always change folkways; when the conflict between law and folkways becomes overtly political, coercion is likely still required. To be clear, even in the absence of politicization, changing social norms in the absence of significant coercive capacity is no easy task. Fostering compliance in places where the state is coercively weak and/or underfunded remains challenging. Thus far, academics and practitioners have largely struggled and failed under such circumstances to increase compliant behavior. But this doesn't mean that compliance in the places we would least expect to find it is impossible, nor do we need to dramatically augment a state's coercive apparatus to raise compliance rates.

This book argues for a more nuanced look at the underpinnings of rule of law and rule-following. It argues that we should question the assumption that knowledge of the law is widely known and understood; it also suggests some strategies by which more accurate legal knowledge can be brought about. More specifically, it suggests that local leaders can sometimes fill the role of lawyers in distributing accurate information about the law and that decentralization of some regulatory responsibilities to interested parties can prove fruitful in terms of locally held legal knowledge. Even if accurate legal knowledge is widespread, this book argues that poverty can still undermine compliance. Poor populations are particularly sensitive to the cost of compliance and, when a population is largely poor, individual-level sensitivities can, when acted upon, lower compliance rates. They can also have spillover effects, fostering inaccurate legal knowledge and leading those who know what the law is to reconsider complying with regulations that so few others follow. Finally, this book suggests that the regulatory arena, long the province of absolutes, might benefit from an infusion of pragmatism. Even coercively weak states can achieve compliance when they focus what resources they have on the goal of a particular regulation, recognize the problems associated with achieving that goals and then design around those problems. When taken together, these findings deepen our academic understanding of the intimate connection between state and society and suggest practical ways in which this connection can be reimagined to better foster rule of law.

Survey Instruments

Conservation Case

"Do you or your family members work in ecotourism?"
1. Yes
2. No
7. Don't Know or Won't Say

"Which of the following categories best describes your family's income last year?"
1. Less than 32,000 NPR/20,000 INR (only enough for food and shelter)
2. 32,000–1 lakh NPR/20,000–60,000INR
3. 1–5 lakhs NPR/60,000–3 lakhs INR
4. More than 5 lakhs NPR/More than 3 lakhs INR
5. Other_____
7. Don't Know or Won't Say

"Do you use wood to cook, for heat in your house or any other purpose?"
1. Yes
2. No
3. Sometimes
7. Don't Know or Won't Say

Nepal Version: "Where do you go to collect wood?"
1. National Park
2. Community Forest
3. Buffer Zone
4. Other
7. Don't Know or Won't Say

India Version: "Where do you go to collect wood?"
1. National Park
2. Government Forest Area
3. Privately Owned Land
4. Other
7. Don't Know or Won't Say

"I'm going to read five sentences to you. If the action described in a sentence is required in the National Park, please answer yes. If the action described in a sentence is not required in the National Park, please answer no."
1. People must stay on roadways at all times.
2. A person must do *puja* if he or she kills any of the animals.
3. People can collect fallen wood.
4. People must not cut down live trees.
5. Once per year the people can pay a fee to cut grass in the forest.
7. Don't Know or Won't Say

"If someone went into the National Park and collected fallen wood, do you think that person would be caught by the authorities?"
1. Yes
2. No
7. Don't Know or Won't Say

"How would you describe the punishment for collecting fallen wood from the National Park?"
1. Harsh
2. Reasonable
3. Not Very Harsh
7. Don't Know or Won't Say

"In your opinion, do people have a duty to protect the forest?"
1. Yes
2. No
7. Don't Know or Won't Say

"In your opinion, do people have a duty to obey the law?"
1. Always
2. Often
3. Sometimes
4. Never
7. Don't Know or Won't Say

"Can you access a community forest?"
1. Yes
2. No
7. Don't Know or Won't Say

"Have you or your family members benefited from living near the National Park?"
1. Yes
2. No
3. Both
7. Don't Know or Won't Say

"How have you or your family benefited from living near the National Park?"

_____

7. Don't Know or Won't Say

"How has living near the National Park harmed you or your family?"

---

   7. Don't Know or Won't Say

"Have you lost crops, livestock or family members to wildlife?"
   1. Yes
   2. No
   7. Don't Know or Won't Say

"Have you received government compensation for these losses?"
   1. Yes
   2. No
   7. Don't Know or Won't Say

"Has the government installed solar street lights in this area?"
   1. Yes
   2. No
   7. Don't Know or Won't Say

"Have you received a new *chulah* (stove) from the government?"
   1. Yes
   2. No
   7. Don't Know or Won't Say

"Have you received treatment at the government medical camps?"
   1. Yes
   2. No
   7. Don't Know or Won't Say

"Have any of your livestock received treatment at the government veterinary medical camps?"
   1. Yes
   2. No
   7. Don't Know or Won't Say

Accurate Legal Knowledge

In order to assess the accuracy of respondents understanding of relevant laws, I read respondents the following series of five possible legal requirements, in either Hindi or Nepali: (1) people must stay on roadways at all times; (2) a person must do *puja* (pray) if he or she kills any of the animals; (3) people can collect fallen wood; (4) people must not cut down live trees; and (5) once per year the people can pay a fee to cut grass in the forest. I then asked them to state that, "Yes," a described behavior is allowed or, "No," a described behavior is not allowed.[1] I use responses to the third item above to assess the accuracy of legal understandings of the specific regulation covered by my research, with a "No" response being accurate in this case. Responses to the remaining questions assess the accuracy of broader legal understandings. Doing so allows me to determine whether accuracy of legal understandings is specific to areas of concern and/or interest or whether those who have accurate understandings of one park regulation have accurate understandings of other, sometimes unrelated, park regulations. Accurate responses to these other questions (1, 2, 4, and 5) are as follows: people need not stay on roadways at all times, they are not required by law to perform a *puja* ceremony if they harm any of the wildlife in the park and they are not allowed to cut down live trees; in addition, in Nepal, but not in India, individuals are legally allowed to cut grass in the park during a once-a-year legal holiday.

Income-Level/Poverty

"Which of the following categories best describes your family's income last year?"

6. Less than 32,000 NPR/20,000 INR (only enough for food and shelter)
7. 32,000–1 lakh NPR/20,000–60,000INR
8. 1–5 lakhs NPR/60,000–3 lakhs INR
9. More than 5 lakhs NPR/More than 3 lakhs INR
10. Other_____

There was also a code for respondents who refused to answer or did not know their income. Then, for data analysis purposes, I used the first category, which roughly corresponds to one dollar per day, to mark those living below the poverty line. I used responses 2, 3, and 4 to mark those living above the poverty line. Finally, I manually categorized responses in category 5 into categories 1–4.

Firewood Need

"Do you use wood to cook, for heat in your house or any other purpose?" Interviewers then placed respondents' answers into one of four categories: (1) "Yes"; (2) "No"; (3) "Sometimes"; and (4) "Don't Know or Won't Say."

Compliance

In order to assess compliance, I asked those respondents who gave a "Yes" or "Sometimes" answer to the "firewood need" question the following question, in either Hindi or Nepali: "Where do you go to collect wood?" Interviewers in Nepal then placed respondents' answers into one or more of the following five categories: (1) "National Park"; (2) "Community Forest"; (3) "Buffer Zone"; (4) "Other"; and (7) "Don't Know or Won't Say." Meanwhile, interviewers in India placed respondents' answers into one or more of the following five categories: (1) "National Park"; (2) "Government Forest Area"; (3) Privately Owned Land; (4) "Other"; and (7) "Don't Know or Won't Say." I developed each of these location-specific lists during preliminary fieldwork, as well as during the pilot for this survey; they roughly correspond to the answers I received on either side of the border during the early phases of the project. The fact that the only substantial "Other" response that I received was "Purchase" indicates that these categorizations are accurate. Also, while concerns about the self-reported nature of this data are not unfounded, my experience has been that respondents on both sides of the border are quite forthcoming about where they collect wood, regardless of the legality of doing so in those locations. The fact that so many of my respondents on both sides of the border admit to collecting wood in the national parks suggests that self-reported compliance data is not as problematic, at least in this case, as one might expect.

Fear

Moving on to possible confounding variables, I assess whether respondents are fearful about the punishment associated with non-compliance by asking them the following question: "If someone went into the National Park and collected fallen wood, do you think that person would be punished by the authorities?" Interviewers then categorized responses into: (1) "Yes"; (2) "No"; and (3) "Don't Know or Won't Say." I followed this question with another designed to assess respondents' perceptions of the punishment associated with non-compliance: "How would you describe the punishment for collecting fallen wood from the National Park?" Interviewers offered respondents the following options: (1) "Harsh"; (2) "Reasonable"; (3) "Not Very Harsh"; and (4) "Don't Know or Won't Say."

Duty

In order to assess whether respondents believed they had a duty to comply, I asked two separate questions. First: "In your opinion, do people have a duty to protect the forest?" Interviewers then placed respondents' answers into the following categories: (1) "Yes"; (2) "No"; and (3) "Don't Know or Won't Say." I also asked: "In your opinion, do people have a duty to obey the law?" Interviewers asked respondents to pick one of the following categories: (1) "Always"; (2) "Often"; (3) "Sometimes"; (4) "Never"; and (5) "Don't Know or Won't Say." For purposes of data analysis I separate responses 1 and 2 from responses 3 and 4, with the former indicating a duty to obey the law.

Community Forest Access

In order to assess Community Forest access I asked respondents in Nepal: "Can you access a community forest?" Interviewers then placed responses into one of the following three categories: (1) "Yes"; (2) "No"; and (3) "Don't Know or Won't Say." I did consider trying to measure this variable by calculating the distance to the nearest Community Forest from each village, but I eventually decided that this seemingly more objective measure is more problematic than the subjective measure I used due to variation in access to transportation. For those who must travel on foot, which is the majority of the population, Community Forest access is quite proscribed. However, for those who have a bicycle or a motorcycle, a more distant Community Forest is still accessible to them. Thus, asking respondents whether they have access gets closer than the distance calculation to measuring whether or not they can use Community Forest wood to cook or heat their homes.

Schools Case

"Do you or your family own land?"
1. Yes
2. No
7. Don't Know or Won't Say

"Do you or your family own a business?"
1. Yes
2. No
7. Don't Know or Won't Say

"Do you or your family work for the government?"
1. Yes
2. No
7. Don't Know or Won't Say

"Can you read and/or write?"
1. Yes
2. No
7. Don't Know or Won't Say

"In terms of your age, which one of the following categories is appropriate?"
1. 18–24
2. 25–34
3. 35–44
4. 45–54
5. 55+
6. Other_____
7. Don't Know or Won't Say

"In terms of education, have you?"
1. Not Attended School
2. Attended School Occasionally
3. Completed High School
4. Attended University
5. Completed University
6. Attended or Completed Graduate School
9. Other_____
7. Don't Know or Won't Say

"How many teachers are on staff at this school?"

_____

"What is the total enrollment (of students) at this school?"

_____

"Which of the following categories best describes this school's revenue last year?"
1. Less than 32,000 rupees
2. 32,000–1 lakh rupees
3. 1–5 lakhs rupees
4. More than 5 lakhs rupees
5. Other_____
7. Don't Know or Won't Say

"What fees do students pay to gain admission to this school?"

_____

"Once admitted to this school, what fees do students pay to attend this school on a yearly basis?"

_____

"What percentage of your students are Indian and what percentage are Nepali?"

_____

"In your experience, what student-teacher ratio do schools in this area maintain?"
1. <1:25
2. 1:25 to 1:34
3. 1:35 to 1:44
4. 1:45 to 1:54
5. 1:55 to 1:64
6. >1:64
7. Don't Know or Won't Say

"I'm going to read a series of statements to you, some of which are required by law and some of which aren't. Please answer yes after you hear a statement that is required by law and no after a statement that is not required by law."
1 Schools must provide one teacher for every 40 students. Yes/No
2. Schools must ensure that all students have clean clothing to wear to school. Yes/No
3. Schools must provide one teacher for every 30 students. Yes/No
4. Schools must provide every student with a functioning pen or pencil. Yes/No
5. Schools must provide separate toilets for boys and girls. Yes/No
7. Decline to respond/no response.

"In your opinion, does having a student-teacher ratio that is greater than 1:30 (1:40 in Nepal) create problems for either students or teachers?"
1. Yes
2. No
7. Don't Know or Won't Say

"In your opinion, do schools have a duty to maintain a low student-teacher ratio?"
1. Yes
2. No

7. Don't Know or Won't Say

"If a school has a higher student-teacher ratio than 1:30 (1:40 in Nepal), do you think that school will be caught by the authorities?"
1. Yes
2. No
7. Don't Know or Won't Say

"If a school has a higher student-teacher ratio than 1:30 (1:40 in Nepal) and is caught by the authorities, do you think that school will be punished by the authorities?"
1. Yes
2. No
7. Don't Know or Won't Say

"How would you describe the punishment for schools that have a higher student-teacher ratio than 1:30 (or 1:40 in Nepal)?"
1. Harsh
2. Reasonable
3. Not Very Harsh
7. Don't Know or Won't Say

"Is it in a school's best financial interests to have a low student-teacher ratio?"
1. Yes
2. No
7. Don't Know or Won't Say

"Have government regulations regarding student-teacher ratios caused financial harm to schools?"
1. Yes
2. No
7. Don't Know or Won't Say

"Do parents of students demand low student-teacher ratios?"
1. Yes
2. No
7. Don't Know or Won't Say

"Do parents remove their children from schools with high student-teacher ratios and place them in schools with lower ratios?"
1. Never
2. Sometimes
3. Often
4. Always
7. Don't Know or Won't Say

"Has the enrollment in this school increased or decreased since the government started the points-based scoring system for private schools?"

1. Increased
2. Stayed the same
3. Decreased
7. Decline to Respond/No Response

"Has this school ever been recognized on Rastriya Shiksha Diwas?" (India only)

1. Yes
2. No
7. Don't Know or Won't Say

"In your opinion, do private schools have a duty to obey the law?"

1. Yes
2. No
7. Don't Know or Won't Say

"After observing as many classrooms as possible in this school, choose a statement that best fits with your observations:"

1. None of the classrooms contained fewer than 30/40 students.
2. Some of the classrooms contained fewer than 30/40 students.
3. About half of the classrooms contained fewer than 30/40 students.
4. Most of the classrooms contained fewer than 30/40 students.
5. All of the classrooms contained fewer than 30/40 students.

Accurate Legal Knowledge

In order to assess the accuracy of respondents understanding of relevant laws, I read respondents the following series of five possible legal requirements, in either Hindi or Nepali: (1) schools must provide one teacher for every 40 students; (2) schools must ensure that all students have clean clothing to wear to school; (3) schools must provide one teacher for every 30 students; (4) schools must provide every student with a functioning pen or pencil; and (5) schools must provide separate toilets for boys and girls. I then asked them to state that, "Yes," a described behavior is allowed or, "No," a described behavior is not allowed. I use responses to the first and third item above to assess the accuracy of legal understandings of the specific regulation covered by my research, with a "Yes" response to the first being accurate in Nepal and a "Yes" to the third being accurate in India.

Income-Level/Poverty

In order to assess the resources available at a given school, I asked respondents: "Once admitted to this school, what fees do students pay to attend this school on a yearly basis?" For data analysis purposes, I divided my data into those schools who charged above median tuition and those that charged below.

Compliance

In order to assess compliance, I observed the proportion of classrooms at each school that were in compliance with the relevant teacher-student ratio regulation, which varied slightly by country. I then picked one of the following statements: (1) none of the classrooms contained fewer than 30/40 students; (2) some of the classrooms contained fewer than 30/40 students; (3) about half of the classrooms contained fewer than 30/40 students; (4) most of the classrooms contained fewer than 30/40 students; (5) all of the classrooms contained fewer than 30/40 students. I considered a rating of 4 or 5 to be compliant behavior for purposes of analysis.

Fear

I assess whether respondents are fearful about the punishment associated with non-compliance by asking them the following question: "If a school has a higher student-teacher ratio than 1:30, do you think that school will be caught by the authorities?" Responses of "Yes," "No," and "Don't Know or Won't Say" were possible. I considered a response of "Yes" to indicate fear. I followed this question with another designed to assess respondents' perceptions of the punishment associated with non-compliance: "How would you describe the punishment for schools which have a higher student-teacher ratio than 1:30 (or 1:40 in Nepal)?" Responses of "Harsh," "Reasonable," "Not Very Harsh," and "Don't Know or Won't Say" were possible. I used responses to this question to assess whether the penalty was sufficient to motivate a change in behavior if accurate legal knowledge was already in place. Because I found very little variation in responses to these two questions, I probed the efficacy of parental enforcement via the RTE with the following question: "Do parents of students demand low student-teacher ratios?" Potential responses were "Yes," "No," and "Don't Know or Won't Say." I considered a response of "Yes" to indicate fear of delegated enforcement. I then asked another fear-related question: "Do parents remove their children from schools with high student-teacher ratios and place them in schools with lower ratios?" Potential responses were "Never," "Sometimes," "Often," "Always," and "Don't Know or Won't Say." I coded responses of "Often" and "Always" as fear of delegated enforcement.

Duty

In order to assess whether respondents believed they had a duty to comply, I asked two separate questions. First: "In your opinion, do schools have a duty to maintain a low teacher-student ratio (below 30 in India or 40 in Nepal)?" (1) "Yes"; (2) "No"; and (3) "Don't Know or Won't Say." A response of "Yes" indicates a duty to comply with the specific law in question. I also asked: "In your opinion, do people have a duty to obey the law?" (1) "Always"; (2) "Often"; (3) "Sometimes"; (4) "Never"; and (5) "Don't Know or Won't Say." For purposes of data analysis I separate response 1 and 2 from responses 3 and 4, with the former indicating a duty to obey the law more generally.

Brick Kilns Case

"Do you or your family own land?"
  1. Yes
  2. No
  7. Don't Know or Won't Say

"Do you or your family own a business?"
  1. Yes
  2. No
  7. Don't Know or Won't Say

"Do you or your family work for the government?"
  1. Yes
  2. No
  7. Don't Know or Won't Say

"Can you read and/or write?"
  1. Yes
  2. No
  7. Don't Know or Won't Say

"In terms of your age, which one of the following categories is appropriate?"
  1. 18–24
  2. 25–34
  3. 35–44
  4. 45–54
  5. 55+
  6. Other_____
  7. Don't Know or Won't Say

"In terms of education, have you?"
  1. Not Attended School
  2. Attended School Occasionally
  3. Completed High School
  4. Attended University
  5. Completed University
  6. Attended or Completed Graduate School
  9. Other_____
  7. Don't Know or Won't Say

"Approximately how many people work at this brick kiln?"

_____

"What is the average price at which bricks from this kiln are sold?"

_____

"Approximately how many bricks are made at this brick kiln per week?"

_____

"Which of the following categories best describes this brick kiln's revenue last year?"
 1. Less than 1 lakh rupees/60,000 INR
 2. 1–5 lakhs rupees/60,000–3 lakhs INR
 3. 5–10 lakhs rupees/3–6 lakhs INR
 4. More than 10 lakhs rupees/6 lakh INR
 5. Other_____
 7. Don't Know or Won't Say

"What villages do your workers come from?"

_____

"How far away are the villages that your workers come from?"
 1. Less than 5 km away
 2. Between 5 km and 10 km away
 3. Between 10 km and 20 km away
 4. Between 20 km an 50 km away
 5. More than 50 km away
 7. Don't Know or Won't Say

"What percentage of the workers at this brick kiln is Indian and what percentage is Nepali?"

_____

"What is the average worker's take-home wages at this brick kiln?"

_____

"Is this brick kiln registered with the government?"
 1. Yes
 2. No
 7. Don't Know or Won't Say

"Has this brick kiln ever been given a green flag by the government?"
 1. Yes
 2. No
 7. Don't Know or Won't Say

"In your opinion, do brick kiln bosses have a duty to hire their workers family members if they have a need for additional workers?"
 1. Yes
 2. No
 7. Don't Know or Won't Say

"I'm going to read a series of statements to you, some of which are required by law and some of which aren't. Please answer yes after you hear a statement that is required by law and no after a statement that is not required by law."
 1. Employers must provide workers with food and shelter in addition to pay. Yes/No
 2. Employers must ensure that workers have clean clothing to wear. Yes/No

3. Employers must not hire workers under age 18. Yes/No
4. Employers must pay workers at least monthly, but can pay them more frequently. Yes/No
5. Employers must give preference to hiring the family members of current workers. Yes/No
7. Don't Know or Won't Say

"In your experience, do brick kilns in this area hire people who are under 14 years old?"
1. Always
2. Often
3. Sometimes
4. Rarely
5. Never
7. Don't Know or Won't Say

"In your opinion, is a person who works before turning 14 years old helped or harmed by working?"
1. Only Helped
2. Both Helped and Harmed
3. Only Harmed
7. Don't Know or Won't Say

"In your opinion, does employing people who are under 14 years old create problems for society?"
1. Yes
2. No
7. Don't Know or Won't Say

"In your opinion, do brick kilns have a duty to hire only adults (people who are over 14 years old)?"
1. Yes
2. No
7. Don't Know or Won't Say

"If a brick kiln employs workers who are under 14 years old, do you think that brick kiln will be caught by the authorities?"
1. Yes
2. No
7. Don't Know or Won't Say

"If a brick kiln employs workers who are under 14 years old and is caught by the authorities, do you think that the bosses will be punished by the authorities?"
1. Yes
2. No
7. Don't Know or Won't Say

"How would you describe the punishment for bosses who hire workers who are under 14 years old?"
1. Harsh
2. Reasonable

3. Not Very Harsh
7. Don't Know or Won't Say

"If a brick kiln employs workers who are under 14 years old and is caught by the authorities, do you think that the owners will be punished by the authorities?"
1. Yes
2. No
7. Don't Know or Won't Say

"How would you describe the punishment for owners who employ workers who are under 14 years old?"
1. Harsh
2. Reasonable
3. Not Very Harsh
7. Don't Know or Won't Say

"Is it in a brick kiln's best financial interests to hire workers who are under 14 years old?"
1. Yes
2. No
7. Don't Know or Won't Say

"Have government regulations prohibiting workers who are under 14 years old caused financial harm to brick kilns?"
1. Yes
2. No
7. Don't Know or Won't Say

"In your opinion, should people who are under 14 years old have a right to work for pay?"
1. Yes
2. No
7. Don't Know or Won't Say

"Why is it important for people who are under 14 years old to have a right to work for pay?"

_____

"In your opinion, should businesses have a right to hire workers who are under 14 years old?"
1. Yes
2. No
7. Don't Know or Won't Say

"Why is it important for businesses to have a right to hire workers who are under 14 years old?"

_____

"Do parents demand that brick kilns hire their under-14-year-old children?"
1. Yes
2. No
7. Don't Know or Won't Say

"Have NGOs tried to raise awareness about the problems associated with 'child labor' in this area?"

1. Never
2. Sometimes
3. Often
4. Always
7. Don't Know or Won't Say

"Has the number of under-14 workers at brick kilns in this area increased or decreased over the last three years?"

1. Increased
2. Stayed the Same
3. Decreased
7. Don't Know or Won't Say

"In your opinion, do bosses at brick kilns have a duty to obey the law?"

1. Yes
2. No
7. Don't Know or Won't Say

"In your opinion, do owners at brick kilns have a duty to obey the law?"

1. Yes
2. No
7. Don't Know or Won't Say

"After observing as many workers as possible at this brick kiln, choose a statement that best fits with your observations:"

1. None of the workers appears to be under age 10.
2. Some of the workers appear to be under age 10.
3. About half of the workers appear to be under age 10.
4. Most of the workers appear to be under age 10.
5. All of the workers appear to be under age 10.

Accurate Legal Knowledge

In order to assess the accuracy of respondents understanding of relevant laws, I read respondents the following series of five possible legal requirements, in either Hindi or Nepali: (1) employers must provide workers with food and shelter in addition to pay; (2) employers must ensure that workers have clean clothing to wear; (3) employers must not hire workers under age 18; (4) employers must pay workers at least monthly, but can pay them more frequently; (5) employers must give preference to hiring the family members of current workers. After each statement I asked them to answer that, "Yes," a described behavior is allowed or, "No," a described behavior is not allowed. I used responses to the third item above to assess the accuracy of legal understandings of the specific regulation covered by my research, with a "No" response representing accurate legal knowledge, since it is legal for employers to hire children over the age of 14.

Income-Level/Poverty

In order to assess the resources available at a given kiln, I asked respondents: "Which of the following categories best describes this brick kiln's revenue last year?" (1) Less than 1 lakh rupees/60,000 INR; (2) 1–5 lakhs rupees/60,000–3 lakhs INR; (3) 5–10 lakhs rupees/ 3–6 lakhs INR; (4) more than 10 lakhs rupees/6 lakhs INR; (5) Other_____ _____; (7) Don't Know or Won't Say. For data analysis purposes, I used responses to this question and to questions about the average brick price a kiln was able to fetch at market to determine resources/wealth and profitability.

Compliance

In order to assess compliance, I observed the number of individuals working at a given kiln who appeared to be 10 years old or younger. I then picked one of the following statements: (1) None of the workers appears to be under age 10; (2) Some of the workers appear to be under age 10; (3) About half of the workers appear to be under age 10; (4) Most of the workers appear to be under age 10; (5) All of the workers appear to be under age 10. I considered a rating of 1 to be compliant behavior for purposes of analysis.

Fear

I assess whether respondents are fearful about the punishment associated with non-compliance by asking them the following question: "If a brick kiln employs workers who are under 14 years old, do you think that brick kiln will be caught by the authorities?" Responses of "Yes," "No," and "Don't Know or Won't Say" were possible. I considered a response of "Yes" to indicate fear. I followed this question with another designed to assess respondents' perceptions of the punishment associated with non-compliance: "How would you describe the punishment for bosses/owners who hire workers who are under 14 years old?" Responses of "Harsh," "Reasonable," "Not Very Harsh," and "Don't Know or Won't Say" were possible. I used responses to this question to assess whether the penalty was sufficient to motivate a change in behavior if accurate legal knowledge was already in place.

Duty

In order to assess whether respondents believed they had a duty to comply, I asked two separate questions. First: "In your opinion, do brick kilns have a duty to hire only adults (people who are over 14 years old)?" (1) "Yes"; (2) "No"; and (3) "Don't Know or Won't Say." A response of "Yes" indicates a duty to comply with the specific law in question. I also asked: "In your opinion, do brick kiln bosses/owners have a duty to obey the law?" (1) "Always"; (2) "Often"; (3) "Sometimes"; (4) "Never"; and (5) "Don't Know or Won't Say." For purposes of data analysis I separate response 1 and 2 from responses 3 and 4, with the former indicating a duty to obey the law more generally.

Cross-Border Balance Table

Note: While the sample is imbalanced on Land Ownership and Literacy, t-tests suggest no relationship between any of these variables and compliance with wood-taking prohibitions in either India or Nepal. The Land Ownership imbalance is well documented and related to imperfect land redistribution in India; it is almost certainly not an artifact of the sample. Literacy rates may appear higher in Nepal within this sample for two reasons. First, this is self-reported literacy data. Second, it contains both a higher percentage of women in India and a lower proportion of women in Nepal than are found in the broader population, and women are both less likely to be literate and, in my experience, to say they are literate; conversely, men are generally more likely to report literacy, even when this is not fully accurate.

Table A2.1 Balance Table for Large-N Survey Sample in Conservation Case

Variable	India	Nepal	p-value	SE
Age	3.201	3.295	0.097	0.036
Income (Low-High)	1.297	1.326	0.171	0.015
Education	1.800	1.908	0.059	0.034
Gender (M-F)	0.500	0.475	0.187	0.014
Land Ownership	0.611	0.811	0.000	0.012
Literacy	0.488	0.710	0.000	0.014

Forest Canopy Density Analysis

There are plausible concerns that self-reported variation in compliance with wood-collection prohibitions may not reflect realities of wood collection on the ground. To address this question, we use Landsat imagery to qualitatively assess the state of the forests in the study area.[1] In particular, we evaluated the Forest Canopy Density (FCD) index in and around the Chitwan and Valmiki parks using imagery obtained on May 1, 2013, the closest panel to the time of survey implementation that had minimal cloud cover.

FCD is a popular diagnostic for forest health, developed during a multiyear study conducted by the Japan Overseas Forestry Consultants Association (JOFCA) and International Timber Organization (ITTO) (JOFCA 1997; Rikimaru 1996; Rikimaru & Miyatake 1997; Rikimaru, Roy & Miyatake 2002; Roy, Miyatake & Rikimaru 1997). It combines standard vegetation, bare soil, and shadow indices with thermal signals in order to produce an index that is sensitive to the canopy, rather than simply vegetation. Validation exercises via neural networks, linear regression, and maximum likelihood classifiers performed in the Barandabhar forest corridor in the Chitwan Valley indicate that FCD is qualitatively reliable while being easy to implement (Joshi et al. 2006; see also Bera, Saha & Bhattacharjee 2020; Deka, Tripathi & Khan 2013; Falensky et al. 2020; Kwon et al. 2012; Mothi Kumar et al. 2018; Panta & Kim 2006; Sahana, Sajjad & Ahmed 2015).

We implemented the FCD model in a set of Python routines following the methods described in JOFCA (1997); Rikimaru (1996); Joshi et al. (2006); Rikimaru & Miyatake (1997); Rikimaru, Roy & Miyatake (2002); Roy, Miyatake & Rikimaru (1997), with slight modifications described below.[2] Prior to analysis, the thermal band was converted to surface temperature and all other bands were converted to top of atmosphere reflectance, including correction for sun angle, using coefficients in the metadata file. No further atmospheric correction was performed. We stretched the data in two different ways, with little effect on the final map. The method documented in JOFCA 1997; Rikimaru 1996; Joshi et al. 2006; Rikimaru and Miyatake 1997; Rikimaru, Roy and Miyatake 2002; and Roy, Miyatake and Rikimaru 1997 recommends stretching by two standard deviations about the mean, but for our final map we stretched interactively using histograms of the reflectance.

We calculated the Advanced Vegetation Index (AVI), Bare Soil Index (BSI), and Advanced Shadow Index (ASI)—also called the Corrected Shadow Index or CSI—according to the usual formulae (JOFCA 1997; Rikimaru 1996; Joshi et al. 2006; Rikimaru & Miyatake 1997; Rikimaru, Roy & Miyatake 2002; Roy, Miyatake & Rikimaru 1997). The documented algorithm (JOFCA 1997) uses a maximum filter when calculating the ASI, but we found that made little difference in this case. Prior to further processing we perused the values of each index along transects from the imagery in which we could visually identify inhabited and forest areas from Google Earth photographs, and chose thresholds below which (for AVI and ASI) and above which (for BSI and temperature) the signal was clearly non-forested region. We also identified a region of cirrus contamination in the northwest corner of the region of interest, evident in the B10 imagery.

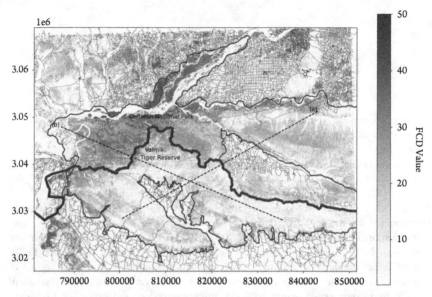

Figure A3.1 Modeled Forest Canopy Density in India and Nepal with Transects Marked

The FCD model combines the AVI and BSI into a standardized vegetation index (SVD), combines the ASI and surface temperature into a scaled shadow index (SSI), and then derives the FCD index from the SVD and SSI. Most literature references describe using singular value decomposition (svd) to derive both the SVD and SSI as least-square linear combinations of their two component indices. We chose instead to plot AVI vs. BSI and temperature vs. ASI pixel-for-pixel, and use our knowledge of the thresholds to manually select a line onto which we projected the pixel values. Doing the projection manually allowed us to ignore and mask pixels that our threshold analysis had identified as inhabited land, water, and cirrus cloud, avoiding need for the careful pre-masking and mean subtraction required by the svd method if one wishes to ensure it does not fit unwanted pixels.

In the body of the book, in Chapter 5, Figure 5.2 shows an FCD image of the western region of both Chitwan and Valmiki National Parks, overlaid with local roads and borders. The India-Nepal border is in bold and park boundaries are marked in thinner lines. In Figure A3.1, we display the FCD values along two transects, labeled "a" and "b." Distance along these transects is plotted in kilometers, referenced to the international border.

Transect "a" was chosen for the fact that it crossed unprotected, populated areas that are near each park; it was also chosen to represent a "worst case" comparison for Chitwan, in that the transect crosses areas of Chitwan that have some of the lowest FCD values in the park. Transect "b" was chosen for the fact that it cuts across large swaths of varied forest land in both Chitwan and Valmiki.

The locations at which the border and park boundaries intersect the transects are shown respectively, in Figure A3.2, as thick and thin dashed lines. As one can see from the analysis, there is a marked cross-border difference for transect "b" and less pronounced cross-border difference for transect "a."

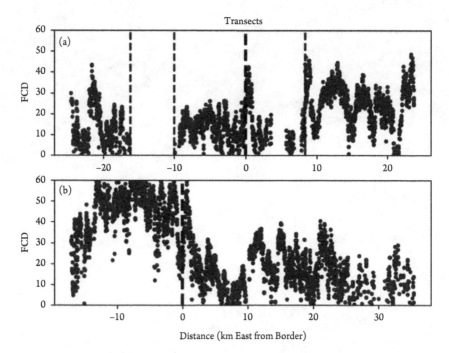

Figure A3.2 Modeled Forest Canopy Density in India and Nepal along Transects

In short, the FCD analysis confirms that the survey and observational data are not spurious and there was likely markedly different behavior occurring on opposite sides of the border, particularly considering the fact that population density was and is greater on the Nepal side of the border. We should be cautious, however, about the inferences we draw from this data. Cross-border variation in FCD is likely only partially driven by the behavior of average people, who tend to take very minor amounts of wood from these forests, particularly as compared to the criminal gangs that engage in logging in this area. Thus, for purposes of this book, which seeks to explain the behavior of ordinary people, we can conclude that survey and observational data regarding their behavior are supported by FCD analysis.

Notes

Chapter 1

1. This is something they are positioned to do, despite uncertainty about the law, because they know that a higher payment is likely to constitute compliance.
2. The IRS audit rate for the 2014 fiscal year stood at 0.85 percent and typically hovers at about 1 percent of all individual returns.
3. This is not as true of the socio-legal compliance literature. See Winter and May 2001.
4. Note that this may not be true in all cases. In the 2013 US audit targeting controversy, the IRS was accused of disproportionately enforcing the tax code against right-wing organizations, seemingly at the direction of IRS agents who pursued their own agenda rather than the state's. After probing the matter, however, the FBI found little evidence to support this claim. See also Hacker and Pierson (2016).
5. Interestingly, the lack of developing world evidence may stem from a bias in academia itself. When preparing to conduct this research, I spoke with legal academics who stated quite plainly that law schools are not interested in hiring individuals who study compliance in the context of the developing world. The same is largely true of political science and sociology departments.
6. These customary norms are often cultural in origin.
7. For a balance table, including relevant demographic variables, please see Table A2.1 in Appendix 2.
8. These numbers are low because they include many individuals who hold inaccurate legal understandings.
9. In this particular case, it's hard to imagine how delegated regulation might be implemented, since there are no obvious interested parties to which a government might delegate. Parents often request that their children be employed at brick kilns, and managers are always looking for ways to reduce costs.

Chapter 2

1. Charles Peirce, in his 1878 piece "How to Make Our Ideas Clear," is the acknowledged originator of the concept of pragmatism, but I start with James, in part, because he articulated the concept at such length and depth.
2. This is, of course, setting aside the important and relevant point, made by some, that there is no distinction between graffiti and art: graffiti *is* art. For the purposes of this paragraph and the argument here, I go with a majoritarian approach and consider

graffiti to be the visual markings and designs that many people would call graffiti and art to be visual markings and designs that many would call art.

3. The fine at the time of writing was 500 rupees, which is about $5. This may not seem like much, but it is the equivalent of a couple days' work for most Nepalis, where GDP per capita in 2017 was only $835.

Chapter 3

1. I use my own survey data because government district-level data on income are either not collected or missing across all districts in which I conduct research.

2. Paschim and Purba Champaran.

3. Chitwan, Parsa, Makwanpur, and Nawalparasi.

4. Nepal Census (2011).

5. India Census (2011) and Nepal Census (2011).

6. "[A]ll the lowlands from the Kali Eastward to the Teesta, rendering either the foot or the ridge of the lowest Rang of Hills, the common boundary through that line." IOR/Home/Misc/515, 1814–1816 Nepalese War, Vol 58, No. 116.

7. When Nepal solicited a peace treaty with the East India Company to end the Anglo-Nepal War, the negotiations were repeatedly suspended because of the King's "extreme aversion to cede the whole of the Terrai or lowlands which the Governor General had demanded." IOR/Home/Misc/515, Record of B. J. Jones to Indian Board, December 1816.

8. "In our eastern terai no Sirdars can live. No one will accept an appointment there even upon double pay. The Gorkhas are masters there for 6 months only in the year. The Tharoos are the masters for the other 6 months." IOR/L/PS/6/512, August 6, 1860. Nepal Residency. Colonel G. Ramsay. Resident. Letter to Cecil Beadon Esq. Sec.y to the gov.t of India in the Foreign Department, For William.

9. H/MISC/655, in a letter from J. Adam to E. Gardner, July 22, 1815. J. Adam suggests that the reason the Maharajah of Nepal didn't want to let the Terai go was that much of the monarchy's land and land held by soldiers and other elites was located there. They were willing to risk all to keep their personal real estate.

10. H/MISC/655. Correspondence between J. Adam and E. Gardner through 1815.

11. Letter from Ross D. Mangles (Secret Committee to Governor General of India), February 9, 1858, London, India Political Department Collection: Cession of the Oude Terai to Nepal, L/PS/6.

12. Ibid., quoting Article II from the "Treaty of Segowlee."

13. India Political Department Collection: Cession of the Oude Terai to Nepal, L/PS/6.

14. At the time of data collection, the Indian Ministry of the Environment had not notified any area of Valmiki National Park as either Critical Wildlife Habitat or Critical Tiger Habitat, though it would almost certainly be consider to be both of these if the issue is ever brought before the ministry.

15. It is also not clear that villagers living is the area surrounding Valmiki have any claims whatsoever to minor forest produce. While many are of Tharu descent, considered a Scheduled Tribe, and, thus, potentially able to legally collect minor forest produce, almost no one in this area can claim to have been forest dwelling in 1980, as all settlements I was able to locate were in the agricultural plains surrounding the forest and very few people in this area would be able to prove, as required, pre-1980 occupation of specific tracts of forest land.

16. https://www.hindustantimes.com/india/for-bihar-s-tribals-jungle-rights-matter-more-than-jungle-raj/story-3Iq62hxJKpsuM04DWsmjHJ.html.

17. It is prohibited: "To cut, fell, remove, obstruct, trim the trees, plants, bushes or any other forest products or to perform any activity to be drying up the forest products, to set fire or to harm in any form." Chitwan National Park Rules (1974).

18. Nepal previously used panchayats (five-member bodies) for local governance, but disbanded with the system in 1990. Village Development Committees were then used from 1990 through 2017. In 2017, after data collection for this book was complete, the Gaunpalika system was put in place.

19. I measure compliance at the individual level via self-reporting, but I verify my country-wise results with observational data collected over the course of three months in similar locations on either side of the order.

20. I did so before inquiring about their legal knowledge in order to avoid any priming effects.

21. This anecdote is real and comes from a woman I met while on a local bus in Nawalparasi District, in Nepal. I did not ask her to relate this story. She shared it of her own accord and I am relating it here because it is illustrative, but it was not collected in a research capacity.

22. Pearce and Tombs (1990, 1997, 1998); Parker (2002); Molnar et al. (2004).

23. The financial capacity of regulated entities to comply with existing or proposed laws has been shown to affect the design of regulatory programs in the United States (Thornton et al. 2008; Huber 2011).

24. I measure compliance via indirect self-reporting in the conservation case and by observation in the private schools and brick kilns cases.

25. I also consider Chitwan's Buffer Zone Management Committee to have accurate legal information, but I found its reach to be so limited that I could not properly test my hypotheses in locations in which it had and had not disseminated accurate legal information.

26. Some User Groups use Community Forests as sources of medicinal plants, in addition to sources of firewood. Other User Groups have gone so far as to set up revenue-generating businesses that rely on the preservation of the Community Forest. One such User Group offers elephant rides through the jungle to tourists.

27. I chose to conduct this experiment solely in Nepal because accurate analysis and interpretation of the data from a cross-border experiment would be extremely challenging. Survey data had already established cross-border variation. Thus, I proceeded in Nepal alone in order to explore the effectiveness of certain legal knowledge dissemination techniques in a place where legal knowledge has been shown to

have a significant effect on compliance while also minimizing potential latent variation among the populations of particular villages. Importantly, I have no reason to believe that it would be any less effective near Valmiki.

28. This design is imperfect from a strict experimental point of view. Individuals in this region live in villages and it is almost impossible to provide information to a significant number of villagers and expect that the information will not be shared with other villagers within a short time frame. In close-knit environments like a village of a few hundred people where information is shared rapidly, it is impossible to conduct three different and independent interventions and expect no contamination. Hence, while the design is imperfect, it does allow assessment of how villagers gain legal knowledge, particularly since all three villages had similar baseline legal knowledge.

29. Two tangential points may be of interest here. The first is that the Indian and Nepali states, despite minimal capacity, have managed to generate these motivations, suggesting that state capacity may not be to blame in the many situations throughout the world in which weak states do not manage to generate rule of law. The second is that individuals are motivated to comply, even if they hold inaccurate understandings of what might constitute compliance, suggesting that distribution of accurate information in areas plagued by non-compliance, when combined with consistent state action, might make a difference in overall compliance rates.

30. Anatole France (1894): "La majestueuse égalité des lois, qui interdit au riche comme au pauvre de coucher sous les ponts, de mendier dans les rues et de voler du pain."

31. I use the word "manageable" here because the cost of deterring or motivating individuals away from poverty-driven non-compliance would, generally speaking, be small relative to both GDP and state resources.

32. Interview conducted at Gitanagar, Nepal, on February 23, 2013.

33. Interview conducted at Jagatpur, Nepal, on December 15, 2012.

34. As Nepal was never formally colonized, individuals, businesses, and organizations in India might comply (or not comply) with a regulation that relates to the colonial experience differently from their Nepali counterparts because of the well-documented historical baggage that flows from colonization.

35. That said, I have chosen the subject material of each of these cases because it is an area that is of current concern to a large number of individuals in both India and Nepal. Examining securities laws, in comparison, would only be important and topical to a small subset of the Indian and Nepali populations.

36. To do so, I trained and managed two teams of approximately ten interviewers, one on each side of the border. Each individual spoke the dominant language in the area, Bhojpuri/Tharu, in addition to Nepali or Hindi (depending upon the context). Since surveys were conducted simultaneously on both sides of the border, I also hired a local manager to handle day-to-day problems on the Indian side of the border.

37. In each village, survey teams started from a common point (a crossroads, a well, etc.) and fanned out in multiple directions, stopping at every seventh house to conduct an interview. Interviewers were instructed to interview men and women in roughly equal proportions and to consciously seek to interview individuals of varying ages.

38. These measures can be found in Appendix 1.

39. These measures can be found in Appendix 1.

40. I held this focus group in Jagatpur VDC, Nepal—a village that is adjacent to both Chitwan National Park and a Community Forest, in addition to being two km from park headquarters.

41. While the survey responses I get in response to such questions are almost certainly unreliable in terms of absolute numbers regarding both compliance, since many of the responses required are subjective, surveys are still the appropriate way to proceed because I was not looking for absolute numbers; I was looking for relative numbers and I have no reason to believe that ordinary individuals on either side of the India-Nepal border would respond to the same questions in systematically different ways unless, of course, they actually observe different behavior. Also, I've found individuals to be quite forthcoming about their activities inside and outside of the park and many individuals readily admitted to behavior that would constitute non-compliance.

42. Here I use respondents' reports that they have access to a Community Forest as a proxy for their knowledge of the legal understanding that wood collection in community forests is allowed under the law and preferable to collection in Chitwan National Park.

43. I found it remarkably easy to observe individuals complying with or—as was more often the case in Valmiki—breaking park regulations.

Chapter 4

1. In this descriptive statistics chapter I include all responses to a particular question. In later chapters, the data associated with certain individuals, those who failed or refused to answer particular questions may be excluded from analysis for incompleteness. These individuals and their responses are included here to give the fullest picture possible of the survey population.

2. For purposes of this project, these include cooking food and heating one's home with firewood as a fuel.

3. In this descriptive statistics chapter I include all responses to a particular question. In later chapters the data associated with certain individuals, those who failed or refused to answer particular questions may be excluded from analysis for incompleteness. These individuals and their responses are included here to give the fullest picture possible of the survey population.

4. In this descriptive statistics chapter I include all responses to a particular question. In later chapters the data associated with certain individuals, those who failed or refused to answer particular questions may be excluded from analysis for incompleteness. These individuals and their responses are included here to give the fullest picture possible of the survey population.

Chapter 5

1. Winter and May (2000).
2. Sanction of Valmiki Tiger Reserve APO from the National Tiger Conservation Authority, 2012–2013.
3. Sanction of Valmiki Tiger Reserve APO from the National Tiger Conservation Authority, 2014–2015.
4. Bereiter & Scardamalia (1985); Bransford, Franks, Vye and Sherwood (1989); Spiro et al. (1987, 1988); Spiro and Jheng (1990); Brown et al. (1989).
5. Spiro et al. (1992).
6. The implication or this respondent's statement, to my mind, based upon the longer interview, is that if everyone is collecting wood, then it must not be illegal.
7. In this particular case she is right.
8. In this case, it's not clear that having one's house too close to a road is illegal per se—at least outside of Kathmandu, where road-widening has often involved the state taking back land on which illegal encroachments have been built—but, it is true that the state, in this case the Nepali state, retains a quasi-eminent domain right that it exercises regularly when widening and paving roads. My respondent took the fact that she had to move her house (which was located in the Terai, not in Kathmandu), tear it down, and reconstruct it elsewhere as punishment for her own illegal action, not as the state exercising a right to remove even a legally constructed house.
9. These villages were, as mentioned in the Introduction, randomly selected from the broader Nepal sample for the leadership experiment.

Chapter 6

1. By non-interference I mean that state actors, despite the fact that they have little right to interfere in Community Forests unless User Groups are determined to be mismanaging them, are actually staying out of Community Forests and not using their position of power to harass those collecting wood there.
2. Given that involvement in ecotourism is, by some standards, borderline significant, some further research on this particular variable would be useful. This is particularly true as there is more ecotourism on the Nepal side of the border than on the Indian side in this particular region and, in theory, involvement in ecotourism might lead to more accurate understandings of the law. Due to the low levels of involvement in ecotourism among my respondents (less than 5 percent), I am unable to do so here.
3. Bamberg and Schmidt (1999) report similar behavior when observing reactions to new transport options. Students in a university town in Germany responded positively to policy interventions aimed at reducing car use when these interventions either lowered the cost of public transport use or made public transport more convenient.
4. Interestingly, the lack of developing world evidence may stem from a bias in academia itself. When preparing to conduct this research, I spoke with legal academics who

stated quite plainly that law schools are not interested in hiring individuals who study compliance in the context of the developing world. The same is largely true of Political Science and Sociology Departments. If this doesn't point to a hole in the literature, I'm not sure what does.

5. Up until recently this border region has been plagued, both in India and Nepal, by Maoist insurgencies. During this period the state almost ceased to exist at the local level. In the intervening time, the Nepali and Indian states have re-entered this region, but only minimally and signs of the state remain few and far between.

6. The financial capacity of regulated entities to comply with existing or proposed laws has been shown to affect the design of regulatory programs in the United States (Thornton et al. 2008; Huber 2011).

7. I run these t-tests on data for all respondents who report a need for wood. Because those who report a need for wood are significantly more likely to be poor than those who do not, this analysis likely underestimates the compliance gap between those living above and below the poverty line.

8. The fact that rates of reported compliance are not zero on the Indian side of the border for those living below the poverty line raises a question about whether my respondents are really being driven to non-compliance by their poverty and lack of access to other fuel. An examination of the fuels my respondents on both sides of the border report using suggests that those living on the Indian side of the border appear to have greater access to a wood/gas alternative for both cooking and heating: sugar cane leaves. Almost none of my respondents on the Nepal side of the border report using sugar cane leaves as fuel, and this is hardly surprising given that there is little to no sugar grown in this region of Nepal. However, just across the border in India, approximately 38 percent of my respondents report using sugar cane leaves to meet at least some of their fuel needs. This is also not surprising, as sugar is grown on a commercial scale in Paschim Champaran, Bihar, and sugar cane leaves are often discarded and available for locals with proximity to sugar production operations to use as fuel.

9. These numbers are surprisingly high, given the low level at which the states on either side of the border engage in enforcement. I plan to explain this phenomenon in a separate paper, but I will mention here that I believe the generally capricious enforcement of regulations and laws in both India and Nepal, coupled with frontline bureaucrats' abilities to extract bribes for non-enforcement from citizens who can ill afford to pay them, leads to a general fear of the state that individuals take with them to almost any regulatory context regardless of the level of enforcement in the particular set of circumstances in which they find themselves.

Chapter 7

1. This is the legal mandate for primary schools in India. The maximum ratio in secondary schools in India is 1:35. Only primary schools were surveyed for this research (on both sides of the border).

2. Banerjee et al. (2010) find that parents of children enrolled in government schools in Uttar Pradesh often did not know applicable regulations, nor that some of them were members of Village Education Committees, but I believe parents who are sending their children to private school are differently motivated. Those who send their children to government school have acquiesced to the default. In contrast, most who send their children to private school do so because they know that government schools provide very little in the way of education and that teachers rarely show up to class. This level of investigations, particularly when combined with the fact that they made a decision to pay for private school and then chose a school, demonstrates that they are already engaged in making active choices about their children's education. They are also spending their own money when making these choices. It stands to reason that some will find out about applicable regulations and use these to their advantage if they are unhappy with the performance of the school they have chosen.

3. I was unable to locate a small number of schools that were on government lists of private schools in the area. These schools are no longer at their listed address and, from what I could tell from asking individuals at or around those addresses, these schools have closed.

4. Though I did visit and secure compliance data from every functioning brick kiln in this area, I was not able to interview every manager. In particular, the managers of four different kilns located quite close to Raxaul Bazaar refused to speak to me when they heard the topic of my study. Though none of these kilns appeared to employ child labor, these managers were concerned that their proximity to a large town and a main highway would mean that they would be first to be punished if for some reason my results were to find their way into government hands. Though I assured these individuals that I was collecting all data anonymously and that they had nothing to fear, as I was prohibited from handing over my data to the government by the Berkeley IRB, this was little consolation.

5. Due to the small number of data points in this set, neither of these comparisons is statistically significant.

Chapter 8

1. Illiteracy means that "implicit general deterrence," as described by Thornton et al. (2005), does not exist.

2. In some ways this delegation principle is analogous to the "private right of action" that is often made available in the United States. Farhang (2006).

3. This proposal assumes a baseline level of affluence that is not present in the poorest and most remote parts of South Asia. In such places, any cost outlay at all would likely be beyond most families' means. If the state wished to still proceed with micro-grid installation in such places, it would have to shoulder most of the cost itself.

Appendix 1

1. You can find the specific wording of this and all other survey questions in the appendix.

Appendix 3

1. Landsat 8 level 2 products were obtained from the USGS website (http://earthexplorer. usgs.gov). The region of interest is in path 142, row 041, and we further limited our area to the region bounded by 27.25–27.7 East Longitude and 83.85–84.55 North Latitude. The closest clear day imagery in time to the field data acquisition were taken on May 1, 2013, and we used bands B2, B3, B4, B5, B6, and B10. Subsequent calculations and overlays were performed after projecting to the local coordinate reference system (CRS), EPSG 32644.
2. Geometric conversions, raster display, and feature overlays were implemented with the GeoPandas and Rasterio modules, along with Shapely and Osmnx-extracted base maps. International and Nepal park borders were obtained from the Database of Global Administrative Areas (GADM), and the Valmiki park boundaries were digitized from OpenStreetMaps using Contextily with Rasterio.

References

Afridi, Farzana. 2011. "The Impact of School Meals on School Participation: Evidence from Rural India." *Journal of Development Studies*, 47:11: 1636–1656.

Agrawal, Arun. 1999. *Greener Pastures: Politics, Markets, and Community among a Migrant Pastoral People*. Durham, NC: Duke University Press.

Agrawal, Arun, A. Chhatre & R. Hardin. 2008. "Changing Governance of the World's Forests." *Science*, 320: 1460–1462.

Agrawal, Arun & Elinor Ostrom. 2001. "Collective Action, Property Rights, and Decentralization in Resource Use in India and Nepal." *Politics & Society*, 29:4: 485–514.

Akerlof, George A. 1970. "The Market for 'Lemons.'" *Quarterly Journal of Economics*, 84:3: 488–500.

Alm, James, Betty R. Jackson & Michael McKee. 1992a. "Institutional Uncertainty and Taxpayer Compliance." *American Economic Review*, 82:4: 1018–1026.

Alm, James, Betty R. Jackson & Michael McKee. 1992b. "Estimating the Determinants of Taxpayer Compliance with Experimental Data." *National Tax Journal*, 65:1: 107–114.

Andreoni, James, Brian Erard & Jonathan Feinstein. 1998. "Tax Compliance." *Journal of Economic Literature*, 36:2 (June): 818–860.

Arnott, R. & J. E. Stiglitz. 1988. "The Basic Analytics of Moral Hazard." *Scandinavian Journal of Economics*, 9:3: 383–413.

Aumann, Robert. 1976. "Agreeing to Disagree." *Annals of Statistics*, 4:6: 1236–1239.

Aurbach, Adam. 2019. *Demanding Development: The Politics of Public Goods Provision in India's Urban Slums*. Cambridge: Cambridge University Press.

Baland, Jean-Marie, Pranab K. Bardhan, & Samuel Bowles. 2007. *Inequality, Cooperation, and Environmental Sustainability*. Princeton, NJ: Princeton University Press.

Baland, J. M. & J. P. Platteau. 1996. *Halting Degradation of Natural Resources: Is There a Role for Rural Communities?* New York: Food and Agriculture Organization.

Bamberg, Sebastian & Peter Schmidt. 1999. "Regulating Transport: Behavioral Changes in the Field." *Journal of Consumer Policy*, 22: 479–509.

Banerjee, Abhijit V., Rukmini Banerji, Esther Duflo, Rachel Glennerster & Stuti Khemani. 2010. "Pitfalls of Participatory Programs: Evidence from a Randomized Evaluation in Education in India." *American Economic Journal: Economic Policy*, 2:1: 1–30.

Banerjee, Abhijit, Arun G. Chandrasekhar, Esther Duflo & Matthew O. Jackson. 2016. "Gossip: Identifying Central Individuals in a Social Network." Working Paper.

Barbier, E. & J. Burgess. 2001. "Tropical Deforestation, Tenure Insecurity, and Unsustainability." *Forest Science*, 47:4: 497–509.

Bardach, Eugene & Robert A. Kagan. 1982. *Going by the Book: The Problem of Regulatory Unreasonableness*. Philadelphia: Temple University Press.

Barr, C. 2000. "Profits on Paper: The Political Economy of Fiber, Finance and Debt in Indonesia's Pulp and Paper Industries." Bogor, Indonesia: CIFOR.

Beck, Kirk A., James R. P. Ogloff & A. Corbishley. 1994. "Knowledge, Compliance, and Attitudes of Teachers toward Mandatory Child Abuse Reporting in British Columbia." *Canadian Journal of Education*, 19:1: 15–29.

Becker, Gary S. 1968. "Crime and Punishment: An Economic Approach. " *Journal of Political Economy*, 76: 169–217.

Bera, B., S. Saha & S. Bhattacharjee. 2020, "Estimation of Forest Canopy Cover and Forest Fragmentation Mapping Using Landsat Satellite Data of Silabati River Basin (India)." *Journal of Cartography and Geographic Information*, 70: 181–197.

Bereiter, Carl & Marlene Scardamalia. 1985. "Cognitive Coping Strategies and the Problem of 'Inert Knowledge.'" In *Thinking and Learning Skills 2: Research and Open Questions*, ed. Susan Chipman, J. Segal & Robert Glaser. Hillsdale, NJ: Lawrence Erlbaum Associates.

Bhavnani, Ravi, Michael G. Findley & James L. Kuklinski. 2009. "Rumor Dynamics in Ethnic Violence." *Journal of Politics*, 71:3: 876–892.

Blackman, Allen & Randy Bluffstone. 2021. "Decentralized Forest Management: Experimental and Quasi-Experimental Evidence." *World Development*, 145: Article 105509.

Blackman, A., L. Corral, E. Lima & G. Asner. 2017. "Titling Indigenous Communities Protects Forests in the Peruvian Amazon." *Proceedings of the National Academy of Sciences of the United States of America*, 114: 4123–4128.

Bluffstone, Randy, A. Dannenberg, P. Martinsson, P. Jha & R. Bistra. 2020. "Cooperative Behavior and Common Pool Resources: Experimental Evidence from Community Forest User Groups in Nepal." *World Development*, 129: Article 104889.

Blumenthal, Marsha, Charles W. Christian & Joel Siemrod. 2001. "Do Normative Appeals Affect Tax Compliance? Evience from a Controlled Experiment in Minnestoa." *National Tax Journal*, 54:1: 125–138.

Boittin, Margaret L. 2013. "New Perspectives from the Oldest Profession: Abuse and the Legal Consciousness of Sex Workers in China." *Law & Society Review*, 47:2: 245–278.

Bowman, D., C. Heilman & P. B. Seetharaman. 2004. "Determinants of Product-Use Compliance Behavior." *Journal of Marketing Research*, 41:3: 324–338.

Braithwaite, John & T. Makkai. 1994. "Trust and Compliance." *Policing and Society*, 4:1: 1–12.

Braithwaite, J., T. Makkai & V. Braithwaite. 2007. *Regulating Aged Care: Ritualism and the New Pyramid*. Cheltenham: Edward Elgar.

Bransford, J. D., J. J. Franks, N. J. Vye & R. D. Sherwood. 1989. "New Approaches to Instruction: Because Wisdom Can't Be Told. In *Similarity and Analogical Reasoning*, ed. S. Vosniadou & A. Ortony. Cambridge: Cambridge University Press.

Brehm, John & James Hamilton. 1996. "Non-Compliance in Environmental Reporting." *American Journal of Political Science*, 40:2: 444–477.

Brown J. S., A. Collins & P. Duguid. 1989. "Situated Cognition and the Culture of Learning." *Education Researcher*, 18: 32–42.

Carnes, G. A. & Andrew D. Cuccia. 1996. "An Analysis of the Effect of Tax Complexity and Its Perceived Justification on Equity Judgments." *Journal of the American Taxation Association*, 18: 40–56.

Carothers, Thomas. 1998. "The Rule of Law Revival." *Foreign Affairs*, 77(2), 95–106.

Coase, R. H. 1960. "The Problem of Social Cost." *The Journal of Law & Economics*, 3: 1–44.

Coleman, Stephen. "The Minnesota Income Tax Compliance Experiment: State Tax Results." St. Paul: Minnesota Department of Revenue, April 1996.

Contreras-Hermosilla, A. 1997. "The 'Cut and Run' Course of Corruption in the Forestry Sector." *Journal of Forestry*, 95:12: 33–36.

Contreras-Hermosilla, A. 2000. "The Underlying Causes of Forest Decline." CIFOR Occasional Paper 30. Bogor, Indonesia: Center for International Forestry Research.

Contreras-Hermosilla, Arnoldo, Richard Dornbosch & Michael Lodge. 2007. "The Economics of Illegal Logging and Associated Trade." Roundtable on Sustainable Development, Paris, January 8–9, 2007.

Cook, Brian J. 1988. *Bureaucratic Politics and Regulatory Reform*. New York: Greenwood.

Deka, J., O. Prakash Tripathi & M. L. Khan. 2013, "Implementation of Forest Canopy Density Model to Monitor Tropical Deforestation." *Journal of Indian Society for Remote Sensing*, 41:2: 469–475.

Dewey, John. 1924. "Logical Method and Law." *Cornell Law Review*, 10:1: 17–27.

Dewey, John. 1938. *Experience and Education*. New York: Macmillan Company.

Dixit, A. 2003. "Trade Expansion and Contract Enforcement." *Journal of Political Economy*, 111:6: 1293–1317.

Dreze, Jean & Aparajita Goyal. 2003. "Future of Mid-Day Meals." *Economic & Political Weekly*, 38:44: 4673–4683.

Dunning, Thad. 2012. *Natural Experiments in the Social Sciences: A Design-Based Approach*. Cambridge: Cambridge University Press.

Elster, Jon. 1989. *The Cement of Society: A Study of Social Order*. Cambridge: Cambridge University Press.

Falensky, M. A. et al. 2020. "Application of Forest Canopy Density (FCD) Model for the Hotspot Monitoring of Crown Fire in Tebo, Jambi Province." *Jurnal Geografi Lingkungan Tropik*, 4:1: 59–67.

Farber, Daniel A. 1988. "Legal Pragmatism and the Constitution." *Minnesota Law Review*, 72: 1331–1378.

Farhang, Sean. 2006. *The Litigation State: Public Regulation and Private Lawsuits in the U.S.* Princeton, NJ: Princeton University Press.

Faure, Michael, Anthony Ogus & Niels Philipson. 2009. "Curbing Consumer Financial Losses: The Economics of Regulatory Enforcement." *Law & Policy*, 31: 161–191.

Feest, Johannes. 1968. "Compliance with Legal Regulations." *Law and Sociological Review*, 2:3: 447–471.

Feld, Lars P. & Bruno S. Frey. 2007. "Tax Compliance as the Result of a Psychological Tax Contract." *Law & Policy*, 29:1: 102–120.

Fellner, Gerlinde, Rupert Sausgruper & Christian Traxler. 2013. "Testing Enforcement Strategies in the Field: Threat, Moral Appeal & Social Information." *Journal of the European Economic Association*, 11:3: 634–660.

France, Anatole. 1894. *Le Lys Rouge*. Paris: Calmann-Levy.

Friedman, Lawrence M. 1975. *The Legal System: A Social Science Perspective*. New York: Russell Sage Foundation.

Gachter, Simon. 2007. "Conditional Cooperation: Behavioral Regularities from the Lab and the Field and Their Policy Implications." In *Economics and Psychology: A Promising New Cross-disciplinary Field*, ed. B. S. Frey & A. Stutzer. Cambridge, MA: MIT Press.

Gailmard, Sean. 2010. "Politics, Principal-Agent Problems, and Public Service Motivation." *International Public Management Journal*, 13:1: 35–45.

Gebreegziabher, Z., A. Mekonnen & B. Gebremedhin. 2020. "Determinants of Success of Community Forests: Empirical evidence from Ethiopia." *World Development*, 138: Article 105206.

Gelo, D. 2020. "Forest Commons, Vertical Integration and Smallholders' Saving Response: Evidence from a Quasi-Natural Experiment." *World Development*, 132: Article 104962.

Gerstein, Robert S. 1970. "Privacy and Self-Incrimination." *Ethics*, 80:2: 87–101.

Gerstenfeld, A., & H. Roberts. 2000. "Size Matters: Barriers and Prospects for Environmental Management in Small and Medium-Sized Enterprises." In *Small and Medium-sized Enterprises and the Environment: Business Imperatives*, ed. R. Hillary, 106–118. Sheffield: Greenleaf Publishing.

Gezelius, Stig & Maria Hauck. 2011. "Toward a Theory of Compliance in State-Regulated Livelihoods: A Comparative Study of Compliance Motivations in Developed and Developing World Fisheries." *Law & Society Review*, 45:2: 435–470.

Gibbs, Jack P. 1968. "Crime, Punishment and Deterrence." *Southwestern Social Science Quarterly*, 48: 515–530.

Gibson, Clark C., John T. Williams & Elinor Ostrom. 2005. "Local Enforcement and Better Forests." *World Development*, 33:2: 273–284.

Goncalves, M. P., M. Panjer, T. S. Greenberg & W. B. Magrath. 2012. "Justice for Forests: Improving Criminal Justice Efforts to Combat Illegal Logging." Washington, DC: World Bank Group.

Gormley, Ken G. 1998. "An Original Model of the Independent Counsel Statute." *Michigan Law Review*, 97: 601–695.

Gray, Wayne B. & John T. Scholz. 1991. "Analyzing the Equity and Efficiency of OSHA Enforcement." *Law & Policy*, 13: 185–214.

Grey, Thomas C. 2003. "Judicial Review and Legal Pragmatism." *Wake Forest Law Review*, 38: 473–511.

Greenwald, B. & J. E. Stiglitz. 1987. "Imperfect Information, Credit Markets and Unemployment." *European Economic Review*, 31: 444–456.

Greenwald, B. & J. E. Stiglitz. 1988. "Pareto Inefficiency of Market Economies." *American Economic Review*, 78:2: 351–355.

Guha, Ramachandra. 1989. *The Unquiet Woods: Ecological Change and. Peasant Resistance in the Himalaya*. Delhi: Oxford University Press.

Gunningham, Neil, Robert A. Kagan & Dorothy Thornton. 2003. *Shades of Green: Business, Regulation and Environment*. Stanford, CA: Stanford University Press.

Gunningham, Neil, Robert A. Kagan & Dorothy Thornton. 2004. "Social License and Environmental Protection: Why Businesses Go beyond Compliance." *Law & Social Inquiry*, 29:2: 307–341.

Hacker, Jacob S. & Paul Pierson. 2016. American Amnesia: How the War on Government Led Us to Forget What Made America Prosper. New York: Simon & Schuster.

Hahn, Robert W. & Gordon L. Hester. 1989. "Where Did All the Markets Go? An Analysis of EPA's Emissions Trading Program. *Yale Journal on Regulation*, 6: 109–153.

Hall, Peter & Rosemary Taylor. 1996. "Political Science and the Three New Institutionalisms." *Political Studies*, 44: 935–957.

Hardin, Garrett. 1968. "The Tragedy of the Commons." *Science*, 162:3859: 1243–1248.

Havinga, Tetty. 2006. "Private Regulation of Food Safety by Supermarkets." *Law & Policy*, 28: 515–533.

Hillary, R. 1995. *Small Firms and the Environment: A Groundwork Status Report*. Birmingham: Groundwork Foundation.

Hillman, Robert W. 1998. *Hillman on Lawyer Mobility*. New York: Aspen Publishers, Inc.

Hofmann, Eva, Erik Hoelzl & Erich Kirchler. 2008. "A Comparison of Models Describing the Impact of Moral Decision Making on Investment Decisions." *Journal of Business Ethics*, 80:1: 171–187.

Huber, Bruce R. 2011. "Transition Policy in Environmental Law." *Harvard Environmental Law Review*, 35: 91–130.

Hutchinson, A. & I. Chaston. 1995. "Environmental Perceptions, Policies and Practices in the SME Sector: A Case Study." Paper presented September 23–24, 1994. Bradford: Business Strategy and the Environment Conference.

Hutter, Bridget. 1997. *Compliance: Regulation and Environment.* Oxford: Clarendon Press.

James, William. 1907. *Pragmatism.* Indianapolis, IN: Hackett Publishing.

Jayaraman, Rajshri. 2015. "The Impact of School Lunches on Primary School Enrollment: Evidence from India's Midday Meal Scheme." *Scandinavian Journal of Economics*, 117:4: 1176–1203.

Jensen, G. F. 1969. "Crime Doesn't Pay: Correlates of a Shared Misunderstanding." *Social Problems*, 17: 189–201.

JOFCA, 1997, "Rehabilitation of Logged-over Forests in Asia/Pacific Region, Sub-Project III." Project Report on PD 32/93 Rev.2 (F), prepared by Japan Overseas Forestry Consultants Association for the International Tropical Timber Organization (ITTO).

Joshi, A. L. 1993. "Effects on Administration of Changed Forest Policies in Nepal." *Paper presented at the Workshop on Policy and Legislation in Community Forest*, RECOFTC, Bangkok, Thailand.

Joshi, C., J. De Leeuw, A. Skidmore & I. Van Duren. 2006, "Remotely Sensed Estimation of Forest Canopy Density: A Comparison of the Performance of Four Methods." *International Journal of Applied Earth Observation and Geoinformation*, 8: 84–95.

Kagan, Robert A. 1994. "Regulatory Enforcement." In *Handbook of Regulation and Administrative Law*, ed. D. Rosenbloom & R. Schwartz, 383–422. New York: Marcel Dekker.

Kagan, Robert A., Neil Gunningham & Dorothy Thornton. 2011. "Fear, Duty, and Regulatory Compliance: Lessons from Three Research Projects." In *Explaining Compliance: Business Responses to Regulation*, ed. Christine Parker & Vibeke Nielsen. London: Edward Elgar.

Kagan, Robert A. & John T. Scholz. 1984. "The 'Criminology of the Corporation' and Regulatory Enforcement Strategies." In *Enforcing Regulation*, ed. Keith Hawkins & John M. Thomas. Boston: Kluwer-Nijhoff.

Kagan, Robert A. & Jerome H. Skolnick. "Banning Smoking: Compliance without Enforcement." In *Smoking Policy: Law, Politics, and Culture*, ed. Robert L. Rabin & Stephen D. Sugarman, 69–94. New York: Oxford University Press.

Kahsay, G. A. & H. Medhin. 2020. "Leader Turnover and Forest Management Outcomes: Micro-Level Evidence from Ethiopia." *World Development*, 127: Article 104765.

Kandori, Michihiro. 1992. "Social Norms and Community Enforcement." *Review of Economic Studies*, 59:1: 63–80.

Keeler, Theodore E. 1994. "Highway Safety, Economic Behavior, and Driving Environment." *American Economic Review*, 84:3: 684–693.

Kim, Pauline T. 1998. "Norms, Learning and the Law." *University of Illinois Law Review*, 1999:2: 447–515.

Klepper, Steven, Mark Mazur & Daniel Nagin. 1991. "Expert Intermediaries and Legal Compliance." *Journal of Law and Economics*, 34:1: 205–229.

Klepper, Steven & Daniel Nagin. 1989. "The Deterrent Effect of Perceived Certainty and Severity of Punishment Revisited." *Criminology*, 27:4: 721–746.

Kleven, Henrik, Martin Knudsen, Claus Kreiner, Soren Pedersen & Emanuel Saez. 2011. "Unwilling or Unable to Cheat? Evidence from a Randomized Tax Audit Experiment in Denmark." *Econometrica*, 79: 651–692.

Ko, K., J. Mendeloff & W. Gray. 2010. "The Role of Inspection Sequence in Compliance with OSHA Standards: Interpretations and Implications." *Regulation & Governance*, 4: 48–70.

Koch, Susanne. 2017. "International Influence on Forest Governance in Tanzania: Analysing the Role of Aid Experts in the REDD+ process. *Forest Policy & Economics*, 83:C: 181–190.

Kwon, T-H. et al. 2012. "Forest Canopy Density Estimation Using Airborne Hyperspectral Data." *Korean Journal of Remote Sensing*, 28:3: 297–305.

Levi, Margaret & Audrey Sacks. 2007. "Legitimating Beliefs: Concepts and Indicators." Afrobarometer Working Paper Series. Cape Town, South Africa: Afrobarometer.

Levin, D. Z., E. M. Whitener & R. Cross. 2006. "Perceived Trustworthiness of Knowledge Sources." *Journal of Applied Psychology*, 91:5: 1163–1171.

Lewis-Beck, Michael & John Alford. 1980. "Can Government Regulate Safety? The Coal Mine Example." *American Political Science Review*, 74: 745–756.

Licht, Amin N. 2008. "Social Norms and the Law: Why Peoples Obey the Law." *Review of Law and Economics*, 4:3: 715–750.

Licht, Amir N., C. Goldschmidt & S. Schwartz. 2006. "Culture Rules: The Foundations of the Rule of Law and Other Norms of Governance." *Journal of Comparative Economics*, 35:4: 659–688.

Makkai, T. & J. Braithwaite. 1996. "Procedural Justice and Regulatory Compliance." *Law and Human Behavior*, 20: 83–98.

May, Peter J. 2005. "Regulation and Compliance Motivations: Examining Different Approaches." *Public Administration Review*, 65:1: 31–44.

May, Peter J. & Søren Winter. 2000. "Reconsidering Styles of Regulatory Enforcement: Patterns in Danish Agro-Environmental Inspection." *Law and Policy*, 22 (April): 143–173.

Mazar, Nina, On Amir & Dan Ariely. 2008. "The Dishonesty of Honest People: A Theory of Self-Concept Maintenance." *Journal of Marketing Research*, 45: 633–644.

McCubbins, Matthew D., Roger G. Noll & Barry R. Weingast. 1987. "Administrative Procedures as Instruments of Political Control." *Journal of Law, Economics and Organizations*, 3:2: 243–277.

McKean, Margaret. 1992. "Success on the Commons: A Comparative Examination of Institutions for Common Property Resource Management." *Journal of Theoretical Politics*, 4:3: 247–281.

Milgrom, Paul. 1981. "An Axiomatic Characterization of Common Knowledge." *Econometrica: Journal of the Econometric Society*, 49:1: 219–222.

Min, Brian & Miriam Golden. 2014. "Electoral Cycles and Electricity Losses in India." *Energy Policy*, 65: 619–625.

Miteva, D. & S. Pattanayak. 2021. "Ecosystem Services, Protected Areas, and Decentralization: Example from Indonesia of Conservation Evaluation 2.0." *World Development*.

Molnar, Augusta, Sara J. Scherr & Arvind Khare. 2004. *Who Conserves the World's Forest? A New Assessment of Conservation and Investment Trends*. Washington, DC: Forest Trends & Ecoagricultural Partners.

Mothi Kumar, K. E. et al. 2018. "Forest Canopy Density Assessment Using High Resolution LISS-4 Data in Yamunanagar District, Haryana." *International Archives of the Photogrammetry, Remote Sensing and Spatial Information Sciences*, XLII-5: 285–288.

Moynihan, Patrick D. 1998. *Secrecy: The American Experience*. New Haven, CT: Yale University Press.

Muir, William K. 1973. *Law and Attitude Change*. Chicago: University of Chicago Press.

Murphy, James J. & John K. Stranlund. 2007. "A Laboratory Investigation of Compliance Behavior under Tradable Emissions Rights: Implications for Targeted Enforcement." *Journal of Environmental Economics and Management*, 53:2: 196–212.

Nagendra, Harini, Mukunda Karmacharya & Birendra Karna. 2005. "Evaluating Forest Management in Nepal: Views across Space and Time." *Ecology & Society*, 10:1: 24.

Nonet, Philippe & Philip Selznick. 1978. *Law and Society in Transition: Toward Responsive Law*. New York: Harper & Row.

Okumu, B. & E. Muchapondwa. 2020. "Welfare and Environmental Impact of Incentive Based Conservation: Evidence from Kenyan Community Forest Associations." *World Development*, 129: Article 104890.

Orfield, Gary, Franklin Monfort & Rosemary George. 1987. *School Segregation in the Early 1980s: Trends in the States and Metropolitan Areas*. Washington, DC: Joint Center for Political Studies.

Orfield, Myron W. Jr. 1987. "The Exclusionary Rule and Deterrence: An Empirical Study of Chicago Narcotics Officers," *University of Chicago Law Review*, 54:3: 1016–1069.

Ostermann, Susan L. 2016. "Rule of Law against the Odds." *Law & Policy*, 38:2: 101–123.

Ostrom, Elinor. 1990. *Governing the Commons*. Cambridge: Cambridge University Press.

Ostrom, Elinor. 1992. *Crafting Institutions for Self-Governing Irrigation Systems*. San Francisco: Institute for Contemporary Studies.

Pager, Devah, Bruce Western & Bart Bonikowski. 2009. "Discrimination in a Low Wage Labor Market: A Field Experiment." *American Sociological Review*, 74 (October): 777–799.

Palmer, Jason & Rita van der Vorst. 1996. "Are 'Standard Systems' Right for SMEs?" *Eco-Management and Auditing*, 3:2: 91–96.

Panta, M. & K. Kim. 2006. "Spatio-temporal Dynamic Alteration of Forest Canopy Density Based on Site Associated Factor: View from Tropical Forest of Nepal." *Korean Journal of Remote Sensing*, 22:5: 313–323.

Parker, Christine. 2002. *The Open Corporation: Effective Self-regulation and Democracy*. Cambridge: Cambridge University Press.

Parker, Christine. 2013. "The War on Cartels and the Social Meaning of Deterrence." *Regulation and Governance*, 7:2: 174–194.

Parker, Christine & Vibeke Nielsen. 2011. "Deterrence and the Impact of Calculative Thinking on Business Compliance with Regulation." *Antitrust Bulletin* 56:2: 337–426.

Pearce, Frank & Steve Tombs. 1990. "Ideology, Hegemony and Empiricism: Compliance Theories and Regulation." *British Journal of Criminology*, 30: 432–443.

Pearce, Frank & Steve Tombs. 1997. "Hazards, Law and Class: Contextualizing the Regulation of Corporate Crime." *Journal of Social and Legal Studies*, 6: 79–107.

Pearce, Frank & Steve Tombs. 1998. *Toxic Capitalism: Corporate Crime and the Chemical Industry*. Aldershot: Ashgate/Dartmouth.

Pendleton, Michael R. 2007. "The Social Basis of Illegal Logging and Forestry Law Enforcement in North America." In *Illegal Logging: Law Enforcement, Livelihoods and the Timber Trade*, ed. Luca Tacconi, 17–42. London/Sterling: Earthscan.

Petts, J. 1999. "The Regulator-Regulated Relationship and Environmental Protection: Perceptions in Small and Medium Sized Enterprises." *Environment and Planning*, 18:2: 191–206.

Petts, J. 2000. "Small and Medium Sized Enterprises and Environmental Compliance." In *Small and Medium Sized Enterprises and the Environment*, ed. R. Hillary Sheffield: Greenleaf.

Piaget, Jean. 1967. *Biologie et Connaissance* (Biology and Knowledge). Paris: Gallimard.

Pimental, David. 2014. "Culture and the Rule of Law: Cautions for Constitution-Making." *Fordham International Law Journal Online*, 37.

Piquero, Alex R., Raymond Paternoster, Greg Pogarsky & Thomas A. Loughran. 2011. "Elaborating the Individual Difference Component in Deterrence Theory." *Annual Review of Law and Social Science* 7: 335–360.

Pires, Roberto. 2008. "Promoting Sustainable Compliance: Styles of Labour Inspection and Compliance Outcomes in Brazil." *International Labour Review* 147:2–3: 199–229.

Pogarsky, Greg. 2009. "Deterrence and Decision Making: Research Questions and Theoretical Refinements." In *Handbook on Crime and Deviance*, ed. Marvin D. Krohn, Alan J. Lizotte & Gina Penley-Hall, 241–258. Berlin: Springer.

Polinsky, A. Mitchell. 1989. *An Introduction to Law and Economics*. Boston: Little, Brown and Company.

Posner, Eric A. 2000. "Law and Social Norms." *Virginia Law Review*, 86: 1781–1819.

Posner, Richard. 1995. *Overcoming Law*. Cambridge, MA: Harvard University Press.

Posner, Richard. 2005. *Law, Pragmatism, and Democracy*. Cambridge, MA: Harvard University Press.

Prendergast, Canice. 2007. "The Motivation and Bias of Bureaucrats." *American Economic Review*, 97:1: 180–196.

Priest, George L. 1981. "A Theory of the Consumer Product Warranty." *Yale Law Journal*, 90: 1297–1352.

Prothro, James R. & Donald W. Matthews. 1963. "Political Factors and Negro Voter Registration in the South." *American Political Science Review* 57:2: 355–367.

Prothro, James & Donald Matthews. 1966. *Negroes and the New Southern Politics*. New York: Harcourt, Brace & World.

Pruckner, Gerald J. & Rupert Sausgruber. 2013. "Honesty on the Streets—A Natural Field Experiment on Newspaper Purchasing." *Journal of the European Economic Association*, 11: 661–679.

Radin, Margaret Jane. 1989. "Reconsidering the Rule of Law." *Boston University Law Review*, 69: 781–819.

Radin, Margaret Jane. 1991. "Pragmatist and Poststructuralist Critical Legal Practice." *University of Pennsylvania Law Review*, 139:4: 1019–1058.

Radner, Roy & Joseph E. Stiglitz. 1984. "A Non-Convexity in the Value of Information." In *Bayesian Models in Economic Theory: Studies in Bayesian Econometrics*, Vol. 5 ed. M. Boyer & R. Kihlstrom. New York: Elsevier Science, 1984.

Rees, Joseph V. 1994. *Hostages of Each Other: The Transformation of Nuclear Safety since Three Mile Island*. Chicago: University of Chicago Press.

Ribot, Jesse, Arun Agrawal & Anne Larson. 2006. "Recentralizing While Decentralizing: How National Governments Reappropriate Forest Resources." *World Development*, 34:11: 1864–1886.

Ribot, J. 2008. "Building Local Democracy through Natural Resource Interventions: An Environmentalist's Responsibility." Washington DC: World Resources Institute.

Rikimaru, A. 1996. "Landsat TM Data Processing Guide for Forest Canopy Density Mapping and Monitoring Model." In International Tropical Timber Organization (ITTO) Workshop on Utilization of Remote Sensing in Site Assessment and Planning for Rehabilitation of Logged-Over Forest, Bangkok, Thailand, 1–8. ALSO: in [1] as "Attachment 1: Landsat TIM Data Processing Guide for Forest Canopy Density Mapping and Monitoring Model."

Rikimaru, A. & S. Miyatake. 1997. "Development of Forest Canopy Density Mapping and Monitoring Model Using Indices of Vegetation, Bare Soil and Shadow." *Proceedings of the 18th Asian Conference on Remote Sensing*, E6 1–6, Kuala Lumpur, Malaysia.

Rikimaru, A., P. S. Roy & S. Miyatake. 2002, "Tropical Forest Cover Density Mapping." *Tropical Ecology*, 43:1: 39–47.

Ross, S. 1973. "The Economic Theory of Agency." *American Economic Review*, 63:2: 134–139.

Rothschild, M. & J. E. Stiglitz. 1976. "Equilibrium in Competitive Insurance Markets: An Essay on the Economics of Imperfect Information." *Quarterly Journal of Economics*, 90:4: 629–649.

Roy, P. S., S. Miyatake & A. Rikimaru. 1997. "Biophysical Spectral Response Modeling Approach for Forest Density Stratification." In *Proceedings of the 18th Asian Conference on Remote Sensing*, JSB 1–6, Kuala Lumpur, Malaysia.

Sahana, M., H. Sajjad & R. Ahmed. 2015. "Assessing Spatio-temporal Health of Forest Cover Using Forest Canopy Density Model and Forest Fragmentation Approach in Sundarban Reserve Forest, India." *Modeling Earth Systems and Environment*, 1:49: DOI 10.1007/s40808-015-0043-0.

Sandmo, Agnar. 2005. "The Theory of Tax Evasion: A Retrospective View." *National Tax Journal* 58: 643–663.

Schmalensee, Richard & Robert N. Stavins. 2017. "The Design of Environmental Markets: What Have We Learned from Experience with Cap and Trade?" *Oxford Review of Economic Policy*, 33:4: 572–588.

Schmidt, Caroline A. & Constance L. McDermott. 2015. "Deforestation in the Brazilian Amazon: Local Explanations for Forestry Law Compliance." *Social & Legal Studies*, 24:1: 3–24.

Scholz, John T. & Wayne B. Gray. 1990. "OSHA Enforcement and Workplace Injuries: A Behavioral Approach to Risk Assessment." *Journal of Risk and Uncertainty*, 3: 283–305.

Scholz, John T. & Neil Pinney. 1995. "Duty, Fear, and Tax Compliance: The Heuristic Basis of Citizenship Behavior." *American Journal of Political Science*, 39:2: 490–512.

Scott, James C. 1987. *Weapons of the Weak: Everyday Forms of Peasant Resistance*. New Haven, CT: Yale University Press.

Shavell, Steven. 1980a. "An Analysis of Causation and the Scope of Liability in the Law of Torts." *Journal of Legal Studies*, 9: 463–516.

Shavell, Steven. 1980b. "Strict Liability versus Negligence." *Journal of Legal Studies*, 9: 1–25.

Sibley, Susan. 2005. "After Legal Consciousness." *Annual Review of Law and Society*, 1 (December): 323–368.

Sills, E., A. Pfaff, L. Andrade & J. Kirkpatrick. 2020. "Engaging Local Governments in Reducing Deforestation: Impacts of a Pilot Program in the Brazilian Amazon." *World Development*, 129: Article 104891.

Siskind, F. B. 1980. *Compliance with Standards, Abatement of Violations and Effectiveness of OSHA Safety Inspections*. Technical Analysis Paper No. 62. Washington, DC: U.S.

Department of Labor, Office of the Assistant Secretary for Policy, Evaluation and Research.

Snortum, John R., Dale E. Berger & Ragnar Hauge. 1988. "Legal Knowledge and Compliance." *Alcohol, Drugs and Driving*, 4: 251–263.

Somanathan, E., R. Prabhakar & B. Mehta. 2009. "Decentralization for Cost-Effective Conservation." *Proceedings of the National Academy of Sciences*, 106:11: 4143–4147.

Sorg, James D. 2005. "A Typology of Implementation Behaviors of Street-Level Bureaucrats." *Review of Policy Research*, 2:3: 391–406.

Spiro, R. J. & J. C. Jehng. 1990. "Cognitive Flexibility and Hypertext: Theory and Technology for the Nonlinear and Multidimensional Traversal of Complex Subject Matter." In *Cognition, Education, Multimedia: Exploring Ideas in High Technology*, edited by D. Nix & R. J. Spiro. Hillsdale NJ: Erlbaum.

Spiro, R. J., W. Vispoel, J. Schmitz, A. Samarapungavan & A. Boerger. 1987. "Knowledge Acquisition for Application: Cognitive Flexibility and Transfer in Complex Content Domains." In *Executive Control Processes*, ed. B. C. Britton. Hillsdale, NJ : Lawrence Erlbaum Associates.

Spiro, R. J., R. L. Coulson, P. J. Feltovich & D. K. Anderson, 1988. "Cognitive Flexibility Theory: Advanced Knowledge Acquisition in Ill-Structured Domains." In *The Tenth Annual Conference of the Cognitive Science Society*. Hillsdale, NJ: Lawrence Erlbaum Associates.

Spiro, R.J., P.J. Feltovich, M.J. Jacobson, & R.L. Coulson. 1992. "Cognitive Flexibility, Constructivism, and Hypertext: Random Access Instruction for Advanced Knowledge Acquisition in Ill-structured Domains. In T.M. Duffy & D.H. Jonassen, Eds., *Constructivism and the Technology of Instruction: A Conversation*. Hillsdale, NJ: Lawerence Erlbaum Associates.

Stiglitz, Joseph E. 1975a. "Information and Economic Analysis." In *Current Economic Problems*, ed. J. M. Parkin and A. R. Nobay, 27–52. Cambridge: Cambridge University Press.

Stiglitz, Joseph E. 1975b. "Incentives, Risk and Information." *Bell Journal of Economics*, 6:2: 552–579.

Stiglitz, Joseph E. 2000. "The Contributions of the Economics of Information to Twentieth Century Economics." *Quarterly Journal of Economics*, 115:4: 1441–1478.

Stiglitz, Joseph E. 2002. "Information and the Change in the Paradigm in Economics." *American Economic Review*, 92:3: 460–501.

Sullivan, Michael. 2007. *Legal Pragmatism: Community, Rights, and Democracy*. Bloomington: Indiana University Press.

Sumner, William Graham. 1907. *Folkways: A Study of the Sociological Importance of Usages, Manners, Customs, Mores, and Morals*. Boston: Ginn & Company.

Tacconi, Luca. 2007. "Illegal Logging: The Extent, Its Impacts and Causes." In *Illegal Logging: Law Enforcement, Livelihoods and the Timber Trade*, ed. Luca Tacconi. London: Earthscan.

Tendler, Judith. 1997. *Good Government in the Tropics*. Baltimore: Johns Hopkins University Press.

Thaler, Richard H. & Cass R. Sunstein. 2008. *Nudge: Improving Decisions about Health, Wealth, and Happiness*. New Haven: Yale University Press.

Thornton, D., N. A. Gunningham & R. A. Kagan. 2005. "General Deterrence and Corporate Environmental Behavior." *Law & Policy*, 27: 262–288.

Thornton, Dorothy, Robert A. Kagan & Neil Gunningham. 2008. "Compliance Costs, Regulation, and Environmental Performance: Controlling Truck Emissions in the US." *Regulation & Governance*, 2:3: 275–292.

Tittle, Charles R. 1969. "Crime Rates and Legal Sanctions." Social Problems, 16: 409–423.

Tittle, Charles R. 1977. "Sanction Fear and the Maintenance of Social Order." *Social Forces*, 55:3: 579–596.

Trubek, David M. 1996. "Law and Development: Then and Now." Proceedings of the Annual Meeting (American Society of International Law), 90: 223–226.

Turpie, J. & G. Letley. 2021. "Would Community Conservation Initiatives Benefit from External Financial Oversight? A Framed Field Experiment in Namibia's Communal Conservancies." *World Development*, 142: Article 105442.

Tyler, Tom R. 1990. *Why People Obey the Law*. Princeton, NJ, and Oxford: Princeton University Press.

Tyler, Tom R. 2006. "Psychological Perspectives on Legitimacy and Legitimation." *Annual Review of Psychology*, 57: 375–400.

van der Wal, M., T. Jaarsma, D. Moser, N. Veeger, W. van Gilst & D. van Veldhuisen. 2006. "Compliance in Heart Failure Patients: The Importance of Knowledge and Beliefs." *European Heart Journal*, 27: 434–440.

van Erp, Judith. 2011. "Naming and Shaming in Regulatory Enforcement." In *Explaining Compliance: Business Responses to Regulation*, ed. Christine Parker & Vibeke Nielsen. London: Edward Elgar.

Varshney, Ashutosh. 2003. *Ethnic Conflict and Civic Life: Hindus and Muslims in India*. New Haven, CT: Yale University Press.

Velez, M. A., J. Robalino, J. Camilo Cardenas, A. Paz & E. Pacay. 2020. "Is Collective Titling Enough to Protect Forests? Evidence from Afro-descendant Communities in the Colombian Pacific Region." *World Development*, 128: Article 104837.

Vermillion, Douglas L. 1997. "Impacts of Irrigation Management Transfer: A Review of the Evidence." *Research Report 11*. Colombo, Sri Lanka: International Irrigation Management Institute.

Villegas, Mauricio G. 2012. "Disobeying the Law: The Culture of Non-Compliance with Rules in Latin America." *Wisconsin International Law Journal*, 29:2: 263–287.

Vygotsky, Lev. 1962. *Thought and Language* (E. Hanfmann & G. Vakar, Trans.). Cambridge, MA: MIT Press.

Wallace, M. B. 1981. *Solving Common-Property Resource Problems: Deforestation in Nepal Ph.D. Thesis*. Cambridge, MA: Harvard University.

Webley, Paul, Henry Robben, Henk Elffers & Dick Hessing. *Tax Evasion*. Cambridge and New York: Cambridge University Press, 1991.

Weingast, Barry R. 1984. "The Congressional-Bureaucratic System." *Public Choice*, 44: 147–191.

Wilson, James Q. & George L. Kelling. 1982. "Broken Windows." *Atlantic Monthly*, 249: 29–38.

Winter, Søren & Peter May. 2001. "Motivation for Compliance with Environmental Regulations." *Journal of Policy Analysis & Management*, 20: 675–698.

Weber, Max. 1958. *The Protestant Work Ethic and the Spirit of Capitalism*. Courier Dover Publications (2003 reprint).

Weil, David. 1996. "If OSHA Is So Bad, Why Is Compliance So Good?" *RAND Journal of Economics*, 27:3 (Autumn): 618–640.

Wilson, Rick K. & Carl M. Rhodes. 1997. "Leadership and Credibility in N-Person Coordination Games." *Journal of Conflict Resolution*, 41:6: 767–791.

Yan, Huiqi, Benjamin van Rooij & Jeroen van der Heijden. 2015a. "Contextual Compliance: Situational and Subjective Cost-Benefit Decisions about Pesticides by Chinese Farmers." *Law & Policy*, 37:3: 240–263.

Yan, Huiqi, Benjamin van Rooij & Jeroen van der Heijden. 2015b. "Symmetric and Asymmetric Motivations for Compliance and Violation: A Crisp Set Qualitative Comparative Analysis of Chinese Farmers." *Regulation & Governance*, early online version, Online ISSN: 1748-5991.

Yapp, C. & R. Fairman, R. 2004. *The Evaluation of Effective Enforcement Approaches for Food Safety in SMEs*. London: Food Standards Agency.

Zago, Susan. 2016. "Riding Circuit: Bringing the Law to Those Who Need It." *Florida A & M University Law Review*, 12:1: 1–53.

Index